The Vision Glorious

Themes and Personalities of the Catholic Revival in Anglicanism

GEOFFREY ROWELL

OXFORD   NEW YORK   TORONTO   MELBOURNE
OXFORD UNIVERSITY PRESS

Oxford University Press, Walton Street, Oxford OX2 6DP

London Glasgow New York Toronto
Delhi Bombay Calcutta Madras Karachi
Kuala Lumpur Singapore Hong Kong Tokyo
Nairobi Dar es Salaam Cape Town
Melbourne Auckland

and associated companies in
Beirut Berlin Ibadan Mexico City Nicosia

Oxford is a trade mark of Oxford University Press

Published in the United States
by Oxford University Press, New York

First published 1983
Reprinted 1983

British Library Cataloguing in Publication Data

Rowell, Geoffrey
The vision glorious.
1. Oxford movement
I. Title
283'.42   BX5100
ISBN 0-19-826443-7

Library of Congress Cataloging in Publication Data

Rowell, Geoffrey.
The vision glorious.
Includes index.
1. Anglo-Catholicism—History.   2. Church of England
—Doctrinal and controversial works.   I. Title.
BX5121.R68   1983   283'.42   83-2369
ISBN 0-19-826443-7

Typeset by Oxprint Ltd, Oxford
and Printed in Great Britain
at the University Press, Oxford
by Eric Buckley
Printer to the University

Preface

THE ONE hundred and fifty years which have elapsed since John Keble preached his Assize Sermon in 1833 have seen transformations in both Church and society going far beyond those which were the occasion of Keble's protest against national apostasy. When the centenary of the Oxford Movement was celebrated in 1933 the heirs of the Tractarians were both theologically creative and a dominant influence in the life of the Church of England. In 1983 the pattern is more complex. The changes in the Roman Catholic Church in the aftermath of the Second Vatican Council, the effect of a second World War and subsequent secularization, the influence of the charismatic movement, the ecumenical advances and no less the ecumenical uncertainties: all these have played their part in leading some to criticize those who would call themselves Catholic within the Church of England as being negative in outlook and theologically stagnant. It has led Anglican Catholics at times to adopt a too narrow designation of what a Catholic understanding of the Church involves and to disparage their Anglican heritage, thus in effect cutting off the branch on which they are sitting. It has meant uncertainty and a loss of direction for others.

This book, written to mark the one hundred and fiftieth anniversary of the Oxford Movement, is intended as a response to those questionings and criticisms by focusing on major themes and personalities of the Catholic revival of the last one hundred and fifty years. It is not a complete history of the movement, nor even a book which sets out to cover all the major controversies and contributions. It has, however, been written in a conviction that at the heart of the movement was a sacramental spirituality; a concern for holiness; a recognition of both imagination and discipline in Christian life; and an awareness of the Church, in its order as in its faith, as being part of the mystery of God's giving of himself in Christ 'for us men and for our salvation'. Much of what those whose names and concerns occur in this book lived by and fought for has become part of the life-blood of the whole Church and this has had an influence far beyond the bounds of the Anglican tradition. But there is a continuing need to be recalled to the heart of the matter and to remember with thanksgiving the witness of the Oxford Movement fathers, their heirs and successors. It is my hope that this book may make its small contribution to the renewal and continuation of their vision.

Keble College,   GEOFFREY ROWELL
Oxford.
All Saintstide, 1982.

Contents

List of plates

(between pp. 120–1)

*John Keble (1792–1866)
John Henry Newman (1801–1890)
Edward Bouverie Pusey (1800–1882)

*'The Oriel Fathers': Manning, Pusey, Newman, and Keble
Altar plate designed by William Butterfield

John Mason Neale (1818–1866) in Eucharistic vestments
*The restoration of liturgical dress

The last celebration of the Feast of the Epiphany at the Margaret Chapel,
    1850
*Pusey preaching in St. Mary's

George Rundle Prynne (1818–1903), Vicar of St. Peter's, Plymouth
Richard Meux Benson (1824–1915), Founder of the Society of St. John the
    Evangelist
John Coleridge Patteson (1827–71), Bishop of Melanesia
Robert Gray (1809–72), Bishop of Cape Town

Edward King (1829–1910), Bishop of Lincoln
Henry Scott Holland (1847–1918), Canon of St. Paul's and Regius Professor
    of Divinity at Oxford

Charles Gore (1853–1932) as Bishop of Worcester
*Reaction to *Lux Mundi*

Frederick George Lee (1832–1902)
Viscount Halifax (1839–1934)

*Reproduced by kind permission of the Bodleian Library, Oxford. All other illus-
trations are from the Hall collection of photographs and other sources in Pusey
House, Oxford, and are reproduced by kind permission of the Principal and Gover-
nors.

I. Introduction

IN 1833 the Derby was won by a horse called Dangerous. It is not recorded whether any regarded this as a sign of the times, but there would have been many members of the Church of England who, had their minds turned in that direction, would have been inclined to do so. The cry 'The Church in danger!' was heard in many quarters in the early 1830s and with some justification. The constitutional position of the Church of England had been weakened, and it seemed likely that it might be weakened still further. The repeal of the Test and Corporation Acts in 1828, the Emancipation of Roman Catholics in 1829, and the passing of the Reform Act in 1832 meant that Parliament was no longer an exclusively Anglican body. The Church of England was no longer in quite the same way the church of the nation. Non-Anglicans were now given access to political power, and that power could be used to legislate for the Church of England. Parliamentary reform meant that the representation of Dissenters in Parliament would be larger than it was likely to have been before the passing of the 1832 Act. A Tory high churchman like Hurrell Froude saw the Reform Act as pouring into the House of Commons 'the turbid waters of sheer mammonry, democracy and republicanism'. Those who regarded Church and State as two sides of a single coin, and held that the state, and the Crown in particular, was bound to uphold the order and polity of the Church of England, could not but be alarmed at these constitutional alterations. Parliament was no longer the lay synod of the Church.

They looked anxiously across the Channel, remembering how the French Church, so closely bound up with the *ancien régime*, had suffered at the hands of the revolutionaries. French priests had found refuge in England and brought tales of revolutionary excesses as well as influencing some Anglicans towards a new understanding of Catholicism. The 1830 revolution, which toppled Charles X, seemed a more immediate portent of political change. Churchmen noted that in France the endowments and property of the Church had been a prime target of attack and reacted nervously to the exposure of the inequalities and excess of Anglican endowments in the *Black Book* and the *Extraordinary Black Book* published by John Wade.

Ancient endowments did not often go hand in hand with the places of greatest pastoral need. The growing industrial towns were often without adequate pastoral provision, whilst amply endowed cathedral canonries were little more than sinecures. Wealthy benefices made an attractive provision for younger sons of established families, and the right to present to such parishes could be bought and sold on the open market. Clergy in more poorly endowed parishes often had to seek an additional cure, sometimes miles away, in order to have an adequate income. Even bishops in the more poorly endowed sees would hold a deanery or canonry in plurality. Little had been done to change the medieval structure of the Church at the time of the Reformation. The King had replaced the Pope, the gentry had replaced the great monastic houses. The centres of power and influence changed but the pattern of church organization did not. The changing society of the England of the industrial revolution did not fit easily into a church meshed into an earlier, agrarian society.

An initial reaction was to provide more churches to meet the needs of the new areas, but even new churches needed money to run them and money frequently came from the charging of pew rents: the poor were banished to benches at the back. It was soon found that more than the provision of new church buildings was necessary.

Anglicans had no forum in which the challenges to the Church and the need for reform might be discussed. The Convocations of clergy had been suppressed as effective leglislative bodies at the beginning of the eighteenth century. Discussion was therefore necessarily informal and often channelled through the committees of religious societies. In such a situation it was not unexpected that a focus of concern should be the University of Oxford. The university was Anglican, as Parliament had been until 1832. The fellows of its colleges were Anglican clergy who, inheriting ancient medieval statutes, remained unmarried as long as they held their fellowships. The colleges were small societies with something of the inheritance and potential of monastic communities for those who wished to see them in that way. At a time when theological colleges were unheard of it was the colleges of the universities of Oxford and Cambridge which were the nurseries of the Church's ministry and the places of education for the leaders of both Church and State. Just as churchmen were worried about the change in the character of Parliament, and so of the state's religious identity, so Oxford churchmen were concerned about pressure to alter the ecclesiastical character of the university. Admission of Dissenters would mean the destruction of the Anglican identity of the university, and a less ecumenical age than our own was quite certain of the errors of both Dissenters and Roman Catholics alike.

If this was the political context of the Oxford Movement, the catalyst was the Government's proposals to suppress and amalgamate certain bishoprics of the Church of Ireland. The Irish Church was an established church just as the Church of England was, but the great majority of the Irish population was Catholic. On many grounds the changes proposed were clearly defensible, but to Oxford Churchmen they seemed like the thin end of a very large wedge. The newly constituted un-Anglican Parliament was claiming the authority to alter the ministry and government of the Church. That raised acutely the question of the identity of the Church of England. The first of the *Tracts for the Times* posed the question to the clergy, 'On what grounds do you stand, O presbyter of the Church of England?'

High doctrines of the church, ministry, and sacraments had in England been very frequently linked with a high Tory doctrine of the state. The seventeenth-century high churchmen had been strongly royalist and defenders of the divine right of kings. The non-jurors, who had gone into schism rather than abjure their oath of allegiance of James II, were looked back to as churchmen who had refused to bow to latitudinarian pressures. Men like Bishop Ken were revered as exemplars of piety and sacramental devotion. The non-jurors' interest in conforming their worship more closely to that of the ancient liturgies was another source of inspiration. Charles I, the martyr-king, provided an additional focus for this traditional high Anglican piety.

The changing character of the state, signalled by the leglislation of the late 1820s and early 1830s, called into question some of the assumptions of this older high churchmanship as well as forcing English churchmen to consider the nature and identity of Anglicanism. How did the Church of England stand in relation to 'popular Protestantism' on the one hand and the Church of Rome on the other? What was the relationship between the Church of England and the church of the first four centuries with which Anglican formularies claimed a special kinship? If the foundations of Anglican theology lay not just in Scripture and a simple 'Bible-Christianity' but in the Catholic creeds and the theological and liturgical tradition of the Early Church, how ought Anglican theology and practice to reflect and continue that heritage? Might it not be possible (or even necessary) for a churchman with a high doctrine of the church, ministry, and sacraments to stand for the separation of church and state? For members of the Church of England that possibility had scarcely been explored, though the small Episcopal Church of Scotland and Episcopalians in America had long lived with this situation. When the young John Henry Newman met Bishop Hobart of New York when Hobart visited Oxford, he confessed himself puzzled as to how Hobart managed to yoke together the high doctrine of the church and republican sentiments.

The asking of questions of identity led to the asking of questions of authority. If bishops were not state functionaries, nor convenient administrators of an ecclesiastical organization, but the successors of the apostles to whom the plenitude of the Church's ministry had been committed, then they had an authority in teaching and in government which was of divine origin. For Newman this meant that a bishop's lightest word was to be obeyed, and he could suggest equally that apostolic bishops were shown to be such by their willingness to be apostolic martyrs. Episcopal authority might be magnified, but in England Anglican bishops were part of the fabric of government, and authority in the Church was still claimed by Parliament. Appeals could be made from church courts to secular courts even in matters of doctrine.

The controversies which beset the Church of England in the nineteenth century are therefore very much controversies which centre on questions of authority: the authority of the Church as an autonomous body over against the state; the limits of the state's authority within a church still recognized as the church of the nation; the nature of the authority to be ascribed to the sources of the Church's teaching—the Scriptures, the Fathers of the Church, and the Prayer Book. As the Catholic Church in Europe in the aftermath of the French Revolution saw the growth of the Ultramontane movement, which stressed the authority of the Papacy over against national churches which could be controlled by secularizing and unsympathetic governments, so the Oxford Movement can be seen in part as a parallel English movement. If the Pope was exalted in Rome, and bishops were exalted by the Tractarians, so the clergy generally affirmed the identity of the Church by becoming more distinctive and set apart. 'In the late eighteenth century', a recent writer has commented, 'the clergyman's role approximated closely to that of the country gentleman, and the clergyman performed a range of functions which were legitimated not by his ordination, but by his status as a country gentleman: a man of integrity and some learning in a society where the majority were illiterate'. A century later the role of the clergy was defined much more closely in terms of liturgical and pastoral skills, reflected in the growth of theological colleges and vocational training and in the increasing re-adoption of clerical dress.[1] As Archbishop Longley's nephew, Henry Lloyd, put it: 'Our behaviour, our dress, our places of resort, our occupations, should always plainly be those of God's clergy.'[2] At the heart of that distinctiveness, as men like Henry Liddon saw, was a deeper spiritual and moral commitment. Theological Colleges became necessary because there was both a higher and different expectation of what a priest should be, and also an awareness that the weakening of the ecclesiastical character of the universities made further training necessary. 'The work of a theological college', wrote Liddon, 'is to mould character as well as to teach truth'. In a secularized university it was accepted that theology was taught academically, but a theological college recognized that 'if a man would teach the power of religious truth, he must personally have felt the need of it'. Theology must be related to both ethics and spirituality.[3]

The changing expectations and understanding of the ministry of the Church were an important part of the impact of the Oxford Movement on the Church. It would be wrong, however, to see these changes as confined to one theological tradition. Recent work has made it clear that a more professional attitude to pastoral care and a greater distinctiveness attributed to the clerical office were changes which characterized all traditions in the Victorian Church.[4] The Evangelical Revival of the eighteenth century had given an important place to the godly minister, and had often led to a more frequent celebration of the sacraments as well as to preaching which touched the heart, clearly distinguished from the moral discourses of eighteenth-century latitudinarianism.

This raises the question of the relationship between the two great movements of religious revival, Evangelicalism and Tractarianism. The polemics of nineteenth-century theology, exacerbated by latent anti-catholicism in British society, led many to view—and indeed to experience—them as two antagonistic movements. More recent scholarship has attempted to re-assess this simple polarity, and has argued that there was more in common than might at first sight be admitted. After all, many of the leading figures of the Oxford Movement, John Henry Newman, Robert Isaac Wilberforce, and Henry Manning had Evangelical backgrounds, though by contrast, Keble and Pusey did not. A stress on the importance of right moral feeling as fundamental to faith was a significant common emphasis. Then, as David Newsome puts it, there was that 'tightest knot which bound the Evangelicals and Tractarians together' in the early years, 'the pursuit of holiness'.[5] In his study, *The Anglican Revival*, the Swedish Archbishop Brilioth pointed to the Irish churchmen, Alexander Knox and his friend Bishop Jebb of Limerick, as notable precursors of the Oxford Movement, who had a warm regard for the personal religion of the Clapham Sect and held in general a highly favourable view of Methodism. Jebb believed that Methodism had been 'the providential means of reviving and diffusing, far beyond its own sphere, that inward, spiritual religion, which is diffused through our liturgy, but which had been before John Wesley's rise, almost entirely banished from our pulpits by the cold, rationalizing, spiritless system of morals'.[6] Knox and Jebb attempted to show that the deep spirituality they observed at the heart of Evangelicalism was also the core of the common prayer and corporate life of the Church. Knox wrote that 'to be *evangelical* is to FEEL that the Gospel is the POWER of God unto salvation'.[7] Like Coleridge he wanted to emphasize that 'Christianity is not a theory or a speculation, but a life; not a philosophy of life, but a life and a living process.'[8]

The mention of Coleridge is a reminder that a stress on Christianity as vital religion rather than theological speculation was not confined to Evangelicals, and so to detect a common stress by Evangelicals and Tractarians on spirituality, the pursuit of holiness, moral conversion, and the priority of faith is by no means to indicate a unique dependence or closeness. Both Evangelicalism and Tractarianism relate to that wider change of sensibility that we call Romanticism, with its exploration of the subjective and the place of imagination and deep feeling in relation to both faith and reason. Moreover, Evangelicalism itself was a complex and changing phenomenon. There was a theological division between Arminians and Calvinists. There were Evangelicals who were strong supporters of the Establishment and others who made common cause with Dissent. There were millenarians looking with apocalyptic ardour for the fulfilment of the prophecies concerning the End. In his celebrated·

article on Church Parties in 1853 Conybeare could detect three distinct groups among Low Churchmen: the Evangelicals, the Recordites and what he called 'the Low and Slow'. By the latter part of the nineteenth century, as Dr Jay has commented, '"Evangelical" could be used with equal validity to describe a churchman of firm commitment to the Establishment, a close co-operator with Dissent, or any rabid anti-Ritualist.'[9]

When contemporaries, some of whom indeed detected certain close links between Evangelicalism and Tractarianism, commented on what distinguished the two movements it was on the doctrine of the church, ministry, and sacraments that they largely focused. Gladstone wrote at the end of his life that 'the Evangelical clergy were the heralds of a real and profound revival, the revival of spiritual life'. But that spiritual life was conceived of primarily in terms of individual conversion. 'There was no corresponding recognition of the Divine kingdom . . . of the great congregation, of the perpetual, indestructible existence of the Church of God.' The idea of the Church was, Gladstone suggested, often reduced to little more than language about 'our venerable Establishment'.[10] In a much earlier letter of 1842 Gladstone wrote of 'those great Catholic principles which distinguish our Church from many other Protestant bodies: such, for instance, as the doctrine of grace in Baptism, of the real sacramental Presence in the Eucharist, of absolution, of universal or Catholic consent, of the Apostolical foundation of the Episcopate, and of its being the source of lawful Church power and of a valid ministry'.[11] From an Evangelical point of view William Goode could write in 1853:

Both the Roman and Tractarian systems are founded upon one and the same fundamental error; namely, that the true Church of Christ must be a body of individuals united together by external and visible bonds of union and communion, under the government of those ordained in succession from the Apostles as their bishops and pastors. From this primary false principle springs an abundant harvest of errors. Truth is sacrificed to unity. The 'priesthood' are exalted to a place not belonging to them, and the ministry of service is turned into a ministry of *lordly government*. . . . The spiritual kingdom of Christ, of which hearts are the subjects, and His word and the unseen influences of His Spirit the ruling and directing authorities, is turned into an earthly kingdom, whose subjects are all those who submit themselves to certain human authorities and hold themselves bound by certain human laws.[12]

For Goode the Church was the invisible communion of true believers; for the Tractarians the Church, its order and sacraments, were, as Newman put it, 'keys and spells' by which, through the providence of God, men were brought into the presence of God's saints. The visible church was not just a convenient organization, it was a sacrament in its common life, in the ordering of its ministry, and in the pattern of its worship. The outward and visible could not be discarded as irrelevant to the inward and spiritual.

Religion must be realised in particular acts in order to its continuing alive. . . . There is no such thing as abstract religion. When persons attempt to worship in this (what they call) more spiritual manner, they end, in fact, in not worshipping at all. . . . What will the devotion of the country people be, if we strip religion of its external symbols, and bid them seek out and gaze upon the Invisible? Scripture gives the *spirit*, and the Church the *body*, to our worship; and we may as well expect that the spirits of men might be seen by us without the intervention of their bodies, as suppose that the Object of faith can be realised in a world of sense and excitement, without the instrumentality of an outward form to arrest and fix attention, to stimulate the careless, and to encourage the desponding. . . .[13]

A sermon of 1836, preached by John Keble to his parishioners at Hursley, gives us another good example. In this Keble's sacramental doctrine of the Church is linked to his Tory reverence for the order and hierarchy of established institutions in society. He reproved Christians who maintained that faith is an entirely personal and individual matter and who argued that there was no need of outward ministrations; Pastors, Churches, Sacraments are good things in their way, but not to be insisted on as necessary to salvation'. The kingdom which Christ proclaimed, Keble declared, was 'a real visible company, united within itself by rules and ordinances, and varying in the ranks and degrees of its members; spiritual indeed and heavenly in its origin, and in the powers which quicken and move it, but having an outward frame and operations just as open to men's notice as any society in this world'. 'Christ's Holy Catholic Church', he continued, 'is a real outward visible body, having supernatural grace continually communicated through it by succession from the Apostles, in whose place the bishops are'.[14]

This concern with the importance of the order, continuity, and sacraments of the Church was closely bound up with the question of Anglican identity. That identity the Tractarians found affirmed in the writings of the Anglican divines of the seventeenth century, men who looked back to the substantial identity of the Church of England with the church of antiquity and who affirmed that the doctrine of the Church of England was that expressed in the catholic consent of the early centuries. The two great series of texts, the *Library of the Fathers* and the *Library of Anglo-Catholic Theology*, edited and published by the Tractarians witnessed to this, the former being translations of the major patristic writings, the latter being the works of the most notable seventeenth-century divines. Newman recognized that the doctrine of the Church for which they stood might be viewed as no more than a paper theory. The *via media* of a reformed Catholicism between Romanism and popular Protestantism might be held to have no genuine, positive existence. So he wrote in the *Lectures on the Prophetical Office of the Church*:

The *via media*, viewed as an integral system, has scarcely had existence except on paper, it has never been reduced to practice, but by piecemeal; it is known not positively but negatively, in its differences from rival creeds, not in its own properties. . . . It still remains to be tried whether what is called Anglo-Catholicism, the religion of Andrewes, Laud, Hammond, Butler and Wilson, is capable of being professed, acted on, and maintained on a large sphere of action and through a sufficient period. . . .[15]

Newman at this period believed, and it was a belief shared by others in the Movement, that Anglicanism had a special mission, to represent a theology 'Catholic but not Roman', which was marked by 'calmness and caution' though giving no encouragement to 'lukewarmness and liberalism'.[16]

Concern with the Church of the early centuries led the Tractarians, and Newman in particular, to a study of the writings of the Fathers. If the Church had a teaching rôle, the nature of that teaching was to be found in the creeds and councils of the early Church and the theological writings of the early centuries. The seventeenth-century divines had drunk deeply at the well of patristic theology; the Tractarians did the same. The theological vision of the Oxford Movement was in large measure a rediscovery and reinterpretation of patristic theology. The typological exegesis of Scripture and the strong sacramentalism of the Fathers commended themselves to men who already had begun to criticize the evidence theology of the eighteenth century, under the influence of the work of Bishop Butler and the rediscovery of the symbolic and imaginative character of language in the literature of Romanticism. In particular the Greek Fathers influenced the Tractarians, as they had influenced the seventeenth-century Anglicans before them. Newman spoke in the *Apologia* of how 'the broad philosophy of Clement and Origen carried him away'. His study of the Arian controversy made him a disciple of Athanasius, and Athanasian doctrine and phraseology stamped itself powerfully on his sermons and theological writing.[17] From the Greek Fathers he learnt of the transcendent mystery of the God who exceeds all our human theological conceptions of him and whose revelation of himself is necessarily by means of economies or dispensations adapted to our limited human understanding. We are led on to an ever deeper apprehension of the truth, and that truth which is revealed to us never ceases to be at the same time a mystery. The truth of God cannot be cut and squared to the dimensions of a dogmatic system. 'Creeds and dogmas', Newman stated, 'live only in the one idea that they are intended to express'.[18] Pusey wrote in 1838 that in his view the Fathers had 'altogether a deeper way of viewing things than moderns', one 'much more penetrated with a consciousness of the mysterious depth of every work and way of God'. If the Scriptures were the fountain of Christian doctrine, the Fathers were the channel through which that doctrine flowed down to later ages of the Church.[19] Again Keble wrote in Tract LXXXIX that the characteristically mystical interpretation of Scripture by the Fathers was rooted in a deep sense of the Divinity of Christ and of the communion of saints.[20]

Keble's reference to the communion of saints is a pointer to an important characteristic of the Tractarian appeal to the Fathers. That to which they appealed was catholic consent, not the works of the Fathers as individuals. Bishop Jebb in, writing of the nature and place of tradition in the Church, appealed especially to the Vincentian canon of doctrine: that which had been believed at all times, everywhere and by all. Newman wrestled with what this might mean, first in his controversy with the Abbé Jager, and then later, and with different conclusions, in his *Essay on Development*. Pusey insisted that the Church appealed 'not to the Fathers individually, or as individuals, but as witnesses; not to this or that Father, but to the whole body, and agreement of Catholic Fathers and ancient Bishops'.[21] Again, in his unpublished *Lectures on Types and Prophecies*, Pusey praised the Fathers for 'their vivid perception of the relations of the several Ch[ris]tian truths (one with another)', so being enabled to 'glide imperceptibly from the mention of the one to the other'.[22] There is a strong sense of the organic nature of Christian truth and of the importance of the Fathers as primary witnesses to that sense. Newman, who wrestled continually with the question of how it was reasonable for a man to believe more than he could understand and to attain to a certitude of faith in a world of probabilities, could speak in the *Lectures on the Prophetical Office of the Church* of every word of revelation being 'the outward form of a heavenly truth, and in this sense a mystery or sacrament'. 'Accordingly, when a candidate for Baptism repeats the Articles of the Creed, he is confessing something incomprehensible in its depth, and indefinite in its extent.'[23] That is because for Newman 'religious truth is . . . like the dim view of a country seen in the twilight, with forms half extricated from the darkness, with broken lines, and isolated masses'. What we are able to receive and to express is 'small and superficial' compared with that truth to which it is intended to lead us and into which we are to grow continually.[24] Liberalism in theology, which Newman and the Tractarians attacked so vehemently, failed to recognize the organic nature of Christian faith, grounded as it was in God's self-revelation. It treated Christian doctrines piecemeal.

In Pusey's *Lectures on Types and Prophecies* we find again this sense of Christian doctrine as a great and mysterious whole which here and now we know only in part. 'By striving over-much at clearness, and practically admitting only what they could make, as they thought, intelligible to themselves', Pusey writes, 'men have narrowed' the Creed 'far below that of the ancient Church, or of our own in former days'. 'It is not', he tells us, 'in proportion to the clearness of our perception, that mysteries have their force'; rather 'greatness and indistinctness commence together', so that it is 'not the things which we know clearly, but the things which we know unclearly' which 'are our highest birth-right'.[25] It is very much of a piece with what later on in the century Gerard Manley Hopkins wrote to his friend Robert Bridges: 'You do not mean by a mystery what a Catholic does. You mean an interesting uncertainty. . . . But a Catholic by mystery means an incomprehensible certainty.'[26] Pusey, like Newman, is aware that the conviction of faith 'is of a compound character and made up of various emotions'. 'In Divine things, awe, wonder, the absorbing sense of infinity, of purity, or of holiness, infuse conviction more directly than reasoning; nay reasoning in that it appeals to one faculty only, and that for a time is erected into a judge, and so, as it were, sits superior, constantly goes directly counter to the frame of mind wherein belief is received.' So it is that the Fathers carry conviction because of their sense of awe and wonder:

Works which like S. Basil or S. Ambrose . . . exhibited God's works with a sort of wondering awe, do in fact convince much more than those which, like Paley, make conviction their professed object, and recall our minds from the contemplation of those works to reflect on their own convincingness. We are not formed to seek conviction but to have it. It is brought to us in the way of duty. In all practical matters we live in belief and through acting on belief, believe in the things of God, and thereby attain a higher kind of belief and an insight into our belief.[27]

As Newman recognized, 'life is not long enough for a religion of inferences'. Faith is a principle of action: to act, he says, 'we must assume, and that assumption is faith'.[28]

For the Tractarians the Fathers were primary witnesses to the reality of the *consensus fidelium* (agreement of the faithful) and so to the organic character of Christian tradition. Their very unsystematic character was something to be valued. Their use of typology, of image and symbol rather than syllogism, witnessed to the reserve and mystery which necessarily characterized Christian faith. Their writing demonstrated the essential reverence which man must have in the presence of God, whereas the logical deductions of systematic theology could lead to little more than a hubris which placed man's intellect at the centre, and a rationalism which failed to kindle the imagination and move the heart. One of Newman's chief charges against the Roman Church in the *Lectures on the Prophetical Office* is that it had over-systematized the Christian faith, and when he comes much later as a Roman Catholic to write on the doctrine of Papal Infallibility he remained reluctant to view papal authority as being primarily concerned with the building of a doctrinal edifice. It had rather the function of a corrective recalling to a truth already in a measure known and dimly discerned. Newman put it thus in a letter of 1868 to J. S. Flanagan: 'what the Apostle is in his own person, that the Church is in her whole evolution of ages, *per modum unius*, a living, present treasury of the Mind of the Spirit of Christ'.

Thus the Apostles had the *fullness* of revealed knowledge, a fullness which they could as little realize to themselves, as the human mind, as such, can have all its thoughts present before it at once. They are elicited according to the occasion. . . .

But how could such a knowledge, partly explicit partly implicit, and varying day by day as to what was the one and what the other, be transmitted to the Church after them? Thus: I believe the Creed . . . was delivered to the *Church with the gift of knowing its true and full meaning.* A Divine philosophy is committed to her keeping: not a number of formulas such as a modern pedantic theologian may make theology to consist in, but a system of thought, sui generis in such sense that a mind that was possessed of it, that is, the Church's mind, could definitely & unequivocally say whether this part of it, as traditionally expressed, meant this or that, and whether this or that was agreeable to, or inconsistent with it in whole or in part. . . .

I conceive then that the Depositum is in such sense committed to the Church or to the Pope, that when the Pope sits in St. Peter's chair, or when a Council of Fathers & doctors is collected round him, it is capable of being presented to their minds with that fullness and exactness, under the operation of supernatural grace, (so far forth and in such portion of it as the occasion requires,) with which it habitually, not occasionally, resided in the minds of the Apostles;—a vision of it, not logical, and therefore consistent with errors of reasoning and of fact in the enunciation, after the manner of an intuition or an instinct. Nor do those enunciations become logical, because theologians afterwards can reduce them to their relations to other doctrines, or give them a position in the general system of theology. To such theologians they appear as deductions from the creed of formularized deposit, but in truth they are original parts of it, communicated per modum unius to the Apostles' minds, & brought to light to the minds of the Fathers of the Council, under the temporary illumination of Divine grace.[29]

This was, Newman told Flanagan, the view he had entertained for many years.

In the vigorous polemic of the letters concerning the Tamworth Reading Room Newman was concerned to attack the narrow limitations of utilitarian epistemology. 'Logic', he wrote, 'makes but a sorry rhetoric with the multitude; first shoot round corners and you may not despair of converting by a syllogism'. 'After all, man is *not* a reasoning animal; he is a seeing, feeling, contemplating, acting animal. He is influenced by what is direct and precise.'[30] This was an important consideration in the Tractarian understanding of sacraments, rites, and ceremonies, and in the close connection that they saw between theology and spirituality. That again was something they valued in the Fathers.

Professor Chadwick has commented that 'the pastoral and devotional power in the Movement proved to be far more effective, in the long run, than its intellectual power. If it altered *lex credendi*, it altered it first by transforming *lex orandi*.'[31] When Newman told Blanco White as early as 1828 that words as such did not have the same force as feelings and that intellect could never be equated with ethos it was this relationship he was attempting to articulate. Ethos was concerned with moral apprehension, with the totality of religious vision, and so with prayer and with sacrament. Of these intellect was but the handmaid.[32] So Newman could expound the way in which he conceived that religious truth was communicated in a long letter to Sir James Stephen in 1835:

No mode of teaching can be imagined so public, constant, impressive, permanent, and at the same time reverential than that which makes the forms of devotion the memorial and declaration of doctrine—reverential because the very posture of the mind in worship is necessarily such. In this way Christians receive the Gospel literally on their knees, and in a temper altogether different from that critical and argumentative spirit which sitting and listening engender. The New Testament forcibly enjoins and countenances this mode of teaching by making certain ordinances, not only significant of Christian doctrines, but even exalting them into Sacraments.[33]

At the heart of Tractarian spirituality and at the centre of Tractarian theology was the doctrine of the Incarnation issuing in the doctrine of the Divine indwelling. This comes over strongly in Newman's *Lectures on Justification* in which he spoke of the gift that is promised to us by God as being 'nothing short of the indwelling in us of God the Father and the Word Incarnate through the Holy Ghost', so that to be justified is 'to receive the Divine Presence within us, and be made a Temple of the Holy Ghost'.[34] In Newman the influence of Athanasius and the Greek Fathers is marked. Participation by grace in the Divine nature is man's end and goal.

The titles which belong to the Divine Word by nature, are by grace given to us, a wonderful privilege. . . . The means by which these titles become ours are our real participation of the Son by His presence within us, a participation so intimate that in one sense He can be worshipped within us as being His temple or shrine.[35]

In *The Doctrine of the Incarnation of our Lord Jesus Christ in its relation to mankind and to the Church*, one of the major theological works of the Oxford Movement, Robert Isaac Wilberforce spoke of God's presence in Christ as the beginning of the Christian's regeneration, the union of all believers in the one Body of Christ as the second stage, and the third the influence of the Word on every individual heart. Truth and holiness are not only imparted to the Church but infused by the Spirit into the heart of every believer. 'This gift of knowledge, like that of holiness, is both an imparted and an infused or *"engrafted"* gift: bestowed from without upon the faithful, as an object of contemplation; and communicated likewise to the body of the Church, as an internal principle of teaching and guidance.'[36] If we turn to some of Manning's Anglican sermons we find again a stress on the centrality and significance of the divine indwelling. In a sermon on 'The gift of abundant life' Manning writes of the Holy Spirit:

The Incarnation is the channel of His influence, of His Presence. He dwells in man as He never dwelt before: by unity of substance with the Word, by very presence through the Word in us. This is the interior life and reality of the True Vine.[37]

'In each one of us', Manning says, 'the Spirit dwells, not by division, or mere emanation, or effect, but by personal presence, inhabitation, and life . . . and the gift of life is not a power, a principle, but a very and true Person dwelling in us'.[38] The 'deep mystery of our own renewed being flows out of the mystery of Christ's incarnation'.

He took our manhood and made it new in Himself, that we might be made new in Him. He hallowed our manhood, and carried it up into the presence of His Father as the first sheaf of the coming harvest, and the first-fruits of a new creation. And we shall be made new creatures through the same power by which He was made man—by the overshadowing of the Holy Ghost.[39]

And Pusey also stressed the same theme.

What the soul is to the body, *that*, God is to the soul. The life of the body is the soul, the Life of the soul is God. . . . Through God indwelling the soul, we have our spiritual life eternal begun in us; we think all the good thoughts we have. Our good is not merely our's, not chiefly or primarily our's, but His. . . . But then what an existence, aweful for the very greatness of the love of God! What a tingling closeness of God! 'Christ *in* you, the hope of glory.'[40]

As the renewing and transfiguring gift of God was no less than 'God's Presence and His very Self and Essence all-Divine', so the very heart of the Church's life was that same reality. 'The whole Church is a sacrament of His presence', wrote Manning, 'and in all parts of it, the man that seeks Him in purity of heart shall see Him with open face'.[41] The sacrament by which men and women are made members of the Church, and so receive the renewing grace and life of God, is Baptism. The new life of Baptism and its regenerating power is one of the key themes of the Tractarians. It was a doctrine which for them emphasized the priority of God's grace as a gift to be objectively claimed. As Robert Wilberforce put it:

The flame requires to be kindled from without, that it may burn within. There must be an external action to which the inward movement must respond. Renovation must have its root in Regeneration. There must be a gift antecedent to our efforts. This gift is that first union with Christ, whereon all communication of graces from Him to us depends. Out of this beginning arises the whole system of the Christian life. And this heavenly impulse is expressly declared in Scripture to be extended to us in Baptism.[42]

The doctrine was far from being a mechanical one, demanding no personal appropriation and no real growth in the spiritual life. 'We cannot', wrote Wilberforce, 'wonder if it be allowed to be inoperative, when children are not instructed in the nature of the gift which they have received.' But 'those who think most highly of Baptism regard it only as the appointed means for that union with Christ, whereby men may obtain strength to serve Him. Baptism neither exempts devout men from the necessity of a watchful life, nor careless men from the necessity of conversion. It is a reason why the watchfulness of the one should be more unvaried, and the conversion of the other more complete.'[43] Pusey, in his Tract on Baptism (LXVII), provided the first full exposition of Tractarian baptismal theology. 'The difficulty of explaining baptismal regeneration is twofold', he wrote, 'first from its being a mystery; secondly, from men being in these days inclined to lower that mystery'. He spoke approvingly of the words of the Catechism, which say that in Baptism 'I was made a member of Christ, the child of God, and an inheritor of the kingdom of heaven', words which echo for him 'the warm undefined language of the Eastern churches', just as the benefits of Baptism are defined in more Augustinian terms: 'a death unto sin, and a new birth unto righteousness'. Pusey argued that the questions so frequently put about how infants can be born again, and be said to live spiritually, and in what this spiritual life consists and how infant and adult baptism are to be related, are all questions which can end in denying not only the reality of any sacramental grace but also the doctrine of the Incarnation from which that grace derives. Following the ancient Church, and, he believed, Anglican teaching of the past, Baptism means that we are 'engrafted into Christ, and thereby recieve a fuller principle of life, afterwards to be developed and enlarged by the fuller influxes of his grace; so that neither is Baptism looked upon as an infusion of grace distinct from incorporation into Christ, nor is that incorporation conceived of as separate from its attendant blessings'.[44] As Pusey made clear in a letter of 1836, the regeneration of Baptism is indeed a new birth, which implies 'a new nature, existence imparted; and this is actual, not metaphorical, and by virtue of the Incarnation of our Lord Who took our nature that He might impart His to us'.[45] So he could write:

Baptismal regeneration, as connected with the Incarnation of our Blessed Lord, gives a depth to our Christian existence, an actualness to our union with Christ, a reality to our sonship to God, an interest in the presence of our Lord's glorified Body at God's right hand, a joyousness amid the subduing of the flesh, an overwhelmingness to the dignity conferred on human nature, a solemnity to the communion of saints who are the fullness of Him who filleth all in all, a substantiality to the indwelling of Christ, that to those who retain this truth the school which abandoned it must needs appear to have sold its birthright.[46]

Once again we catch echoes of the doctrine found in the Greek Fathers, that we may become by grace what Christ is by nature.

The Gorham Judgment of 1850, when the Judicial Committee of the Privy Council ruled against the decision of the church courts which had upheld Bishop Phillpotts's right to decline to institute a clergyman who denied the doctrine of baptismal regeneration, was traumatic for Tractarians. Not only was it seen as a flagrant instance of Erastianism, it also struck at the very heart of their sacramental theology as it related to Baptism. Evangelical critics of the Tractarians were concerned about what they understood as an *ex opere operato* doctrine of sacramental grace, which could become either mechanical or magical. But the roots of Tractarian doctrine are patristic not scholastic. In Christology and in sacramental theology the source from which they drank deepest was the Alexandrian tradition with its emphasis on the supreme condescension and self-giving of God in order that man may be transfigured into his likeness.[47]

As with Baptism so with the Eucharist. John Keble in his tract of 1857, *On Eucharistical Adoration*, speaks of the Eucharist as 'the very crown and fountain' of all God's gifts, in which 'is bestowed on each receiver by way of most unspeakable participation and union, that gift which is God Himself, as well as having God for its Giver'.

'Christ in us,' not only Christ offered for us; a 'divine nature' set before us, of which we are to be made 'partakers.' Must we cease adoring when He comes not only as the Giver, but as the Gift; not only as the Priest, but as the Victim; not only as 'the Master of the Feast,' but as 'the Feast itself?'[48]

Keble argued that the Eucharist 'implies such a union of condescension and power for the deification . . . of each one of us, as the very Incarnation and Cross exhibited for the salvation and redemption of all mankind'. As 'the Person of Jesus Christ our Lord, wherever it is, is to be adored', so Christ is 'to be adored in that Sacrament, as there present in a peculiar manner', for the Sacrament is both 'the standing monument of the Incarnation, and extension of it'.[49] It is worth noting, however, that Keble, as indeed other Tractarians, seems to have moved towards this doctrine. As Dr Härdelin comments in the course of his careful survey of Tractarian Eucharistic teaching, from the evidence which can be gleaned from the 1820s 'we may conclude that both Keble and Newman rejected the idea that the eucharistic gift was given through the instrumentality of the elements, or was necessarily connected with their reception'.[50] As the Movement developed during the 1830s doctrine became more definite and the doctrine of the Real Presence was clearly affirmed. Both the seventeenth-century divines and, above all, the Fathers were appealed to in support of it. Transubstantiation, however, as a way of expressing that Real Presence, was generally repudiated. It seemed to the Tractarians to attempt to explain what was necessarily a mystery, and to be an instance of improper 'rationalism' in theology. As Newman could put it: 'Transubstantiation, as held by Rome, involves in *matter of fact* profane ideas . . . a substitution of something earthly for a heavenly mystery.'[51] Endeavouring to avoid what they thought were 'physical' or 'carnal' interpretations of the Eucharist they spoke most happily of a 'spiritual' presence, a manner of speaking which was not intended to denote anything '*less* than real', but rather 'the most real and intense mode of presence,'since it means a presence not merely external and visible, but an inward life-giving presence to the regenerate man, whose own body is "not only material but spiritual"'.[52] Indeed the inner spiritual nature of man, known only through the outward bodily and material presence, is an analogy to which they frequently refer.

Two sermons of Pusey, of 1853 and 1871, are characteristic in their exposition of the doctrine of the Real Presence. In 1853 Pusey states:

The presence of which our Lord speaks has been termed sacramental, supernatural, mystical, ineffable, as opposed *not* to what is real, but to what is natural. The word has been chosen to express, not our knowledge, but our ignorance; or that unknowing knowledge of faith, which we have of things divine, surpassing knowledge. We know not the manner of his presence . . . but it is a presence without us, not within us only; a presence by virtue of our Lord's words, although to us it becomes a saving presence, received to our salvation, through our faith. It is not a presence simply in the soul of the receiver, as 'Christ dwells in our hearts by faith' (Eph. 3:17); or as, in acts of spiritual, apart from sacramental, communion, we, by our longings, invite him into our souls. But while the consecrated elements . . . remain in their natural substances, still, since our Lord says, 'This is my body,' 'This is my blood,' the Church of England believes that 'under the form of bread and wine,' so consecrated, we 'receive the body and blood of our Saviour Christ.' And since we receive them, they must be there, in order that we may receive them. We need not then (as the school of Calvin bids men) 'ascend into heaven, to bring down Christ from above' (Rom. 10:6). For he is truly present, for us truly to receive him to the salvation of our souls, if they prepared by repentance, faith, love, through the cleansing of his Spirit, for his coming.[53]

The sermon of 1871 is entitled simply 'This is My Body'. Grace, Pusey tells us, 'is a communication of God to the soul, making it "a partaker of the Divine nature", communicating that Nature to us in a true, real, though ineffable manner; uniting us with God, and re-tracing in us some image and likeness to Himself'.[54] Grace operates above but not against nature, and so the miracle of the Eucharistic presence 'is above, but . . . is no more against our senses, than those equally miraculous operations of (God's) love, whereby He, through His infused grace or the outpouring of His Spirit, converts the averted soul, and, uniting, binds it to Himself with the indissoluble bond of love, or turned the fiery persecutor . . . into the devoted Apostle, whose life was the life of Christ within him'.[55] And so Pusey went on to speak of the grace given in the Eucharist, weaving into his discourse a whole wealth of patristic references. The Eucharistic gift is the summation of the longing for God in the human heart, a longing implanted by God Himself. 'The indwelling of God *in* the soul is the first-fruits of the Incarnation.' To indicate something of what this meant Pusey cited Cyril of Alexandria.

I [i.e. the Son of God] took mortal Flesh: but, having dwelt in it, being by nature Life, because I am of the Living Father, I have re-elemented it ('ανεστοιχείωσα) wholly into Mine own life.—As then, although I was made Flesh, again I live through the living Father, retaining in myself the natural excellence of Him Who begat Me, so also he who, by the participation of My Flesh receiveth Me in himself, shall live, being wholly and altogether trans-elemented (μεταστοιχειούμενος) into Me, Who am able to give life, because I am of the life-giving Root, as it were, that is, God the Father.[56]

In the Eucharist, Pusey concluded, quoting St Ephraem, Christ both feeds us and commingles 'Himself with us and us with Him' in such a way as never to loose His hold on us. Once again we note the influence of the Eastern Fathers on Tractarian theology.

Much more might be said about the theological vision and inspiration of the Tractarians, and more will undoubtedly emerge in what follows as we look more individually and personally at the contribution of the Tractarian leaders and at their successors in what became a Catholic revival, which transformed the face of Anglicanism by recalling it to its roots in Scripture and Tradition. That there was a conservative, defensive side to the Oxford Movement is undoubted. Changes in contemporary society were too far-reaching for some of the causes which they sought to champion to be realistically defensible. Critical scholarship needed a greater sympathy than they were willing to accord it. Much of the religious polemic of the nineteenth century is narrow and dated, and some of it was certainly a fiddling whilst Rome burned. Yet it was far from being simply a reactionary movement, suffused with a warm glow of Romanticism. It was more theologically creative than that, and it was so primarily because it drew so deeply from the Fathers both in the matter and the manner of its theologizing.

II. John Keble and the High Church tradition

ON SUNDAY 14 July 1833 the Assize Sermon was preached in the University Church in Oxford by John Keble. He took as his theme 'National Apostasy'. That sermon was for John Henry Newman, recently returned to England after his Mediterranean travels, 'the start of the religious movement of 1833'. J. B. Mozley, a young undergraduate at Magdalen, declared the sermon to be 'the first regular remonstrance against the measures of the infidel party here, the first decided and printed protest from a minister of the Church in his proper and peculiar station'.[1]

The occasion of the sermon was the Irish Church Temporalities Bill, whereby the Whig Government of Earl Grey sought to re-organize and rationalize the bishoprics of the Church of Ireland and their endowments. The reasonableness of the measures proposed was not the central issue. In the context of the relationship of Church and state, of Parliamentary change, and of the granting of rights to Dissenters and Roman Catholics, the bill represented to churchmen like Keble a sacrilegious interference with church order by the secular power. Where order was attacked faith was at stake. A nation which 'for centuries acknowledged, as an essential part of its theory of government', that it was a Christian nation, was 'also a part of Christ's Church, and bound, in all her legislation and policy, by the fundamental rules of that Church'. If such rules are treated lightly, and cast aside by 'a fashionable liberality', is 'Apostasy', Keble asked his hearers, 'too hard a word to describe the temper of that nation?'[2]

Those who responded to the Assize Sermon as a symbol of protest on behalf of the Church—and not all churchmen who heard it saw it as such—did so as much because of the preacher as for what he had to say. John Keble's reputation as a man who had gained a double First, as the poet who was the author of *The Christian Year*, and as a priest whose pastoral gifts and holiness of life deeply influenced those who came in contact with him, ensured that his words had greater force. Dean Church described him as 'the true and primary author' of the Oxford Movement, and he brought to that Movement an upbringing in the tradition of Anglican high churchmanship as well as his poetic sensitivity.

John Keble was born in 1792 at Fairford in Gloucestershire, the son of another John Keble, who was the parish priest of the village of Coln St. Aldwyns three miles away. He grew up in the Gloucestershire countryside with a deep love of natural beauty, and an appreciation of plants and flowers and the changing seasons. The famous medieval stained glass of Fairford parish church, with its saints and biblical scenes, stamped on his mind the significance of symbol and imagery as channels of religious truth. The faith that he was taught by his father was moulded by the great Caroline divines of the seventeenth century. He reverenced the memory of Charles I as a martyr-king, who had died rather than compromise the faith and order of the Church of England. In a University sermon of 1831, preached on the anniversary of Charles's execution, Keble commented that: 'it must ever seem quite as natural, that the Church of England should keep this day, as it is that Christ's universal Church should keep the day of St. Stephen's martyrdom'.[3] The devotion of the non-jurors, and the sacramental piety and pastoral example of the seventeenth-century poet-priest, George Herbert, were other powerful influences. The books which Keble would recommend to those who sought his spiritual guidance and advice were, with the exception of the *Imitation of Christ*, the devotional works of the high Anglican tradition of the seventeenth and eighteenth centuries, blending theological reflection with prayer and pastoral concern: Jeremy Taylor's *Holy Living* and *Golden Grove*, the *Preces Privatae* of Bishop Lancelot Andrewes, John Kettlewell's *A Companion for the Penitent*, the *Sacra Privata* of Bishop Thomas Wilson of Sodor and Man, and William Law's *Serious Call to a Devout and Holy Life* and *Christian Perfection*.

In 1806 Keble went up to Oxford at the then usual age of 14, becoming a member of Corpus Christi College. Four years later he took a double first-class degree and the following year was elected to a fellowship at Oriel College, one of the most coveted academic honours in Oxford at the time. In 1815 he was ordained deacon, and a year later priest, serving country parishes near Fairford, but still keeping in touch with Oriel. In 1817 he was called back to Oriel as a college tutor, and brought to that office a strong pastoral sense, new to Oxford but which was to imprint itself on the educational

'The nucleus of the whole controversy', he writes, 'was undoubtedly the question of church authority: not so much the question as to the reach and limits of that authority . . . as . . . the question . . . with whom church authority resides.'[8] Keble saw Hooker as a defender of episcopacy and the doctrine of the apostolic succession, not going as far as later writers like Laud, Hammond, and Leslie, but laying the foundations for them and being in essential agreement with them.[9] He praised Hooker's strong sacramentalism; his sense of the mystery of the Incarnation, and that which he saw as consequent upon the doctrine of the Incarnation, 'the real, substantial Participation of Christ by His saints'.[10] From Hooker's sacramentalism Keble passed to his reverence for the ordinances, customs, and ceremonies of the Church, and saw Hooker as exemplifying the theological understanding of the early Fathers, and the Christian Platonism of the Greek Fathers in particular, which so influenced the Anglican tradition. What he has to say on this is worth quoting at length.

The truth is, Hooker's notion of ceremonies appears to have been the legitimate result of a certain high and rare course of thought, into which deep study of Christian antiquity would naturally guide a devout and reflective mind. The moral and devotional writings of the Fathers shew that they were deeply inbued with the evangelical sentiment, that Christians as such are living in a new heaven and a new earth; that to them 'old things are passed away,' and 'all things are becoming new;' that the very inanimate creation itself also is 'delivered from the bondage of corruption into the glorious liberty of the children of God.' Thus in a manner they seem to have realized, though in an infinitely higher sense, the system of Plato: everything to them existed in two worlds: in the world of sense, according to its outward nature and relations; in the world intellectual according to its spiritual associations. And thus did the whole scheme of material things, and especially those objects in it which are consecrated by scriptural allusion, assume in their eyes a sacramental or symbolical character.

   This idea, as it may serve to explain, if not to justify, many things, which to modern ears sound strange and forced in the imagery of the Fathers and in their interpretations of Scripture; so it may be of no small use in enabling us to estimate rightly the ceremonials of the Church. The primitive apostolical men, being daily and hourly accustomed to sacrifice and dedicate to God even ordinary things, by mixing them up with Christian and heavenly associations, might well consider every thing whatever as capable of becoming, so far, a means of grace, a pledge and token of Almighty presence and favour: and in that point of view might without scruple give the name of μυστήρια or sacraments to all those material objects which were any how taken unto the service of religion; whether by Scripture, in the way of type or figure; or by the Church, introducing them into her solemn ritual. . . . God omnipresent was so much in all their thoughts, that what to others would have been mere symbols, were to them designed expressions of His truth, providential intimations of His will. In this sense, the whole world, to them, was full of sacraments.[11]

Keble recognized that the context in which Hooker wrote meant that he had been more cautious in his attitude to ceremonies than Keble himself would have wished. He has no doubt, however, of the Patristic quality of Hooker's theology in this as in other matters, so that, as he puts it, 'Hooker's sympathy with the fourth century rather than the sixteenth is perpetually breaking out, however chastened by his too reasonable dread of superstition.'[12]

Keble's edition of Hooker was completed in 1841, but already in *The Christian Year* the sense of man existing in two worlds was evident:

> Two worlds are ours: 'tis only Sin
> Forbids us to descry
> The mystic heaven and earth within
> Plain as the sea and sky.

This understanding was part of his heritage from the theological tradition of classical Anglicanism, and was mediated in particular by the doctrine of analogy as expounded by Bishop Butler. But in Keble's hands it was re-shaped under the influence of Romanticism, and the theological doctrine became closely linked with a poetic theory. In his lectures as Professor of Poetry he linked the reverence which must characterize the response of faith with the nature of poetry: 'One most essential feature of all poetry is a due reserve, which always shrinks from pouring forth everything, worthy or unworthy, without selection or modesty. A certain reverence must be observed: as with sacred things, so here, everything must be touched upon with due reserve.'[13] The Romantic poets, Keble suggests, proclaim a depth in the natural order which is neglected by the scientific investigator, in the same way as the Fathers discern a depth in Scripture by their typological and allegorical interpretation. The Romantic poets, by reminding their readers of the mystery of creation, are a safeguard against an idolatry of the material world. In a similar way the Fathers free us from the imprisonment of the letter to enable us to live in the presence of the mystery of God's working of our salvation. We can progress, Keble said, from 'the way of regarding external things . . . as fraught with imaginative associations' to seeing in them 'parabolical lessons of conduct, or as a symbolical language in which God speaks to us of a world out of sight'.[14] We move from the poetical, the symbolizing tendency, to the moral—the employment of that capacity to bring about the betterment of human life—and finally to the mystical. This last, Keble believed, was 'the Christian, or Theological use of it, . . . the reducing of it to a particular set of symbols and associations, which we have reason to believe, has, more or less, the authority of the great Creator Himself'.[15] It is interesting, and perhaps not wholly out of place, to set this progression alongside Kierkegaard's account of religious life moving from the aesthetic, through the ethical to the religious.

It was Keble's own poetry, and particularly *The Christian Year*, which made him widely known. There were almost fifty editions between 1827 and Keble's death in 1866, and through it many were led to a renewed appreciation of symbol and imagery, and to the Prayer Book pattern of fast and festival. Keble's method was to build on a theme text from one of the readings of the day and draw out the symbolism both of Scripture and the natural order. The traditional high Anglican suspicion of 'enthusiasm' meant that Keble's work was viewed cautiously at first; Hurrell Froude thought that Keble might be taken for a Methodist. In fact the poems, though rather dated to late-twentieth-century taste, bear the impress of many characteristics of classical Christian spirituality, as well as the special qualities of joy, gentleness, and humility which were so personally attractive in John Keble.

The poem, 'New Every Morning is the love', now well known as a hymn, could be said to be Keble's version of Jean-Pierre de Caussade's 'sacrament of the present moment'.

> If on our daily course our mind
> Be set to hallow all we find,
> New treasures still, of countless price,
> God will provide for sacrifice.
>
> The trivial round, the common task,
> Will furnish all we ought to ask,—
> Room to deny ourselves; a road
> To bring us daily nearer God.[16]

The created world is seen as 'charged with the grandeur of God', transfigured by God's glory, for those with eyes to see and hearts open to the gracious working of the Spirit.

> When round Thy wondrous works below
> My searching rapturous glance I throw,
> Tracing Thy Wisdom, Power, and Love,
> In earth or sky, in stream or grove.[17]

In his poem on the Catechism Keble returned to a favourite theme, the inadequacy of human words to express the mystery of God whether in prayer or in doctrinal statement.

> And if some tones be false or low,
>   What are all prayers beneath
> But cries of babes, that cannot know
>   Half the deep thought they breathe?
>
> In His own words we Christ adore,
>   But Angels, as we speak,
> Higher above our meaning soar
>   Than we o'er children weak.[18]

In his poems concerned with moments of revelation other indications of this same emphasis appear. The natural order of creation can, for those with eyes to see, become that which proclaims God's glory:

> Thou who hast given me eyes to see
> And love this sight so fair;
> Give me a heart to find out Thee,
> And read Thee everywhere.[19]

Scripture, likewise, is a mirror reflecting the glory of God:

> Hold up thy mirror to the sun,
> And thou shalt need an eagle's gaze,
> So perfectly the polish'd stone
> Gives back the glory of his rays:
>
> Turn it, and it shall paint as true
> The soft green of the vernal earth,
> And each small flower of bashful hue
> That closest hides its lowly birth.

> Our mirror is a blessed book,
>   Where out from each illumin'd page
> We see one glorious Image look
>   All eyes to dazzle and enrage,—
>
> The Son of God: and that indeed
>   We see Him as He is, we know,
> Since in the same bright glass we read
>   The very life of things below.[20]

The mirror of God's glory is both dazzling and accurate, and the demand for the certainty of perfect knowledge proves to be a demand which if met would overwhelm, and to which the true response is that of adoration.

> Is there, on earth, a spirit frail,
>   Who fears to take their word,
> Scarce daring, through the twilight pale,
>   To think be sees the Lord?
> With eyes too tremblingly awake
> To bear with dimness for His sake?
> Read and confess the hand divine
> That drew thy likeness here so true in every line.
>
> For all thy rankling doubts so sore,
>   Love thou thy Saviour still,
> Him for thy Lord and God adore,
>   And ever do His will.
> Though vexing thoughts may seem to last,
> Let not thy soul be quite o'er cast;—
> Soon will He shew thee all His wounds and say
> 'Long have I known thy name—know thou my face alway.'[21]

It is the pure in heart who see God, and it is the saints of God who through grace shine with the light of God. They are 'earth's gems' caught by the fire of heaven, or, as Keble put it in a later poem, 'the Saviour in His people crown'd'. In a vivid image Keble compares the coruscating light of the waterfall, which unites myriads of drops of water in a single current, with the individual yet corporate brilliance of the communion of saints.

> Go where the waters fall
>   Sheer from the mountain's height!

> Mark how, a thousand streams in one,
> One in a thousand, on they fare,
> Now flashing to the sun,
> Now still as beast in lair. . . .

In the same way individual Christians can seem as separate as the drops of water cascading in the waterfall, but it is the common water of baptismal life which sustains them and bears them onwards to a common destiny.

> If of the Living Cloud they be
> Baptismal drops, and onward press
> Toward the Living Sea
> By deeds of holiness,
>
> Then to the Living Waters still
> (O joy with trembling!) they pertain,
> Join'd by some hidden rill,
> Low in Earth's darkest vein.[22]

This poem dates from 1844, and from the same year comes one which indicates the place which Marian devotion came to have in Keble's understanding of the communion of saints, though it was a poem that, on the advice of Keble's friends, was not originally published in the volume, *Lyra Innocentium*, for which it was intended.

> Mother of God! O, not in vain
> We learn'd of old thy lowly strain,
> Fain in thy shadow would we rest,
> And kneel with thee, and call thee blest;
> With thee would "magnify the Lord",
> And if thou art not here adored,
> Yet seek we, day by day, the love and fear
> Which bring thee, with all saints, near and more near.
>
> What glory thou above hast won,
> By special grace of thy dear Son,
> We see not yet, nor dare espy
> Thy crowned form with open eye.

If the heavenly glory of the Virgin is now hidden from human eyes, and only the mother at Bethlehem or Nazareth is given to us, yet

Mary's bearing of Christ in whom Godhead and manhood are substantially united gives her the highest of places in the Church's veneration of the saints of God.

> Thenceforth, Whom thousand world adore,
> He calls thee Mother evermore;
> Angel nor Saint His face may see
> Apart from what He took of thee.
> How may we choose but name thy name,
> Echoing below in high acclaim
> In holy Creed? Since earthly song and prayer
> Must keep faint time to the dread anthem there.

The Angelus prayer, 'Hail, Mary, full of grace!' is our appropriate response, as it was Gabriel's greeting, to Mary the image of the Church.

> . . . unforbidden may we speak
> An Ave to Christ's Mother meek.
> (As children with "good morrow" come
> To elders in some happy home:)
> Inviting so the saintly host above
> With our unworthiness to pray in love.
>
> To pray with us, and gently bear
> Our falterings in the pure bright air.[23]

If this poem dates from 1844, already in the poem for the Annunciation in *The Christian Year* some seventeen years earlier Keble could write the couplet:

> Ave Maria! thou whose name
> All but adoring love may claim. . . .

The later poem is more explicit in its affirmation of the place of Mary in Christian doctrine and devotion, and in claiming the prayers of the saints, and of the Virgin in particular, but the devotion is already there in the earlier one. The background is both the early Fathers and the seventeenth-century divines, though Keble goes beyond a writer like Bishop Bull, who is on the one hand willing to ascribe any honour to the Virgin which does not derogate from God, but on the other hand will not allow invocation, and can state that 'the Virgin herself was more blessed by conceiving Christ in her heart by faith, than by conceiving Him in her womb'.[24]

Newman said of Keble that 'he did for the Church of England what none but a poet could do: he made it poetical'.[25] Keble might have said that through poetry he attempted to re-awaken a sacramental sense. He believed that poetry had a cathartic function, but in the early centuries of the Church 'the mysteries of divine Truth had supplied the place of poetry'.[26] The sacramental operation of the grace of God in the prayer and worship of the Church was the means of a deeper healing than poetry could provide. In an age when the sacramental grace was neglected poetry once again became a means of expressing man's spiritual need, and could become the way by which men and women were led to a rediscovery of sacramental religion. So Keble wrote at the conclusion of his *Lectures on Poetry*:

We must go back to the very beginning and foundation of all Poetry. Our conclusion was, that this divine art essentially consisted in the power of healing and restoring overburdened and passionate minds. It follows that the more deeply any feeling penetrates human affections, and the more permanently it influences them, the closer are its relationships and associations with Poetry.[27]

The deepest feelings of all are religious, and so religion necessarily makes use of poetry, for poetry 'supplies a rich wealth of similes whereby a pious mind may supply and remedy, in some sort, its powerlessness of speech; and may express many things more touchingly, many things more seriously and weightily, all things more truly, than had been possible without this aid'.[28] The poet by moving men's hearts with image and simile is not merely creating arbitrary pictures of a fantasy world but also leading men to a deeper awareness of the nature of their own existence and of the world which they inhabit.

The various images and similes of things, and all other poetic charms, are not merely the play of a keen and clever mind, nor to be put down as empty fancies: but rather they guide as by gentle hints and no uncertain signs, to the very utterances of Nature, or we may more truly say, of the Author of Nature.... In short, Poetry lends Religion her wealth of symbols and similes; Religion restores these again to Poetry, clothed with so splendid a radiance that they appear to be no longer merely symbols, but to partake (I might almost say) of the nature of sacraments.[29]

Furthermore, Keble went on, the poet and the man of faith share a common conviction that there is more to life than what meets the eye, that we are part of a greater whole than we can fully recognize.

Those who, from their very heart, either burst into poetry, or seek the Deity in prayer, must needs ever cherish with their whole spirit the vision of something more beautiful, greater and more lovable, than all that mortal eye can see. Thus the very practice and cultivation of Poetry will be found to possess, in some sort, the power and guiding and composing the mind to worship and prayer: provided indeed the poems contain nothing hurtful either to religion or morality.[30]

Both the poet and the man of faith are called to a whole-hearted commitment and attentiveness. And so Keble warns that 'no poet will ever be great who does not constantly spend time and toil in studying the beauty of earth and sky so as to make every detail of the whole bear upon the object of his own love and enthusiasm'. No more 'will any one make the slightest progress in holiness and piety who is content with the empty praises of good books or good men and makes no attempt to imitate them in his own life'.[31] From the poetry of the heart fostered by such discipline Keble looked to see a re-kindling of the Christian imagination, and he himself notably contributed to it.

The allusive quality and symbolic character of poetry made it for Keble a powerful vehicle of Christian truth. Keble knew well the inadequacy of human language to convey the mystery of God. He was suspicious of the easy religion of slogans and the equally easy religion of superficially stirred emotions, both of which he saw as characteristic of much of the popular Evangelicalism of his day. He was no less critical of a rationalist theology in which moral truth became a matter of syllogisms. Faith was indeed of the heart as well as of the head, but it was not of a heart worn upon the sleeve. When Keble prepared Charlotte Yonge, the novelist, for confirmation, he warned her of two dangers: of speaking too freely and easily of church matters—the ecclesiastical gossip which failed to recognize and respect the holiness of the church and its worship—and of loving Christian symbolism merely for its beauty and its poetry. It was a failure to exercise a due 'reserve' that had led on the one hand to the over-definition of Christian doctrine which Keble saw in the Roman Catholic doctrine of transubstantiation as an explanation of the reality of Christ's Presence in the Eucharist, and on the other hand, in reaction to this doctrine, to denials of any Real Presence in the Eucharist at all. In his *Sermon on Primitive Tradition* he makes his point quite clearly:

> Transubstantiation on the one hand . . . the denial of Christ's real presence on the other. . . . The two errors in the original are perhaps but rationalism in two different forms; endeavours to explain away, and bring nearer to the human intellect, that which had been left thoroughly mysterious both by Scripture and tradition. They would turn the attention of man from the real life-giving miracle to mere metaphysical or grammatical subtleties, such as our fathers never knew.[32]

Keble protested against many of the academic theologians of his day for their 'habit of resolving the high mysteries of the faith into mere circumstances of language, methods of speaking adapted to our weak understanding, but with no real counterpart in the nature of things'.[33] We must be alert, he says, to the danger of 'slighting divine mysteries because we cannot comprehend and explain them', and he is never tired of reminding his hearers that it is only the pure in heart who see God. Theology is properly doxology, worship, and so there must always be a sense of awe and wonder in our approach to God, whether as theologians or as Christian believers. Theology and spirituality must be closely joined. Keble's theology, like that of the Orthodox churches both today and throughout their history, can be properly said to be mystical theology, prayed theology. He would well have understood what the great Byzantine mystic St. Symeon the New Theologian wrote at the turn of the first millennium, speaking of man's knowledge of God:

> We can know God in the same way a man can see a limitless ocean when he is standing by the shore with a candle during the night. Do you think he can see very much? Nothing much, scarcely anything. And yet, he can see the water well, he knows that in front of him is the ocean, and that this ocean is enormous and that he cannot contain it all in his gaze. So it is with our knowledge of God.[34]

If the way of holiness, enabled by the grace of God given most especially in the sacraments, was the way by which God made Himself known, then the worship of the Church was the means by which men and women were led along that way. For an Anglican that meant the Prayer Book, though the Prayer Book seen against the background of the Church of the Fathers. For the ordinary Christian believer, Keble wrote, 'in all great things the Prayer Book is really the voice of the ancient Church'.[35] He came to see, however, that the Prayer Book had deficiencies when compared with the ancient liturgies, and could write in the preface to the second part of Hurrell Froude's *Remains* (1839) that, through the work of William Palmer and Bishop Lloyd, the publication of Cranmer's works and the reprinting of the two Prayer Books of Edward VI, 'our old notions about the perfection of the Liturgy were dispelled'. As Froude put it, it was 'crumbs from the Apostles' table'.[36] Keble's apparent endorsement of Froude's views led Isaac Williams to publish a Tract on the Prayer Book in which he stressed the virtues of the Prayer Book as inculcating penitence and obedience, even though there were losses. Somewhat to his surprise Keble agreed with him. But the losses were there nonetheless, as Williams made clear:

We cannot look into Breviaries and Missals without observing their high choral tone in distinction from our own. To advert to particulars, we have the ancient kyrie eleison but the hallelujahs, . . . the hosannas at the end of the Trisagion, the Gloria Deo at the Gospel (except as observed by traditionary use) are omitted. . . . From the Prayer for the Church Militant we have excluded the more solemn commendation to God and prayer for the dead . . . and in the Prayer of Oblation, the beautiful mention of angelic ministries, as bearing our supplications into the presence of the Divine Majesty, is lost.[37]

Subsequent liturgical change was to restore many of these things.

Keble's theology was particularly concerned with sanctification, and it became increasingly a eucharistically centred theology. This is brought out clearly in an important sermon he delivered in Scotland on the Sunday on which the new Communion Office was introduced in the Episcopal Church. In this he roots Christian sanctification in the offering of the Son in obedience to the Father's will.

Sanctification, in its ordinary, scriptural meaning, seems primarily to refer to the solemn act of God the Son, setting Himself apart to do God's will in his Incarnation and Death, and in the whole economy of salvation. Sanctification, like Righteousness, is the property of Christ our Head: to us His members and to all created things . . . it is vouchsafed . . . in a secondary and derivative sense.[38]

The Eucharist is the special focus of God's work of sanctification. It puts Christians in mind of the work of Christ and is the means whereby they share in His life and action. It no less puts God in mind of the work of Christ, through the 'remembering' of the mighty acts of salvation. It is both sacrifice and sacrament:

'For their sakes I am sanctifying myself, that they also may be sanctified through the Truth' . . . This one saying of Christ conveys apparently in itself the two chief points of the evangelical doctrine concerning the holy and blessed Eucharist: first, that it is His memorial Sacrifice, a means of obtaining God's favour and pardon for all such as truly repent: next that it is a most high Sacrament, a means whereby we are united to Christ, and so made more and more partakers of His righteousness here, and His glory hereafter. 'I sanctify myself': there is the Sacrifice; 'that they also may be sanctified through the Truth': there is the Sacrament.[39]

Because the basis of the Eucharist is Christ's self-offering, God acts in it despite the involuntary defects of rites and ceremonies. Furthermore, if the Eucharist is the appointed way by which we share in the holiness of God and the offering of Christ, then in the Sacrament we may rightly adore Christ's presence. There is no more reason to object to such adoration focused on the Sacrament on the grounds that it is an imprisonment of God than to object to the Incarnation itself. Indeed, the Eucharist is an extension of the Incarnation, and calls us to special worship and adoration, because of the greatness of the benefit God gives us, the fact that it is offered to each one of us personally and individually, and that in the offering of this gift we know the depth of Christ's condescension to us and his willingness to humble Himself.

That, therefore, of which we eat, the same we are most humbly to worship; not the less, but the more, because in so giving Himself to us He is stooping so very low for our sakes. . . . If we really believe that that which He declares to be His own Flesh and Blood is Jesus Christ giving Himself to us under the form of Bread and Wine, how can we help thanking, and therefore adoring, (for to thank God is to adore), the unspeakable Gift, as well as the most bountiful Giver? seeing that in this case both are one.[40]

The importance which John Keble, in common with the other Tractarians, attached to the Eucharist meant an increase in the number of celebrations and a more frequent receiving of communion. Keble considered that this could bring with it dangers from the too light regarding of holy things, and so preferred that more frequent communion should be accompanied by a stricter discipline. In particular he looked for the revival of the discipline of sacramental Confession. In the parish this would help the priest to know intimately the needs of his people: 'we go on working in the dark . . . until the rule of systematic Confession is revived in our Church'.[41] Keble himself was much used as a confessor, and his counsel on penance in his letters is always marked by understanding and charitable concern, reminding us of Fénelon or St. Francis de Sales, though there are also elements of Tractarian strictness. Jeremy Taylor and Kettlewell's *Companion to the Penitent* are recommended as good guides in preparation for Confession. Keble saw sacramental Confession as part of the ordinary ministrations of the village priest to his parish. The parish priest to be a true pastor had to know and guide his people, and therefore to be prepared to lead them gently to speak of the deep matters of faith and of their own spiritual needs. It was his own practice to begin all pastoral visits with prayer in order to overcome embarrassment in talking of such matters. He considered it best to avoid phrases like 'direction' and 'auricular confession' because of their associations. What was important was the spiritual reality of sacramental Confession, and to that men needed to be brought with love and sensitivity. So he could write, albeit in a somewhat sentimental, Victorian vein, that:

. . . a few grains of old English common sense, or rather of Christian prudence and charity, applied to the realities of English life (a grace to be specially prayed for as well as cultivated) . . . will be rewarded, through God's blessing, with many a repetition of that sight, dear to angels, (if one may say so without presumption), of a noble-hearted English peasant on his knees in humble confession, making an unreserved offering of himself, and never dreaming that what he is about is at all out of the common.[42]

Keble was always suspicious of a demand for 'a minute and incessant direction'. That was 'a morbid craving'. He was sensitive to the dangers of hero-worship, of idolizing the confessor, and his own letters of spiritual counsel frequently begin with a heartfelt disclaimer of his own ability and worthiness as a spiritual guide. When his friend Pusey made his confession to him in 1846 Keble not unnaturally shrank from the role of confessor.

As to directing you I know I shall be utterly bewildered, were it only from ignorance and inexperience. You must really think beforehand what is most likely to do you good. Mere suffering is the first and simplest thought: but then there are duties to be done. And have we a right to disqualify ourselves for them? Is it not best to leave it to the Almighty to do so if He see fit, by sickness.[43]

He urged Pusey not to punish himself too sharply, and when Pusey suggested that part of the ascetic discipline he proposed to adopt should include not smiling except when with children or when it seemed a matter of love, Keble commented that not smiling was merely a penalty imposed on others rather than on oneself. He wrote to Pusey:

God be thanked if He has made His precious gifts available to you through the like of me. . . . You must pray for me . . . that I may be contrite—that is really what I want and need. You need not fear my treating myself too austerely: my tendencies and habits, I am sorry to say, lie far too much the other way, and circumstances besides are against it. . . . For my sake, and for all our sakes, be not hard upon yourself—remember what is said about 'often infirmities.'[44]

In the sacrament of Confession and in spiritual guidance, as in theology, Keble was suspicious of the cut and dried statement: he commented to Newman that he had always fancied that Newman was 'over sanguine in making things square, and did not quite allow enough for Bishop Butler's notion of doubt and intellectual difficulty being some men's element and appropriate trial'.[45] So he could write:

As the tender and anxious conscience is won by the expectation of some peculiar, untried repose, to be found in Roman Catholic confessionals only; forgetting that the same treasure of pardon is by God's mercy already within its reach: so the restless argumentative intellect thinks to take refuge in the doctrine of infallibility; not considering, that by a like effort, we might as well, if so disposed, silence our scruples in continuing where God has placed us.

But why should imperfect beings such as we are, depend on assurance of either kind?[46]

Keble firmly believed that it was his duty to remain where God had placed him, and believed no less firmly that the Church in which God had placed him, though imperfect in many respects, was part of Christ's Holy Catholic Church. He believed himself called to serve both its holiness and its catholicity, knowing that that could lead to a way of the Cross within as well as outside the Church. He recognized that, for many who shared his convictions of the Catholic heritage of the Church of England, the state of the Church would appear to be only a 'conditional, temporary footing ... so unsatisfactory, so miserably poor and meagre, so unlike the glorious vision which they have been used to gaze on of the one Catholic Apostolic Church'. Such experience, however, is the lot of every Christian in whatever communion.

Men will not escape from this state of decay by going elsewhere, though they may shut their eyes to the reality of it. Rather, whatever our position be in the Church, since God Almighty has assigned it to us for our trial, shall we not accept it and make the best of it, in humble confidence that according to our faith it will be to us?[47]

Not only was the communion in which he had been placed important to Keble, but his role within the Church was likewise to be accepted in humility. He quoted with approval George Herbert's warning that 'ambition or an untimely desire of high advancement, under colour of doing more good, is a great stumbling block to the holiness of scholars'. God, he believed (and told an Oxford congregation in 1841) 'from time to time prepares persons who are to do Him service in the way of self-sacrifice, by deep retirement, by quiet study and devotion'.[48] That was his own calling: as one who was never promoted to high office in the Church, and yet whose sanctity of life was such that he exercised a continuing influence on the Church of his day; so much so that on his death in 1866 men met to found an Oxford college in memory of him, which would enshrine the principles by which he lived.

Priest, pastor and poet, John Keble was all three, and the way in which he lived out that three-fold calling was perhaps his most important contribution to the Oxford Movement. Some have characterized him as a man of limitations, and in some respects those limitations are obvious. The Assize Sermon reflected an understanding of the Church of England, which was no longer viable in a society being transformed by the social change of the industrial revolution, and the political currents stemming from the French Revolution. Though equally, his sense of the Catholic Church as wider than the

Church of England and with a richer heritage than many contemporary churchmen recognized, redeemed the Oxford Movement from mere conservative parochialism. Other limitations were self-chosen and were an essential part of Keble's understanding of the ascetic discipline that the way of Christian holiness involved. Isaac Williams said of him that 'Keble made humility the one great study of his life' with the result, as Williams saw it, that 'there was such a reality and truth about him that even good men of an opposite school in religion appeared to one as counterfeits, when one was used to him; and one felt oneself hollow from the contrast'.[49] In 1875 the ageing Newman wrote to Pusey of the power of Keble and of the enormous difficulty of adequately characterizing him:

How can I profess to paint a man who will not sit for his portrait? how can I draw out his literary merits, when he considers it his special office to edit, or to translate, or to discourse in a dead language, or to sing hymns?

It was no accident that he is thus difficult to bring under the jurisdiction of the critic. He had as little aim at literary success in what he wrote, as most authors have a thirst for attaining it.[50]

And Newman concluded:

As to Mr Keble, all I venture to say of him in this respect is this:—that his keen religious instincts, his unworldly spirit, his delicacy of mind, his tenderness of others, his playfulness, his loyalty to the Holy Fathers, and his Toryism in politics, are all ethical qualities, and by their prominence give a character of their own, or (as I have called it) personality, to what he has written; but these would have succeeded in developing that personality into sight and shape in the medium of literature, had he not been possessed of special intellectual gifts, which they both elicited and used.[51]

Isaac Williams, looking back to the early days of the Oriel reading parties in the Cotswolds, could speak of Keble's impact on him as that of 'one so overflowing with real genuine love in thought, word, and action' which 'was quite new to me, I could scarcely understand it'. 'Each of us was always delighted to walk with him, Wilberforce to gather instruction for the schools, and the rest of us for love's sake.'[52] If we would look for the secret of Keble's influence it is surely in that combination of magnetism and reserve, the hidden qualities of humility and holiness, that led his contemporaries to venerate him as something close to a saint.

Two years before his death John Keble preached a sermon at the anniversary festival of the theological college at Cuddesdon. He gave it the title 'Pentecostal Fear'. In that sermon he spoke of the gift of the Spirit as the source of all holiness and as the basis of all Christian ministry. The theme of the Christian way as one of divinization, familiar from the Greek Fathers, here appears as central to Keble's own spirituality.

Christ is come, not indeed in the Body, but by a nearer, far nearer Presence— by His Spirit: not only *with* them, but *within* them. In Him they now live a new life, which they have entirely from Him; a life which is both His and theirs; whereby they are so joined to Him as to be verily and indeed partakers of a Divine nature.

Yes, my brethren, this and no less was the mysterious Whitsun privilege and glory of those on whom the Holy Ghost first came down: a glory so high and inconceivable, that the Holy Fathers did not hesitate to call it even Deification, and Christianity, which teaches and confers it, they called 'a deifying discipline.'[53]

It is the gift of the Spirit which is the supreme joy and wonder of the Christian life, and yet it is that same gift which is, to those who recognize its stupendous greatness, truly awesome. Keble exhorted his hearers to see 'the fear of God as a Pentecostal grace', and to recognize 'the greatness, the constant presence, the divinity of the unspeakable Gift by which every duty is done, which causes the duty to become so great and aweful, and which throngs the whole of a man's course alike with glorious opportunities and exceeding dangers'. It is indeed a gift of love, although a love which is no sentimental benevolence, but which co-exists with fear of God. But, he went on, 'perhaps in strictness of language it ought not to be spoken of as fear, but as intense, unspeakable adoration, a bowing down to the Light unapproachable, the Presence of which no creature can be worthy'.[54] It is the light of Transfiguration.

Keble concluded with a contrast between the ministry of two clergy, one of whom believes in the reality of the gift of the Divine life and the holiness that it both brings and demands, and the other who does not.

One man goes about his parish with the ever-present belief, that both he and everyone whom he meets, had the Holy Spirit within him—both he and they by Holy Baptism, he also, in a peculiar sense, by Holy Orders. Another, perhaps, no less earnest in work, is mainly taken up with natural and social differences. One goes into a Church, thinks of Isaiah's vision, says to himself, 'here is the Lord, sitting on His throne, high and lifted up, and His glory filling the place: here are the angels, hither Christ coming in His Sacraments.' To another the place is nothing mysterious; he thinks only of edification and comfortable prayer.[55]

We need have no doubt which was John Keble's own understanding.

III. John Henry Newman: Doctrine and Development

IN HIS University Sermon of January 1832, 'Personal Influence the Means of Propagating the Truth', Newman commented that in the matter of moral character 'it is as impossible to write and read a man (so to express it) as to give literal depth to a painted tablet'.[1] Those who have written of Newman have found themselves confronted with a supreme example of just this problem. His rôle and influence in the Oxford Movement is inseparable from his personal pilgrimage, externally from the Church of England to the Church of Rome and internally *ex umbris et imaginibus in veritatem*, 'from shadows and images into truth'. Wilfrid Ward, his perceptive biographer, noted how the epithets 'mystic', 'controversialist', 'theologian', 'recluse' were each applicable and none altogether accurate or exhaustive.[2] Again, it was psychological rather than logical subtlety which was Newman's primary hallmark. He knew, as he put it in the Tamworth Reading Room Letters, that 'the heart is commonly reached, not by the reason, but by the imagination'. In the *Lectures on the Prophetical Office of the Church* he explored the ways in which that imagination was sustained within the Christian community, probing the interaction of the formal and informal manifestations of tradition and the balance of rôles of prophet, priest, and king within the Church. He suspected accounts of the relationship of faith and reason which were so cut and square that they abstracted human knowing from the human knower, and demanded of believers an intellectual capacity and facility of weighing evidence, which would have made faith a matter of conclusions achievable, if at all, only by the learned. The influence of Newman extended in his own time, and has extended subsequently, far beyond the particular concerns of the Oxford Movement. The ideas matured in Oxford in the 1830s bore fruit in *The Idea of a University* and *The Grammar of Assent*, works which in their different ways challenged fashionable assumptions about education and culture on the one hand and about the genesis and nature of faith on the other. His influence on contemporary Roman Catholicism has been significant, Dr Prickett going so far as to comment that 'through Newman, the Anglican tradition of Coleridge has become part of the heritage of the Roman Catholic Church itself'.[3] Both Newman and Manning as Roman Catholics opposed that liberalism which dissolved faith into the relativities of opinion, but they did so in different ways. Manning represented the Ultramontane emphasis on authority, but without Newman's subtle understanding of the way in which such authority was maintained and exercised within the context of a living, historical community. Newman was aware of the ambiguities of all ecclesiastical power and could write in the important preface to the third edition of the *Lectures on the Prophetical Office of the Church* that 'there may indeed be holiness in the religious aspect of the Church, and soundness in her theological, but still there is in her the ambition, craft, and cruelty of a political power'.[4] Impeccability is not promised to the Church. And so in this respect his understanding of the doctrine of papal infallibility, which he thought it inopportune for the Vatican Council of 1870 to define, was marked by an awareness of the limitations of that doctrine.

I conceive then that the Depositum is in such sense committed to the Church or to the Pope, that when the Pope sits in St. Peter's chair, or when a Council of Fathers & doctors is collected round him, it is capable of being presented to their minds with that fullness and exactness, under the operation of supernatural grace, (so far forth and in such portion of it as the occasion requires,) with which it habitually, not occasionally, resided in the minds of the Apostles;—a vision of it, not logical, and therefore consistent with errors of reasoning & of fact in the enunciation, after the manner of an intuition or an instinct.[5]

Here infallibility is talked of in words such as 'intuition' and 'instinct' which have a personal, not a legal or scholastic, reference. Just as Newman always asks how people actually believe, in what way faith can seek understanding, so he asks how the mind of the Church is actually articulated, and from his study of the history of the Church knows that it is not, in W. G. Ward's celebrated phrase, by 'a papal bull at breakfast every day'.

Wilfrid Ward said of Newman's temper that it was 'akin to that of More and Erasmus, who rejected scholastic subtlety and undue dogmatism, but were, nevertheless, filled with enthusiasm for ancient ways and venerable traditions'. It was an expression of the patristic and Benedictine character, contrasted with that of Manning, who, for all his opposition to the Jesuits, was at one with them in his understanding of authority and discipline.[6] A similar distinction is made by Newman himself in one of his Oratory papers, in which he contrasts Oratorian freedom and Jesuit discipline, the legion and the phalanx, the Athenian and the Spartan. 'Obedience to the official Superior is the prominent principle of the Jesuit; personal influence is that of the Oratorian.'[7] Personal influence and personal communication were central to Newman's understanding of the Christian faith and its communication. To profess the Christian faith was to respond to God's own self-communication in Christ and to live by Christ's Spirit. The call to holiness was inseparable from the call to preach the Gospel. Holiness was for Newman 'the great end of preaching'.[8] Christian faith and life must be conjoined. The unsystematic character of Scripture is a mark of its practical orientation. 'The object of the Written Word' is 'not to unfold a system for our intellectual contemplation, but to secure the formation of a certain character.'[9] So likewise the sacramental worship of the Church, its imagery and symbolism, were 'keys and spells' to enable men and women to enter into an awareness of the mystery of God as the source and goal of their lives.

Unlike Keble and Pusey, Newman's ancestry was not the old High Church tradition of Anglicanism. He was born in 1801, the eldest of six children of a London banker, described by Francis Newman as 'somewhat free-thoughted, fond of seeing what different people had to say for their opinions'.[10] His mother taught her family a simple Bible Christianity. Marked from his early days with both a sceptical intellect and imaginative power, moved by Scott and the *Arabian Nights* as well as challenged by the sceptical writings of Hume and Tom Paine, Newman experienced his first deep spiritual experience in 1816 in what he called his 'great change of thought'. Illness and financial disaster in the family were the context of this conversion when, as he wrote in the *Apologia*, 'I fell under the influences of a definite Creed, and received into my intellect impressions of dogma, which through God's mercy, have never been effaced or obscured'. His schoolmaster at Ealing, the Revd Walter Mayers, had a powerful influence, stressing that the Christian faith was to be embraced as 'a principle of spiritual life and action', and teaching, unlike some contemporary Evangelicals, that there was 'a gradual progress by which the knowledge of divine things' was imparted.[11]

When Newman wrote that this 1816 experience of conversion meant that he received into his mind 'impressions of dogma', what he had gained was a new sense of the reality of God; a conviction that his life was henceforth to be understood in the context of 'two and two only absolute and luminously self-evident beings, myself and my Creator'; and a quality of certitude in faith combined with an Evangelical assurance of election. He took two mottoes from the Evangelical commentator, Thomas Scott, as guides for his Christian living: 'holiness rather than peace' and 'growth the only evidence of life'.[12]

In 1817 Newman went up to Trinity College, Oxford. His intention was to become a barrister after taking his degree. He was a serious and studious undergraduate, disapproving of the wild behaviour of some of his contemporaries, but also showing an unusual interest in music with his playing of the violin. Apart from the normal classical and mathematical Oxford curriculum Newman attended lectures on geology and fed his interest in history by reading Gibbon's *Decline and Fall*. His intellectual capacity was widely recognized, and he was expected to gain an outstanding degree. Overwork, however, brought about a collapse at his finals, a lower second class in classics and a failure in mathematics. It was a failure, however, which he was to redeem a year later by his success in the Oriel fellowship examination, the most demanding intellectual test in Oxford at the time.

Newman entered Oriel as an awkward, shy Evangelical, and an Evangelical moreover whose links were more with the radical millenarian Evangelicalism centred on St. Edmund Hall than with the school of Charles Simeon and William Wilberforce. In Oriel Common Room he found himself a member of a close-knit community of sharp minds and remarkable personalities: Edward Hawkins, initially influential on Newman but later, as Provost, to be one with whom Newman disagreed sharply over the pastoral office of the tutor; Richard Whately, the logician who liked to use young minds as anvils to hammer out ideas; Edward Copleston, the Provost, who had played a large part in Oriel's rise to intellectual eminence; John Keble; Renn Dickson Hampden, with whom twelve years later the Tractarians were to disagree sharply. Thomas Arnold, later Headmaster of Rugby, had only recently vacated his fellowship. It is not surprising that Newman could write to his father that he was now 'a member of "the School of Speculative Philosophy in

England"' and that he had, whenever he wished, 'the advice and direction of the first men in Oxford'.[13] Later influences were to come with the election of Edward Pusey (1823), Hurrell Froude, and Robert Wilberforce (1826).

During the ten years from his election as a fellow of Oriel in 1822 to his Mediterranean journey with the Froudes immediately preceding the year 1833 which marked the beginning of the Oxford Movement, Newman's thought developed in a number of different directions. The logical power of Whately, acting on his own deep religious feeling and sceptical intellect, forced him to probe deeply into the relationship of faith and reason, and the justification of religious belief. From Whately he learnt to see the importance of *a priori* arguments, what he called 'antecedent probability' or 'presumption'. As he put it in a University Sermon of 1839: 'Faith is influenced by previous notices, prepossessions, and (in a good sense of the word) prejudices; but Reason, by direct and definite proof.'[14] Newman argued that 'we do not call for evidence till antecedent probabilities fail'. We are guided by common sense and live inevitably by the wisdom of received opinions. Faith is always seeking understanding, it is not through the arguments of the understanding that we are led to faith, though through a close examination of those arguments we may come to recognize more clearly the universal character of faith. In the Church it is tradition which represents the *sensus fidelium*, and it was Hawkins, who had preached a powerful sermon on tradition the year before Newman was elected to his fellowship, the text of which Newman subsequently read, who brought home to Newman the importance of tradition as the context in which Scripture was to be received and understood. In 1825 he studied Butler's *Analogy*, and this had the effect, Newman records, of 'placing his doctrinal views on a broad philosophical basis, with which an emotional religion could have little sympathy'.[15] As Newman noted in the *Apologia*, Butler laid the foundation on which, under Whately's influence, he was to build, that 'Probability is the guide of life.' This led him, he wrote, 'to the question of the logical cogency of Faith' to which he gave a large part of his intellectual endeavour.[16] But Butler was also important because of his stress on the importance of 'a visible Church, the oracle of truth and a pattern of sanctity, of the duties of external religion, and of the historical character of Revelation'. He pointed Newman to a sacramental understanding of Christianity, an understanding which was reinforced by Keble, who himself had a deep reverence for the work of Butler, though Isaac Williams noted that Keble's influence on Newman was mediated by Hurrell Froude, who gave to Keble's ideas an argumentative force of his own.[17]

In 1823 and 1824 Newman attended the lectures of Charles Lloyd at Christ Church, and though Lloyd does not seem to have had the same influence on him as he did on Pusey, he contributed to freeing Newman from some of his debilitating shyness. Lloyd's liturgical interests were also important in that they brought out the continuity of the Prayer Book services with those of the medieval Church, a point not lost on the young Hurrell Froude. Newman confessed that he both felt 'constrained and awkward in the presence of Lloyd', and yet came to hold him in 'affectionate and grateful memory'. In part this was because of the rivalry between Oriel and Christ Church, which came out in Lloyd's antagonism to Whately, who was in the habit of referring to the Fathers as 'certain old divines'. Looking back Newman recognized Lloyd's Catholic tone of mind and was willing to utilize some of Lloyd's earlier arguments when called upon to defend Tract XC. On Lloyd's untimely death soon after becoming Bishop of Oxford, Newman wrote:

I had the greatest esteem, respect, and love for him as a most warm-hearted, frank, vigorous-minded and generous man. His kindness for me I cannot soon forget. He brought me forward, made me known, spoke well of me, and gave me confidence in myself. . . . I wish he ever had been aware how much I felt his kindness.[18]

A letter of Froude's from 1830 indicates that Lloyd's classes were, along with Keble's influence, the source of the pastoral conception of the tutor's role about which Newman, Froude, and Robert Wilberforce were to come into conflict with Provost Hawkins.[19]

Lloyd also gave approval to Newman's plan of reading the Fathers, who were to become one of the major formative influences upon him. He had first come across references to the Fathers in Joseph Milner's Evangelical Church history, which he read at school, and further knowledge of the history of the patristic period had come from Gibbon. By his own account Milner's work had led him to 'an imaginative devotion' to the Fathers and their times, even before he had read a single one of their writings. The task of writing about ecclesiastical miracles and Apollonius of Tyana in 1825–6 pushed him further in a patristic direction, and at the same time he was pressed by Edward Smedley, the editor of the *Encyclopaedia Metropolitana*, for a substantial study on the second-century Fathers, a study Newman wished to expand to 'the period between the Apostolical Fathers and the Nicene Council ... treated as a whole, embracing the opinions etc of the Church, and so much of Platonism and Gnosticism as may be necessary to elucidate its history'.[20] He asked Pusey, who was in Germany, to obtain copies of the Fathers for him, and he received them in Oxford in October 1827. In June of the following year he began the systematic reading of the Fathers and by the end of that Long Vacation had read and noted the Epistle of Barnabas, the Epistles of Clement of Rome, Ignatius of Antioch, Justin, Tatian, and Athenagoras. The reading of the Fathers seems to have been interrupted by the ensuing academic year, and he wrote plaintively to Harriett in June 1829: 'I am so hungry for Irenaeus and Cyprian—I long for the Vacation.'[21] His journal entries, however, do not give any indication of further patristic reading—though this may well have been continued—until a commission from Hugh James Rose to write a history of the Councils of the Church preparatory to a work on the Articles of Religion stimulated him into the research which was to lead eventually to *The Arians of the Fourth Century* in 1833. In August 1831 he read the ancient church historians on the Arian question and Athanasius's Defence of Nicaea and of Dionysius of Alexandria. He notes that this led him to go back to the discussion of the seventeenth-century Bishop Bull, an indication that his knowledge of the Caroline discussions of the Fathers may be earlier than the 1834 date suggested by Dr Parker.[22] In October of the same year his pupils presented him with thirty-six volumes of the Fathers, including the works of Augustine, Athanasius, Cyril of Alexandria, Epiphanius, Gregory of Nyssa, Origen, Basil, Ambrose, and Irenaeus. It was a touching and appropriate tribute at a time when the dispute over the tutorial system had led to Hawkins stopping Newman's pupils.[23]

In the *Apologia* Newman tells us he cannot trace the precise time when he recognized that 'Antiquity was the true exponent of the doctrines of Christianity and the basis of the Church of England', but he was clear that he was confirmed in this belief by his reading of Bishop Bull's works for his book on the Arians. As he went deeper into the Fathers so he was drawn by the Alexandrian Church.

The battle of Arianism was first fought in Alexandria; Athanasius, the champion of the truth, was Bishop of Alexandria; and in his writings he refers to the great religious names of an earlier date, to Origen, Dionysius, and others, who were the glory of its see, or of its school. The broad philosophy of Clement and Origen carried me away; the philosophy, not the theological doctrine; . . . Some portions of their teaching, magnificent in themselves, came like music to my inward ear, as if the response to ideas, which, with little external to encourage them, I had cherished so long. These were based on the mystical or sacramental principle, and spoke of the various Economies or Dispensations of the External. I understood these passages to mean that the exterior world, physical and historical, was but the manifestation to our senses of realities greater than itself. Nature was a parable; pagan literature, philosophy, and mythology, properly understood, were but a preparation for the Gospel.

Looking at the way in which the Greek Fathers traced the preparation for Christianity in both Judaism and Hellenism to the revelatory activity of the Divine Logos, the Word through whom all things were made, Newman noted the movement from shadows and images into truth.

The process of change had been slow; it had been done not rashly, but by rule and measure, 'at sundry times and in diverse manners', first one disclosure and then another, until the whole evangelical doctrine was brought into full manifestation.

And then that very movement of revelation itself provided a clue to the fuller unfolding of the definitive revelation of Christ in the development of doctrine in the Church.

Thus room was made for the anticipation of further and deeper disclosures, of truths still under the veil of the letter, and in their season to be revealed. The visible world still remains without its divine interpretation; Holy Church in her sacraments and her hierarchical appointments, will remain, even to the end of the world, after all but a symbol of those heavenly facts which fill eternity. Her mysteries are but the expression in human language of truths to which the human mind is unequal.[24]

So Newman wrote looking back on his transforming encounter with the Alexandrian Fathers, whose understanding chimed in with much that he had already learnt from Butler's *Analogy* and Keble's *Christian Year*. In the *Arians of the Fourth Century* Newman presents the history of the Arian controversy not only as a rivalry between the schools of Antioch and Alexandria, but as an instance of the distorting and destructive consequences of the speculative concerns of philosophical argumentation when applied to the mysteries of Divine Revelation. In the Tamworth Reading Room letters he was to write: 'first shoot round corners and you may not despair of converting by a syllogism'. He said of Arianism that it was heresy 'founded in a syllogism' which 'spread itself by instruments of a kindred character'.[25] The skills of disputation are inappropriately tested in theological matters because they annihilate mystery and fail to recognize the transcendence of God over all human concepts. 'Those who would not believe the incomprehensibility of the Divine Essence', he wrote, could only 'conceive of it by the analogy of sense; and using the figurative terms of theology in their literal meaning as if landmarks in their inquiries' supposed 'that then, and then only, they steered in a safe course, when they avoided every contradiction of a mathematical and metaphysical nature'.[26]

Newman believed that 'freedom from symbols and articles is abstractedly the highest state of Christian communion', but not because a liberty to pick and choose without restraint was something desirable, but because creeds and dogmatic definitions immediately became vulnerable to the distortions of formalism. The letter was affirmed without the spirit: creeds, the symbol of faith, disclosing the mystery of God, made it possible for scoffers to mock what they had never understood because they had never received those creeds with the appropriate temper of mind.[27] Newman was to write later on that 'creeds and dogmas live only in the one idea they are intended to express', and to insist that worship and prayer are the true context through which the truth of God is received.[28] In the doctrine of reserve and economy Newman believed that the Alexandrian Fathers had attempted to recognize the ever-present element of mystery—of that which transcends human concepts—in their reflection on the Revelation of God enshrined in Scripture and tradition. As Dr Härdelin puts it clearly:

The doctrine of economy has . . . a double aspect, namely an historical and a symbolical. On the one hand God's economy is His condescension in the history of salvation, and on the other it describes the principle of His activity in accommodating Himself to our nature. He reveals Himself in letters which are a 'veil', and in a Church which is a 'symbol' of eternal realities.[29]

Newman argued that the principle of 'economy' is an integral part of all human communication. In order to lead another to conceive of what is unfamiliar a speaker must present 'large propositions, which he has afterwards to modify, or make assertions which are but parallel or analogous to the truth, rather than coincident with it'. So, whilst it may be admitted that 'the simplest and truest notion' of God, which man can obtain, is 'that internal concentration of His active attributes in self-contemplation, which took place on the seventh-day, when He rested from all the work which He had made', it is only through his activities and created works that God is known.

All those so-called Economies or dispensations which display God's character in action, are but condescensions to the infirmity and peculiarity of our minds, shadowy representations of realities which are incomprehensible to creatures such as ourselves, who estimate everything by the rule of association and arrangement, by the notion of a purpose and plan, object and means, parts and whole. . . . What are the phenomena of the external world, but a divine mode of conveying to the mind the realities of existence, individuality, and the influence of being on being?[30]

Newman was aware that a stress on economy could lead to a position in which all real knowledge of God was denied.

On the mind's first mastering this general principle [he wrote], it seems to itself at the moment to have cut all the ties which bind it to the universe, and to be floated off upon the ocean of interminable scepticism; yet a true sense of its own weakness brings it back, the instinctive persuasion that it must be intended to rely on something, and therefore that the information given, though philosophically inaccurate, must be practically certain; a sure confidence in the love of Him, who cannot deceive, and who has impressed the image of Himself and of His will upon our original nature.[31]

It is not surprising, in the light of Newman's comment that 'the information given, though philosophically inaccurate, must be practically certain', that he in large measure, though not completely, agreed with Mansel's 1858 Bampton Lectures, *The Limits of Religious Thought Examined*, to which F. D. Maurice took such exception. It provoked from Newman the admission that Mansel's 'regulative' truth and his 'economical' language had the same import, and also a short, though unpublished, treatise on 'economy', which provides his most systematic treatment of the idea.[32] He put it more poetically in the *Dream of Gerontius*, when endeavouring to convey the experience of the soul after death.

> And thou art wrapp'd and swath'd around in dreams,
> Dreams that are true, yet enigmatical;
> For the belongings of thy present state,
> Save through such symbols come not home to thee.[33]

In discussing the development of creeds in his work on the Arians Newman takes the doctrine of the Trinity as an example. He points out that, in those religiously brought up, there is a practical devotion to the Trinity and 'an implicit acknowledgement of the divinity of the Son and Spirit', which is antecedent to their theological understanding.

This is the faith of uneducated men, which is not the less philosophically correct, nor less acceptable to God, because it does not happen to be conceived in those precise statements which presuppose the action of the mind on its own sentiments and notions. Moral feelings do not directly contemplate and realize to themselves the objects which excite them. . . . A child feels not the less affectionate reverence towards his parents, because he cannot discriminate in words, nay, or in idea, between them and others.

It is only as the child grows that he becomes self-reflective, intro-spective, and analytical, and can give a reasoned account of his affection for his parents. 'Now his intellect contemplates the object of those affections, which acted truly from the first, and are not purer or stronger merely for this accession of knowledge.'[34] 'As the mind is cultivated and expanded, it cannot refrain from the attempt to analyse the vision which influences the heart, and the Object in which that vision centres; nor does it stop till it has, in some sort, succeeded in expressing in words, what has all along been a principle both of its affections and of its obedience.' This is part of that process which Newman was to describe in *The Idea of a University* as 'unlearning the world's poetry and attaining to its prose', an activity which is absolutely right and proper so long as we recognize its nature and limitations. 'The systematic doctrine of the Trinity', therefore, 'may be considered as the shadow, projected for the contemplation of the intellect, of the Object of scripturally-informed piety: a representation, economical; necessarily imperfect, as being exhibited in a foreign medium, and therefore involving apparent inconsistencies or mysteries.'[35] The creeds, Newman argues, set appropriate limits to the attempt to analyse the vision by which we live, and have a practical character in that they are designed to assist worship and obedience, and the fixing and stimulating of the Christian spirit. Furthermore, whereas Scripture is unsystematic, and is addressed principally to the affections, the creeds serve to concentrate the general spirit of Scripture. The faith which they embody is a principle of action; it can be described as a character of mind rather than a notion, and so 'to attempt comprehensions of opinion, aimiable as the motive frequently is, is to mistake arrangements of words, which have no existence except on paper, for habits which are realities; and ingenious generalizations of discordant sentiments for that practical agreement which can alone lead to co-operation.'[36] In this account of the nature and evolution of doctrinal statements Newman opens up perspectives on faith and the development of doctrinal expression which in later writings, *The Prophetical Office of the Church*, *The Essay on Development*, and *The Grammar of Assent*, he will press much further.

In the final pages of the *Arians* Newman wrote of the resemblance he detected between the church of Athanasius and the English Church in his own day. It was not the only time that the Church of the Fathers was to be used by him as an interpretative mirror for his contemporary situation. 'Then as now, there was the prospect, and partly the presence in the Church, of an Heretical Power enthralling it, exerting a varied influence and a usurped claim in the appointment of her functionaries, and interfering with the management of her internal affairs.' But, Newman encouraged his readers, we 'may rest in the confidence that, should the hand of Satan press us sore, our Athanasius and Basil will be given us in their destined season, to break the bonds of the Oppressor, and let the captives go free'.[37] Newman, who had returned from his Mediterranean tour, and the dark experience of dangerous illness in Sicily, imbued with a sense of providential vocation—'they shall know the difference now that I am back again'—was able to throw himself with vigour into the rousing and rallying of the Church with the publication of the first *Tracts for the Times* following Keble's Assize Sermon of 1833.

High Churchmen in Oxford had already been stirred. William Palmer of Worcester College received an urgent letter from Hugh James Rose, the vicar of Hadleigh, proposing action: 'That something is requisite is certain. The only thing is, that whatever is done ought to be *quickly* done; for the danger is immediate, and I should have little fear if I thought we could stand for ten or fifteen years as we are.'[38] The conference at Rose's rectory at Hadleigh which resulted from these initial efforts produced schemes for committees and associations. Hurrell Froude, the only representative of the younger churchmen who were to be the vanguard of the Tractarian Movement, saw no future in caution. The older high churchmen, he wrote, have 'the old prejudices about the expediency of having the Clergy Gentlemen, *i.e.* fit to mix in good society, and about prizes to tempt men of talent into the Church, and the whole train of stuff which follows these assumptions'.[39] Newman agreed with Froude: apostolical zeal was necessary in defence of an apostolical cause. He wrote to Keble urging that the Oxford name must be used in defence of the Church. He told his friend Christie that he thought Keble's Assize Sermon admirable and approved his 'severe and zealous preface'. He reported to Golightly that he and his friends had resolved 'to unite on this simple principle—"with a view to stir up our brethren to consider the state of the Church, and especially to the practical belief and preaching of the Apostolical Succession"'. He proposed that extracts should be printed from the Epistles of St. Ignatius. He confessed to another friend, Frederic Rogers, that 'Tory as I still am, theoretically and historically, I begin to be a Radical practically.'[40] The *Tracts for the Times* were thus conceived to alert the Church to the danger it faced from an Erastian government, to nerve for action, and to recall the apostolic faith of the Fathers. Of the ninety tracts that were eventually published Newman wrote twenty-seven, by far the largest number. Keble and Pusey contributed eight each, John William Bowden and Archdeacon Harrison five, and Froude and Isaac Williams three. Newman typically commented that the *Tracts* were to be the expression of individual convictions, for 'no great work was done by a system—whereas systems rise out of individual exertions'.[41] The apostolical system was important, but it could only be propagated by apostolical enthusiasm. As always with Newman the vision was to be communicated personally.

The *Tracts* were concerned, he wrote in the preface to the first collected volume, with 'the practical revival of doctrines, which, although held by the great divines of our Church, at present have become obsolete with the majority of her members'. They were intended to demonstrate how the Church had been weakened by

Erastian notions, so that her doctrine wore 'a cold aspect', which could only be converted into living truth held from the heart by a re-assertion of the apostolic foundation of the Church as a divine society. In times of danger, he proclaimed in the first of the *Tracts*, Christian ministers could not afford to rest their authority on their position in the state Establishment, their own personal convictions, or their popular successes, only their apostolic descent could provide a sufficient basis. And, full of his knowledge of the early Church, he wrote that 'we could not wish [our bishops] a more blessed termination of their course, than the spoiling of their good and martyrdom'. It was not time for compromise:

In a day like this there are but two sides, zeal and persecution, the Church and the world; and those who attempt to occupy the ground between them, at best will lose their labour but probably will be drawn back to the latter. Be practical, I respectfully urge you; do not attempt impossibilities; sail not as if in pleasure boats upon a troubled sea.[42]

The time was ripe for the defence of the Church's mysteries against the 'cold spirit', which demanded a 'rigid demonstration for every religious practice and observance'.[43]

The *Tracts* were pungent statements, broadsheets summoning the clergy to a defence of apostolic faith and order, which became theological treatises and catenae of the Fathers and Anglican divines. Newman's vision was communicated even more personally through the sermons he preached as Vicar of St. Mary's, and which reverberated for years in the hearts of his hearers. It was not only what he said but how he said it; it was the man who was the vehicle for the living doctrine. Two accounts from many convey something of his force.

It was when Newman read the Scriptures from the lectern in St. Mary's Church at Oxford that one felt more than ever that his words were those of a seer who saw God and the things of God. Many men were impressive readers, but they did not reach the soul. They played on the senses and the imagination, they were good actors, they did not forget themselves, and one did not forget them. But Newman had the power of so impressing the soul as to efface himself; you thought only of the majestic soul that saw God. It was God speaking to you as He speaks to you through creation; but in a deeper way, by the articulate voice of man made in the image of God and raised to His likeness by grace, communicating to your intelligence, and sense, and imagination, by words which were the signs of ideas, a transcript of the work and private thoughts that were in God.[44]

[Newman] always began as if he had determined to set forth his idea of the truth in the plainest and simplest language, language as men say 'intelligible to the meanest understanding'. But his ardent zeal and fine poetical imagination were not thus to be controlled. As I hung upon his words, it seemed to me as if I could trace behind his will, and pressing, so to speak, against it, a rush of thoughts and feelings, which he kept struggling to hold back, but in the end they were generally too strong for him and poured themselves out in a torrent of eloquence all the more impetuous for having been so long repressed. The effect of these outbursts was irresistible, and carried his hearers beyond themselves at once. . . .

His bearing was neither awkward nor ungraceful, it was simply quiet and calm because under strict control: but beneath that calmness, intense feeling, I think, was obvious to those who had any instinct of sympathy with him.[45]

It was not very surprising that a man who evoked such responses was imitated by undergraduates throughout the university even in the way that he flopped to his knees and in the way in which he held his head.

The first note that sounded in Newman's sermons was a call to holiness, the severe demands of Christian living. Holiness is necessary for future blessedness and heaven would be hell for an irreligious man. A University Sermon of 1831 warns of the way in which each action leaves an imprint on a man's future development.

We cannot keep from forming habits of one kind or another, each of our acts influences the rest, gives character to the mind, narrows its freewill in the direction or good or evil, till it soon converges in all its powers and principles to some fixed point in the unbounded horizon before it.[46]

As he reminded his hearers in another sermon, two lines diverging at a small angle separate to greater and greater distances: 'a slight deviation at setting out may be the measure of the difference between tending to hell and tending to heaven'.[47] The dualism of Augustinian theology is apparent: 'there is no middle or neutral state for any one; although as far as the external world goes, all men seem to be in a middle state common to one and all. Yet, much as men look the same, and impossible as it is for us to say where each man stands in God's sight, there are two and but two classes of men, and these have characters and destinies as far apart in their tendencies as light and darkness.'[48] In the same sermon Newman's sense of the unreality of the material world and his intense individual awareness are also apparent. He invites his hearers to consider the bustle of a great city:

. . . crowds are pouring through the streets; some on foot, some in carriages; while the shops are full, and the houses too, could we see into them. Every part is full of life. Hence we gain a general idea of a splendour, magnificence, opulence, and energy. But what is the truth? Why, that every being in that great concourse is his own centre, and all things about him are but shades. . . . He has his own hopes and fears, desires, judgments, and aims; he is everything to himself, and no one else is really anything. No one outside of him can really touch him, can touch his soul, his immortality; he must live with himself for ever. He has a depth within him unfathomable, an infinite abyss of existence; and the scene in which he bears part for the moment is but like a gleam of sunshine upon its surface.[49]

Each individual lived as such before God, and that could never, for Newman, be equated with comfortable religion or easy rationalization. Until men saw God to be 'a consuming fire' and approached him 'with reverence and godly fear, as being sinners' they were not even in sight of the strait gate.[50] But the God whose holiness is so awesome, is also the source of the Christian's strength. It is the indwelling of the Holy Spirit which is at the heart of the Christian life, and through the Spirit the events of the Gospel have been so illuminated that history has been made doctrine.[51] This is a characteristic stress of Newman, that men are primarily influenced by actions and encounters and direct impressions, rather than by rationally argued conclusions. It is part of what he called the dogmatic principle, whose import he set out so brilliantly in the *Tamworth Reading Room Letters* of 1841. In these he emphasized that deductive scientific knowledge could never have the visionary power of religious faith. Science moved from knowledge of natural phenomena to forming a view about those phenomena, to reasoning about that view, and finally to the position of concluding that the view is true. 'This is why', he wrote, 'science has so little of a religious tendency'.

Deductions have no power of persuasion. The heart is commonly reached, not through the reason, but through the imagination, by means of direct impressions, by the testimony of facts and events, by history, by description. Persons influence us, voices melt us, looks subdue us, deeds inflame us. Many

Page 59
paragraph 1

Sr. Sandra
Schneiders would
not agree with this.
"events and action"

Pope Benedict 16 would
not agree

Roger Haight refers to
"the narrative" as the
foundation. This is
the "proclaimed gospel"
of the 19th and 20th
centuries

a man will live and die upon a dogma: no man will be a martyr for a conclusion.[52]

A University Sermon of 1830 follows a similar line, arguing that Christian faith springs from concrete events and actions, which are anterior to philosophical reflection and speculation.

Revelation meets us with simple and distinct *facts* and *actions*, not with painful inductions from existing phenomena, not with generalized laws or metaphysical conjectures, but with *Jesus and the Resurrection*; and *if Christ be not risen* . . . then is our preaching vain, and your faith also is vain. Facts such as these are not simply evidence of the truth of the revelation, but the media of its impressiveness. The life of Christ brings together and concentrates truths concerning the chief good and the laws of our being, which wander idle and forlorn over the surface of the moral world, and often appear to diverge from each other.

And so it can be said that 'the philosopher aspires towards a divine *principle*; the Christian, towards a Divine *Agent*'.[53]

It is this insistence on event and action as the medium of revelation which lead Newman to view both the Evangelicals, with their talk of a spiritual church and their reduction of faith to mental attitude, and the philosophizing liberals as being in error. The visible church, sacramental actions, and the apostolic authority of the Christian ministry are all bound up together in witnessing to the stand of Christian faith on events that happened in a particular place and at a particular time, which yet disclosed and embodied the gracious, redemptive activity of God. So he opposed vigorously those who degraded the Eucharist 'from a Sacrament to a bare commemorative rite', or who understood Baptism as no more than 'a mere outward form, and sign of profession'. It should be no surprise that those holding such views commonly deny the authority of the apostolic ministry: 'for they who think it superstitious to believe that particular persons are channels of grace, are but consistent in denying virtue to particular ordinances'. Such reductionism made 'the whole scheme of salvation' have 'as intelligible and ordinary a character as the repair of any accident in the works of man'. Faith being robbed of its mystery, the sacraments of their virtue, the priesthood of its commission, it was then 'no wonder that sin itself is soon considered a venial matter, moral evil as a mere imperfection, man as involved in no great peril or misery, his duties of no very arduous or anxious nature'.

In a word religion, as such, is in the way to disappear from the mind altogether; and in its stead a mere cold worldly morality, a decent regard to the claims of society, a cultivation of the benevolent affections, and a gentleness and polish of external deportment will be supposed to constitute the entire duties of that being, who is conceived in sin, and the child of wrath, is redeemed by the precious blood of the Son of God, is born again and sustained by the Spirit through the invisible strength of Sacraments, and called, through self-denial and sanctification of the inward man to the Eternal Presence of the Father, Son, and Holy Ghost.[54]

Sin, grace, and forgiveness are words denoting powerful realities, and the superficiality of a merely emotional religion in no way measures up to them.

All the passionate emotion, or fine sensibility, which ever man displayed, will never by itself make us change our ways and do our duty. Impassioned thoughts, high aspirations, sublime imaginings, have no strength in them. They can no more make a man obey consistently, than they can move mountains. . . . Conscience, and Reason in subjection to Conscience, *these* are those powerful instruments (under grace) which change a man.[55]

But if the Christian is not to take refuge in emotional states, he can draw encouragement from the fact of his incorporation in the communion of saints, the great company from every generation of those made holy by the Spirit of God. 'The Ministry and Sacraments, the bodily presence of Bishop and people, are given us', Newman wrote, 'as keys and spells, by which we bring ourselves' into the presence of the saints. 'The unseen world through God's secret power and mercy, encroaches upon this world, and the Church that is seen is just that portion of it by which it encroaches.'[56]

The Church as a school for saints, built up by apostolic creeds, and ministry, and sacraments, was a vision Newman had derived from his study of the Fathers, and it was the appeal to the undivided Church of the first four centuries which seemed to him characteristic of Anglicanism. As the Church of England strove to remain faithful to that tradition, in distinction from the over-systematization of Roman theology and the idiosyncratic individualism of Protestantism, she witnessed to a *via media*. Having entered a controversy about this with a French Catholic priest, the Abbé Jager, Newman endeavoured to set out the ecclesiology of this *via media* in a series of *Lectures on the Prophetical Office of the Church*, which was published eventually in 1837. In these lectures he had necessarily to consider the nature of tradition, the character of the bonds of corporate believing, and the way in which the Church was able to maintain a common faith throughout the changes of history. As such it was a necessary stage in a progress which led him to consider what was involved in doctrinal development.

Newman was always concerned to examine how men actually believed rather than endeavour to conform them to a theory about how they ought to believe. This was true of the individual's assent of faith and it was also true of the corporate faith of the whole Church. So he insisted that the Church in common with all societies moved by tradition. 'We all go by tradition in matters of this world', and in a hundred and one instances we can point to judgements being made of conduct being unusual or against the rule, when there is in fact no written rule to which we are appealing. The common law tradition of England provided Newman with an excellent example. Even murderers, he says, 'are hanged by custom'. As with the law so with the Church, some tradition has been reduced to writing; but it would be unreasonable to demand that all tradition should be so written down. You could not, in fact, do it, and it would in the end distort. In an analogy he used on many other occasions, he points out that if you meet up with a stranger on a journey, it is quite impossible for him to tell you all his mind at once, even though he would be totally present to you. So with an unwritten tradition in the Church:

It is latent, but it lives. It is silent, like the rapids of a river, before the rocks intercept it. It is the Church's unconscious habit of opinion and sentiment; which she reflects upon, masters, and expresses, according to the emergency. We see then the mistake of asking for a complete collection of the Roman Traditions; as well might we ask for a full catalogue of a man's tastes and thoughts on a given subject. Tradition in its fullness is necessarily unwritten; it is the mode in which a society has felt or acted during a certain period, and it cannot be circumscribed any more than a man's countenance and manner can be conveyed to strangers in any set of propositions.[57]

At this stage Newman believed the Roman Church to be in error in its claim that all the doctrines it now taught were to be found in the primitive Church. Though calling itself apostolic it did not take apostolicity seriously, for it overrode the duty to heed the voice of the Church of antiquity by a claim to the infallibility of present church authority. Newman was always one who believed that in theology, as in many other disciplines, it was cumulative arguments which were the most persuasive. Catholic consent concerning the doctrine of the Incarnation was therefore a powerful argument. This was an ancient consent such as was entirely lacking in the disputes between churches of more recent times; and Newman went so far as to say that 'Ancient Consent is, practically, the only, or the main kind of Tradition which now remains to us', though that 'Ancient consent' is not of 'a mathematical or demonstrative character' but a moral one.

There were other considerations which weighed with Newman at this time in his evaluation of the Church of Rome. He was critical of the endeavour to form a complete and consistent theology to be held with unclouded certainty. The scholastic, legal ethos of Roman theology substituted a technical and formal obedience for the spirit of love, and was out of key with the living spirit of the Christian Gospel.

The proofs of the being of God are not written on the sun and sky, nor the precepts of morality spoken from a Urim and Thummim. To require such definite and clear notions of Truth, is to hanker after the Jewish Law, a system of less mysterious information than Christianity, as well as less generous faith.[58]

Following what he had learnt from the Greek Fathers and from Bishop Butler, he argued that theological language must always be 'economical', 'symbolic', and tentative.

Partial and incomplete knowledge must surely be an inseparable attendant on a theology which reveals the wonders of heaven. The human mind cannot measure the things of the Spirit. Christianity is a supernatural gift, originating and living in the unseen world and only extending into this. It is a vast scheme running out into width and breadth, encompassing us round about, not embraced by us. No one can see the form of a building but those who are external to it. We are within the Divine Dispensation; we cannot take it in with the eye, ascertain its proportions, pursue its lines, foretell their directions and coincidences, or ascertain their limits. We see enough for practice, but not even as much as this with an equal degree of clearness; but one part more clearly than another.[59]

A 'technical religion', Newman argued, destroyed 'the delicacy and reverence of the Christian mind' in the same way that criticism could be fatal to 'poetic fervour and imagination'. Thus we find Newman exhibiting the same suspicion of system, and, in a different manner, the same awareness of the allusiveness of theological statement, as that other nineteenth-century prophet, Søren Kierkegaard. Over-definition, the attempt to circumscribe what must necessarily remain mysterious and what can only be indicated tangentially, ends by destroying the faith it attempts to expound. Again with an echo of Kierkegaard, Newman rather fiercely accused Roman systematization of absolving men from the duty of sacrificing their whole lives to God.

If the imposition of system was alien to faith so the organic unity of faith, devotion, and theology, which constituted the living 'idea' of Christianity, could be destroyed by the unfettered exercise of private judgement. Rightly understood, private judgement represents the exercise of the will and is implied in any notion of human responsibility. To exercise this judgement in matters of religion men are governed by both external and internal means. Their awareness is formed by parents, the community of the Church, Scripture, and, for some, by a knowledge of Christian antiquity. Reason, conscience, the moral sense, imagination, and the affections, are all brought to bear in the exercise of private judgement, and Newman once again shows that he prefers a cumulative to a reductionist argument. We need to recognize the varying elements which contribute to the commitment of faith, rather than reducing it to a simple principle, which is untrue to the complexity of the reality.

Turning to the line of argument commonly propounded, that no true faith can be professed without a careful investigation of the grounds for that faith and an analysis of all that bears upon it, Newman asserted that this lead directly to scepticism. It is also untrue to lived experience.

Every one must begin religion by faith, not by controversy; he must take for granted what he is taught and what he cannot prove; and it is better for himself that he should do so, even if the teaching he receives contains a mixture of error. If he would possess a reverent mind, he must begin by obeying; if he would cherish a generous and devoted temper, he must begin by venturing something on uncertain information; if he would deserve the praise of modesty and humility, he must repress his busy intellect and forbear to scrutinize.[60]

Like Keble, who may have influenced him here, Newman ever viewed intellect as the handmaid of man's moral nature.

Turning to a consideration of the Creed, the essential core of Christian doctrine, Newman argued that the creed was at first—being subservient to the faith which gave it birth—of secondary value, but had now become not only a summary of existing faith but a witness to the character and proportion of the primitive faith. It might be compared to the likeness of a friend, which, 'however incomplete in itself, is cherished as the best memorial of him, when he has been taken from us'. Newman described creeds and conciliar definitions—tradition formally stated and enunciated—as episcopal tradition. But tradition is not limited to such formal statement. There is alongside it, and providing the matrix out of which it emerges, what he called 'prophetic tradition', which is exhibited in many informal ways in which faith is affirmed and handed on:

> ... a certain body of Truth, pervading the Church like an atmosphere, irregular in its shape from its very profusion and exuberance; at times separable only in idea from Episcopal Tradition, yet at times melting away into legend and fable; partly written, partly the interpretation, partly the supplement of Scripture, partly preserved in intellectual expressions, partly latent in the spirit and temper of Christians; poured to and fro in closets and upon the housetops, in liturgies, in controversial works, in obscure fragments, in sermons, in popular prejudices, in local customs.[61]

Coleridge wrote that 'words are not things, they are the living educts of the imagination', and the words of faith are, together with the symbols and sacraments of the Church, the 'keys and spells', as Newman put it, which enable us to enter and dwell in a Christian universe. In their origin they are both to be conceived as the stammering attempts of human language to acknowledge God's presence and activity, and as the chosen economy by which God condescends to our finitude. So Newman was at pains to emphasize:

> Every word of Revelation has a deep meaning. It is the outward form of a heavenly truth, and in this sense a mystery or Sacrament. We may read it, confess it; but there is something in it which we cannot fathom, which we only, more or less, as the case may be, not perfectly enter into. Accordingly when a candidate for Baptism repeats the Articles of the Creed, he is confessing something incomprehensible in its depth, and indefinite in its extent.[62]

The same theme occurs in his Tract on Rationalism in Religion, in which he wrote: 'If by speaking of the Gospel as clear and intelligible a man means to imply that this is the whole of it, then I answer, "No; for it is also deep, and therefore necessarily mysterious".'[63] To speak of Christianity as Revelation implies, rather than denies, that it is also a mystery.

Much of Newman's language and understanding in the *Lectures on the Prophetical Office of the Church* is shaped by his study of the Greek Fathers. His patristic roots are also evident in the 1838 *Lectures on Justification* in which he endeavoured to counter Evangelical suspicions of such doctrines as baptismal regeneration and the apostolic ministry because they were thought to foster notions of human merit and were incompatible with the doctrine of justifying faith. Newman stood against the nominalism of popular Evangelical theology. For him 'justifying faith was not . . . a shadow or phantom, which flits about without voice or power . . . not a mere impression, or gleam upon the soul, or knowledge, or emotion, or conviction, which ends with itself, but the beginning of that which is eternal, the operation of the Indwelling Power which . . . works in us so mightily, so intimately with our will as to be in a true sense one with it.'[64] At the heart of the Christian life is the indwelling of the Holy Spirit, who makes Christ present to the believer, and it is this 'Sacred Presence' which 'is our justification in God's sight', and is inseparable from sanctification. 'Our true righteousness is the indwelling of our glorified Lord.' 'This is to be justified, to receive the Divine Presence within us, and be made a Temple of the Holy Ghost.'[65] So Newman wished to affirm that 'justification comes *through* the Sacraments; is received *by* faith; *consists in* God's inward presence; and *lives* in obedience'.[66]

As Newman had argued for an Anglican *via media* in the *Lectures on the Prophetical Office* as far as ecclesiology was concerned, so he wished to set forth an understanding of justification which avoided the extremes of Protestantism and Romanism. The Protestant view he characterized as justification by faith alone, the Romanist view as justification by obedience alone. He condemned the Romanist view as leading to a belief in the intrinsic merit of human good works apart from the gift of God's forgiveness for the past and of his renewing Spirit for the future. But the Protestant view is also condemned because it spoke of a merely imputed rather than an actual righteousness. A view which made of the scheme of salvation one of names and understandings rather than reality was a betrayal of the

Gospel. Real corruption was met with an unreal righteousness. Sacraments were abolished to introduce 'barren and dead ordinances' which 'for the real participation of Christ, and justification through His Spirit, would, at the very marriage feast, feed us on shells and husks, who hunger and thirst after righteousness'.[67]

Newman was conscious that in much contemporary theology discussion of faith and justification had represented faith 'as a sort of passive quality which sits amid the ruins of human nature, and keeps up what may be called a silent protest, or indulges a pensive meditation over its misery'. It had been abstracted in a way which distorted. 'True faith', he insisted, 'is what may be called colourless, like air or water; it is but the medium through which the soul sees Christ; and the soul as little rests upon it and contemplates it as the eye can see air.' Much discussion of faith is therefore of indications of faith being treated as faith itself, such things as signs of conversion, pious feelings and aspirations. But the Christian's concern is with God and his grace, so that it is left to others to say 'here is faith' or 'there is love', where the Christian can only say, 'this is God's grace', and 'that is His holiness', and 'that is His glory'.[68] And the grace of God known, contemplated, and expressed in Christian worship and in Christian life is nothing less than the imparting of the life of God himself. The indwelling Spirit is a pervading presence like light in a building or like perfume in a cloth, and, 'such an inhabitation brings the Christian into a state altogether new and marvellous, far above the possession of mere gifts, exalts him inconceivably in the scale of beings, and gives him a place and office which he had not before'. 'In St. Peter's forcible language, he becomes "partaker of the Divine Nature" and has "power" or authority, as St. John says, "to become the son of God".'[69]

In the *Lectures on the Prophetical Office* Newman had defended the Anglican position as a *via media*, and he believed that *via media* corresponded to the Church of Antiquity. As he studied that Church of Antiquity, however, and particularly under the pressure which arose as a consequence of his editing, with John Keble, of Hurrell Froude's *Remains*, with their strong criticisms of the Reformers, he began to discern a somewhat different picture in the patristic mirror. In the Monophysite controversy the Chalcedonian definition did not represent a *via media*; in the Donatist dispute in North Africa, Augustine had appealed to the catholicity of the Church, the consensus of the Church throughout the world, against a Church in one particular area claiming that it embodied the purity of the Christian Gospel; in the Arian controversy the semi-Arians did not represent Christian orthodoxy. Truth often seemed to lie in the extremes. Was Wiseman right in pressing Augustine's criticism of the Donatists against the Anglicans? In his study of the development of the conciliar creeds Newman was aware of implicit and unformulated faith coming to doctrinal expression, a process which was one of growth and development. As he became aware of the complexity of the patristic controversies and saw them in a new light, the question was also raised as to whether the Tridentine faith of the Church of Rome might not also be a legitimate development. The matter was made more urgent by pressure from younger adherents of the Movement, such as W. G. Ward, who both lacked Newman's historical sense and were not temperamentally cautious. They sought to embrace the whole of Roman Catholic doctrine whilst remaining Anglicans, and it was under that pressure that Newman wrote Tract XC, 'Remarks on Certain Passages in the Thirty-Nine Articles', which was to prove to be the last of the *Tracts*. It was seen by bishops and university authorities as a subtle attempt to Romanize the Church of England and destroy the usefulness of any specifically Anglican doctrinal tests. For Newman, with his conception of episcopacy derived from Ignatius of Antioch, the repudiation of Tract XC by the bishops was a bitter blow. He wrote in 1848, after his conversion to the Church of Rome:

When the affair of No.90 happened, Manning said 'Shut up your controversy and go to the Fathers, which is your *line.*' Well *they* had been the beginning of my doubts, but I did so. I began to translate St. Athanasius. The truth kept pouring in upon me. I saw in the Semi-arians the Via-medians, I saw in the Catholic Church of the day the identical self of the Catholic Church now;—as you know a friend by his words and deeds, or see an author in his works.[70]

The actions of the Anglican episcopate following Tract XC in such matters as the Anglo-Prussian bishopric at Jerusalem only made stronger the doubts Newman had already come to feel. He was driven back, he said, 'on the *internal or personal Notes of the Church*', the existence of real sanctity within the English Church, a concern which led to the series of *Lives of the English Saints*. In 1843 he preached a University Sermon on 'The Theory of Developments in Religious Doctrine'.

Taking as his text Luke 2:19, 'Mary kept all these things and pondered them in her heart', Newman explored the way in which from humble beginnings a great fabric of divinity had come into being, the consequence of a 'great idea taking hold of a thousand minds by its living force'. 'This world of thought is the expansion of a few words, uttered, as if casually, by the fishermen of Galilee.'[71] The theme of development is expounded in a characteristic way, emphasizing the process of mind by which convictions and intuitions which are implicit come to explicit formulation, drawing on personal analogies of the experience of not truly knowing oneself, or being subject to changes of mood without being able to account for such change. Newman suggests that ideas may be latent in the corporate Christian mind of the Church in the same way, so that 'what was at first an impression on the Imagination has become a system or creed in the Reason'. Newman is here as convinced as he was in the *Arians* that creeds and dogmas, though of great importance, always remain in a sense secondary.

Creeds and dogmas live in the one idea which they are designed to express, and which alone is substantive; and are necessary only because the human mind cannot reflect upon that idea, except piecemeal, cannot use it in its oneness and entireness, nor without resolving it into a series of aspects and relations. And in matter of fact these expressions are never equivalent to it; we are able, indeed, to define the creations of our own minds, for they are what we make them and nothing else; but it were as easy to create what is real as to define it; and thus the Catholic dogmas are, after all, but symbols of a Divine fact, which, far from being compassed by those very propositions, would not be exhausted, nor fathomed, by a thousand.[72]

What is fundamental is the living idea 'from which alone change of heart or conduct can proceed', that which is designated by phrases like 'Christ in us', 'Christ dwelling in us by faith'. The whole purpose of creeds is to perpetuate and lead to that religious impression, which, looked at from the opposite direction, 'acts as a regulating principle . . . upon our reasoning'. Statements such as 'the Word was God' 'are not a mere letter which we may handle by the rules of art at our own will, but august tokens of most simple, ineffable, adorable facts, embraced, enshrined according to its measure in the believing mind'.[73] Once again theology is seen as faith seeking understanding. Newman goes on to speak of the economy and dispensation through which God makes himself known to us, and draws parallels from varying disciplines of human knowledge, from the way in which from limited initial data complex systems of classification properly arise. Mathematics develops various methods or calculi; music from limited notes can be developed into multifarious harmonies. Once again from antecedent probability, this time from the way in which human knowledge grows, Newman argues for the development of doctrine.

In the *Essay on the Development of Christian Doctrine*, begun in 1844, Newman brought together his knowledge of the history of the Church, and his conviction of the fact of development and change, to answer for himself the question whether or not it was possible to understand contemporary Catholic doctrine as an expression of that same living idea which had possessed the hearts and minds of the apostles and the Fathers of the Church. Change had to be recognized; developments had to be distinguished in some way from corruptions; his essay was 'an hypothesis to account for a difficulty'. But although the *Essay* is concerned with change, it is nonetheless true, as Misner comments, that 'the basic theme remains the permanence and identity of faith through all transformations.' Newman attempted to show that 'the analogy of an influential idea, one which impresses itself on many minds in a social setting over a period of years and thus makes its mark in history . . . could serve as a hypothesis to explain both the constancy and the change in a tradition founded by divine revelation'.[74] He came to believe, as Misner puts it again, that 'as a religious society with a creed to be maintained, Christianity must have within it a recognized organ . . . by the authority of which the different members of the social body may be kept in a unity of faith.'

If Christianity be a social religion, as it certainly is, and if it be based on certain ideas acknowledged as divine, . . . and if these ideas have various aspects, and make distinct impressions on different minds, and issue in consequence in a multiplicity of developments, true, or false, or mixed, as has been shown, what influence will suffice to meet and to do justice to these conflicting conditions, but a supreme authority ruling and reconciling individual judgments by a divine right and a recognized wisdom? . . . If Christianity is both social and dogmatic and intended for all ages, it must, humanly speaking, have an infallible expounder.[75]

Newman had already come to see in the contemporary Roman Church the community which bore the living family resemblance to the Church of the Fathers. He was now convinced of its doctrinal authority, and on 8 October 1845 he was received into the Church of Rome by the Passionist priest, Dominic Barberi.

It was almost a fortnight before Pusey and Keble could bring themselves to write to each other. 'Our Church', said Pusey, in an open letter, 'has not known how to use him'.[76] No more, it may be said, did the Roman Church which he joined, but which has, in so many ways in a later generation been influenced by him. His exploration of faith and reason; his understanding of Scripture and the Fathers and of the intimate relation, to which they bear witness, between doctrine and devotion; and the force and power of his preaching shaped the whole Oxford Movement. It is noteworthy that when in later years he republished his Anglican works there were scarcely any changes that he found it necessary to make, a testimony to the continuity of his pilgrimage—which he himself saw as *ex umbris et imaginibus in veritatem* (out of shadows and images into truth)—and in a measure to the catholicity of Anglicanism for which he so long contended.

IV. Edward Pusey: Scholarship and devotion

OF THE three men who emerged as leaders of the Oxford Movement, Newman, Keble, and Pusey, it was Edward Pusey whose name became popularly linked with the Tractarian revival, so that to English mythology, assiduously propagated in the latter half of the century by *Punch*, the name 'Puseyite' became the equivalent of 'Jesuit', within the Church of England. 'That Mr Pewdsey, who is such a friend to the pope'[1] became, particularly after Newman's secession to the Church of Rome in 1845, the leader of the Catholic movement, though it was in many respects a leadership from behind, in that more extreme men made the running and Pusey came to their defence. Not a ritualist himself, doubting with his ascetic instinct whether the times were right for concentrating on the magnificence of churches or the beauty of ceremonial, he was yet willing to defend those who, like him, held a high sacramental doctrine and shared a deep belief in the catholicity of the English Church.

Pusey's contribution was weighty scholarship (though of a historical and antiquarian variety), a profound spirituality, an unwavering belief in the catholicity of the Church of England, and the fostering of the religious life. He did not have Newman's intense power to persuade by beauty of language, and his style was far from clear. Liddon commented with reference to his translations of the Fathers, that his concern to reproduce idiom as well as words in translation reacted unfavourably on his own English style: 'people said that he wrote like a Father of the fourth century'.[2] J. B. Mozley queried how Pusey could 'impress, or raise feeling, or keep up attention' since he had 'none of what we may call the arts and accomplishments of preaching', 'pliability of voice, or command over accent, time, or tone; who did not change from fast to slow, or pause, or look off from his pages; who, instead of facing an audience, in the way in which extempore preachers can do throughout a sermon, and which most preachers try to do more or less', kept 'his eyes fixed down', and sustained an unvarying note throughout a long period of delivery. The answer was, he suggested, the reality, the earnest integrity of the preacher.[3] Other witnesses reinforce Mozley's judgement. Pusey, wrote G. W. E. Russell, 'had absolutely no pretensions to oratorical skill'.

> He read every word, generally from a printed copy, in a low, deep, rather monotonous voice, which, in his later years, was husky and thick. His sermons were immensely long, packed with learning, and exhaustive of the subjects with which they dealt. His style of composition was extremely strange; so crabbed and so quaint that it now reads more like a bad translation from the German than genuine English. But occasionally there were passages of a solemn rhetoric, which rose very near eloquence; and, when he came to practical exhortation—to the searching of the heart's secrets, and the enforcement of repentance—it was like the voice of a god.[4]

Pusey was learned, of that there was no doubt. Born in 1800, the second son of a moderately aristocratic family, he went up to Christ Church from Eton in 1819. He was tutored by Charles Lloyd, later Regius Professor of Divinity and then Bishop of Oxford, who had also been tutor to Sir Robert Peel, and whose lectures on the history of the Prayer Book had a significant influence on Tractarian liturgical concerns. It was Lloyd who was to encourage Pusey to journey to Germany, which made him one of the few English theologians to have first-hand acquaintance with German theological thought. It was Lloyd again who urged that the young Pusey should be appointed to the Regius Chair of Hebrew in 1828 at an astonishingly young age. Pusey took a double First, significantly asking his father, who had offered a commemorative present, for a folio set of the Fathers of the Church.[5] In 1823 he was elected to an Oriel fellowship, the year after Newman, who thus describes his first encounter with Pusey:

> His light curly head of hair was damp with the cold water which his headaches made necessary for comfort; he walked fast with a young manner of carrying himself, and stood rather bowed, looking up from under his eye-brows, his shoulders rounded, and his bachelor's gown not buttoned at the elbow, but hanging loose over his wrists. His countenance was very sweet, and he spoke little.[6]

Years later, on their meeting at Keble's vicarage at Hursley after many years of separation, the same picture flashed into Newman's mind.

His face is not changed, but it is as if you looked at him through a prodigious magnifier. I recollect him short and small—with a round head—smallish features—flaxen curly hair—huddled up together from his shoulders downward—and walking fast.[7]

In 1825, following Lloyd's advice, Pusey went to Germany, going first to Göttingen, where he attended the lectures of Eichhorn, as Coleridge had done some thirty years earlier. From there he moved on to Berlin, where he renewed his acquaintance with Tholuck whom he had first met on a visit to Oxford, and also met Schleiermacher, Hengstenberg, and the church historian, Neander. Liddon noted that Schleiermacher's emphasis on religion as being a feeling of dependence on God made a powerful appeal to Pusey, and even claimed that Pusey owed the beginnings of some features of his devotional life to Schleiermacher's influence.[8] In 1826 Pusey returned for a second visit to Germany, with the especial aim of mastering further Semitic languages, Arabic and Syriac in particular. He worked with great intensity, spending some fourteen to sixteen hours a day in the study of Arabic. When he returned to England in June 1827 he was well acquainted, not only with the Semitic languages, but with the leading German orientalists and theologians and the contemporary currents of theological thought in Germany. The last mentioned was to lead him into controversy with Hugh James Rose, who in 1825 had published an account of German Protestantism, ascribing the growth of rationalist opinions amongst German religionists to the lack of confessions of faith and ecclesiastical discipline and guidance. Pusey had found many of his German friends displeased with Rose's argument, and on his return to England he embarked on his own interpretation of the history of Protestant theological thought in Germany in answer to Rose. Pusey linked the rise of rationalism with the prevalence of a scholasticizing orthodoxy in earlier German theology and the consequent pietist reaction. Although he was aware of the dangers of pietism, where devotional phraseology replaced the living experience, he was warmest in his commendation of men like Arndt and Spener, and held up the latter in particular as an outstanding example.[9]

Pusey had returned home not only to write about German theology but also to marry Maria Barker, to whom he had long been attached, but whom his father had for some years refused to countenance as a wife. He was also ordained to the diaconate on 1 June 1828, preaching his first sermon on the text 'Without holiness no man shall see the Lord', a reminder that he shared with Newman and Keble a primary concern for holiness above all else. Appointment to the Hebrew Chair and canonry followed in 1829. Drawing on what he had learned in Germany, he undertook the massive task of cataloguing the Arabic manuscripts in the Bodleian Library in order to complete the work of his predecessor in the Chair, Alexander Nicoll. The enthusiastic Hurrell Froude had found Pusey 'so uncommonly learned that it is impossible to keep pace with him'.[10] His prodigious learning was widely recognized, and when he joined the Tract writers at the end of 1833, having previously limited his support to encouraging the circulation of the *Tracts*, Newman was clear just how valuable Pusey's open adherence was.[11] He wrote in the *Apologia*:

I had known [Pusey] well since 1827–8, and had felt for him an enthusiastic admiration. I used to call him ὁ μέγας. His great learning, his immense diligence, his scholarlike mind, his simple devotion to the cause of religion overcame me. . . . He at once gave to us a position and a name . . . Dr Pusey was a Professor and Canon of Christ Church; he had a vast influence in consequence of his deep religious seriousness, the munificence of his charities, his Professorship, his family connexions, and his easy relations with University authorities. . . . There was henceforth a man who could be the head and centre of the zealous people in every part of the country, who were adopting the new opinions; and not only so, but there was one who furnished the Movement with a front to the world, and gained for it a recognition from other parties in the University. . . . Dr Pusey was, to use the common expression, a host in himself; he was able to give a name, a form, and a personality to what was without him a sort of mob. . . .[12]

Pusey's first Tract, No. XVIII, was on Fasting. Unlike the earlier *Tracts* its author was identified by his initials, partly because at this stage Pusey wished to proceed cautiously in his endorsement of the *Tracts* as a whole. Fasting, Pusey argued, was an ancient and a godly discipline, witnessing with the daily office to the reality of spiritual things, and training Christians in self-denial. The fast-days of the Church were an indication, he wrote, of 'the peculiar character of our Church, which is not a mere Protestant, but a Primitive Church'.[13]

That 'primitive character' was explored more deeply in the substantial Tract on Baptism, which ran to some 400 pages, and was published in three parts in 1835 (Nos. LXVII, LXVIII, LXIX).

Newman emphasized in his preface to the collected volume of the *Tracts* in which it appears, that it was to be regarded, 'not as an inquiry into one single or isolated doctrine, but as a delineation, and serious examination of a modern system of theology, of extensive popularity and great speciousness, in its elementary and characteristic principles'. That popular view held that God conveyed grace 'only through the instrumentality of the mental energies, that is, through faith, prayer, active spiritual contemplations, or ... communion with God, in contradiction to the primitive view, according to which the Church and her Sacraments are the ordained and direct visible means of conveying to the soul what is in itself supernatural and unseen'.[14] Pusey argued, with reference both to the Fathers and the early liturgies, for the reality of sacramental grace conveyed in Baptism. Just as Anglican doctrine was established by an appeal to Anglican worship, so the liturgies of the universal Church pointed to the faith of that Church.[15] Powerfully influenced by the teaching of the Greek Fathers that salvation is a 'partaking of the divine nature', Pusey maintained that 'a meagre conception of the actualness of our Redeemer's gift in His Sacraments ... has produced a meagre Theology, substituting His teaching for His Person, disclosures of God for the mystery of the Incarnation, "knowledge of the Godhead", for "being perfected in Christ", "the revealed will and glory of God", for the "whole fulness of the Godhead"'. Such an exposition had the effect of emptying the word of God of 'His Word', whereas the teaching of the Fathers, as represented, for instance, by St. Hilary, showed how St. Paul combined 'the reality of the indwelling of the Eternal Son in the Man Christ Jesus, with the reality of His communication of Himself to us, the reality of the mystery of Holy Baptism, and our being thereby *in* Him, with the reality of His Holy Incarnation'. Doctrines thus harmonize together, so closely has Christ 'blended together His Sacraments with His own eternal glory, as with His humiliation, constituting them effluences of both conjointly, as in outward form they represent His lowliness, in inward grace they communicate His "Virtue"'.[16]

Drawing on his knowledge of the Syriac Fathers Pusey stressed the wonder of the living seal of the Spirit impressed in Baptism, which, 'bearing with it the impress of the Divine Nature', was a continual source of renewal for the Christian.[17] Pusey deprecated the contemporary equation of Christian worship with moral exhortation. Baptism was more than a sign urging men to closer conformity to

Christ. As a Christian sacrament it constituted 'the hidden spring of such action', it was no less than 'the power of His Resurrection, derived into us from Him'. The early Church, he noted, 'did not simply commemorate . . . "events which took place 1800 years ago"', but in their worship 'showed Him . . . as even then coming into the world, born, suffering, dying, rising, ascending: they longed for His coming; they suffered in His Passion; they rose with Him from the tomb; they followed His Ascension; they awaited His return to judge the quick and dead, and to receive them to His Kingdom'. 'And so in His Sacraments also, He was with them; He fed them in the Eucharist; He washed away their sins in Baptism; and Baptism was to them, Salvation, and the Cross, and the Resurrection.'[18] Pusey pressed home that sense of liturgical participation in the saving events of the Gospel, which marked the patristic understanding, exploring the rich typology of Baptism in the Fathers and the ancient liturgies. He concluded with an appreciation of the place of typology and of image and symbol in theology, a theme which he was to investigate more fully in his 1836 lectures on 'Types and Prophecies'. The Fathers, he wrote, 'saw intuitively what we attain to by a process of argument'.

We are obliged to detect, by analysis, what was to them transparent; and such 'demonstrations,' as compared with their perception, are much what the operation of the anatomist, in detaching the several sinews and muscles, is to their action in life. We lose also the moral influence of the character of truth resulting from their full, unlaboured persuasion; and the impressiveness of their conviction. Still, even under these disadvantages, it will probably be felt, that this system of the Ancient Church does perceive a harmony in Holy Scripture, to which we are strangers; that there is a beauty in this universal relation of the most distant and minutest things and words of Holy Scripture, with the most central and greatest, even those of Him, our Lord; . . . that it is analogous to His scheme of Creation, in which the lowest things bear a certain relation to the highest, attesting the unity of their Author; that it is agreeable to the connection of His Word with His word, that this should, even in what seems the most incidental and insignificant detail of it, speak of Him, Who spoke it, be penetrated with Him, Who is it's and our Life. . . . Certainly, a gradual abandonment of the types and a less reverential and thoughtful appreciation of the reality, have gone together.[19]

Pusey and the other leaders of the Oxford movement recognized, as Dr Härdelin has put it, that 'the Word is greater than the words, and the Spirit greater than the letters', though that apprehension did not lead them to an agnosticism, or to an abandonment of the dogmatic principle. Pusey criticized Lutheran scholasticism for treating Scripture not as 'a living Word' but as 'a dead repository of barren technicalities'. The Fathers, with their allegorical and typological interpretation of Scripture, showed their awareness of image and symbol as the very means by which God revealed himself to man.[20] As Froude put it:

Figures and metaphors are not chosen by inspired writers, . . . to give elevation to plain matters, but because the matters of which they speak are in themselves so elevated as not to admit of being expressed plainly. It is no part of their object to make plain things difficult but difficult things as plain as they admit of being. Thus . . . the various names and titles, by which Jesus Christ is figured in the Bible . . . are given Him not with a view to perplex and obscure our ideas, on a subject which might otherwise have been more clearly presented to us, but because such obscure and perplexed ideas are the nearest approaches to accuracy of which our faculties are susceptible.[21]

It is a theme which Pusey echoed in his lectures on 'Types and Prophecies' when he stressed that with respect to the mystery of God it is not 'clearness and distinctness, but its greatness' which constitutes 'its majesty and impressiveness': 'greatness and indistinctness commence together'. Wilfrid Ward made the same point with respect to Newman's *University Sermons*.

Clearness of statement, or even of thought, is often not the principal essential for the recognition of deep truth. Rationalism is . . . the clear apprehension of a partial or narrow philosophical system incommensurate with the facts of the world and of human nature. . . . Faith on the other hand is less clear in its apprehension, but it touches deeper and more numerous grounds of belief. It is the *obscure* apprehension of a profound and comprehensive philosophy, while Rationalism is the *clear* apprehension of a narrow and shallow philosophy.[22]

The sacraments, the divinely authorized enacted symbols through which the grace of God touched the lives of men, were thus the vital and archetypal pattern for God's communication of himself to men. The theology of Renn Dickson Hampden, whose appointment as Regius Professor of Divinity the Tractarians so vigorously opposed, seemed to them to be marked equally by a low view of the sacraments and by an attempt to apply rationalist principles to the mystery of faith. In his Bampton Lectures Hampden asserted that sacramental theology had been based on a 'theory of secret influences', and suggested that 'the general belief in Magic in the early ages of the Church' was sufficient to account for the acceptance of such a theory. The theory was one of divine causation, but, Hampden maintained, 'the practical power displayed is the sacerdotal'. What Hampden conceived as the scholastic distortion of Christianity was also apparent, he held, in the elaboration of credal and confessional statements. Whereas, he maintained, 'the Apostles' Creed states nothing but facts', the Nicene and Athanasian Creeds are marked by 'scholastic speculations'.[23] Hampden was critical of the realism of scholastic theology, speaking approvingly of the Nominalists, and linked the elaboration of the scholastic system with the development of ecclesiastical authority. He criticized likewise the influence of the mystical tradition represented particularly by Dionysius the Areopagite, and the speculations of the school of Alexandria, although the main thrust of his argument was against Aristotelianism.

Hampden and the Tractarians shared a caution about theological definition, Hampden because such definition, which was necessarily shaped by the culture of the age to which it belonged, was a distortion of the Gospel, the Tractarians because definition could so easily become an unwarranted prying into the mysteries of God. Where they sharply parted company was in the Tractarian reverence for tradition, sacramental piety, the creeds as the symbol of the faith of the Church, and reverence for the Fathers as interpreters of Scripture and witnesses to the interconnection of theology and spirituality. The project of translating a large number of patristic writings, which issued in *The Library of the Fathers*, undoubtedly gained particular impetus from the Hampden controversy. Part of Hampden's offence in Pusey's eyes was the 'bitter and sarcastic language' which he had used about the Fathers.[24]

Pusey was a prime mover in making the works of the Fathers more widely known, emphasizing the patristic interpretation of Scripture as setting out 'ancient catholic truth' in contrast to 'modern private opinions'. The Church appealed 'not to the Fathers individually, or as individuals, but as witnesses; not to this or that Father, but to a whole body, and agreement of Catholic Fathers and ancient Bishops'. In an age when Dean Gaisford could dismiss the Fathers as 'sad rubbish', the forty-eight volumes which eventually comprised the *Library of the Fathers* had a particular importance. Liddon judged that 'it made thoughtful adherents of the Movement feel that the Fathers were behind them, and with the Fathers that ancient undivided Church', as well as keeping before their minds 'the fact that the Fathers were, in several respects, unlike the moderns, not only in the English Church, but also in the Church of Rome'.[25] Of the works translated a large number are commentaries, notably those of St. John Chrysostom, and a significant place is given to the writings of St. Augustine and St. Athanasius.

Pusey valued the Fathers because they witnessed powerfully to the reality of Divine grace, weaving together doctrine and devotion so that *lex orandi* was seen indeed to be *lex credendi*. That same fusion is evident in Pusey's unjustly neglected sermons, as well as in the work of spiritual direction for which he was valued by many. Owen Chadwick has commented that whereas the word 'ecstatic' would never be used of the writings of Keble and Newman, that word 'springs naturally to the mind of one reading the sermons of Pusey'.[26] Yngve Brilioth did not hesitate to call Pusey the *doctor mysticus* amongst the Tractarians.[27] More recently he has been seen to stand in the tradition of 'fools for Christ's sake', of which Jean-Joseph Surin, whom Pusey valued highly, is an example.[28] The range of writers from which Pusey drew was considerable, as Brilioth points out, stressing how Augustine and the Latin Fathers were for Pusey 'a channel for the piety and the theology of the Greek Church'. Clement of Alexandria, Irenaeus, Gregory Nazianzen, Chrysostom, and Cyril are all prominent, and amongst later writers we find Bernard, Ruysbroek, Tauler, Teresa and John of the Cross, Catherine of Siena, Thomas à Kempis, Bonaventura, and Scupoli—the author of the *Spiritual Combat*, a work valued and edited on Mount Athos in the eighteenth century and in Russia in the nineteenth. There were also more recent Catholic writers such as Surin and Avrillon.[29]

The darkness which Pusey knew following his wife's death in 1839 and the ascetic life he subsequently followed, combined with the strong expressions of self-abnegation in many of his letters, have left many with the impression of a gloomy and morbidly unhealthy piety. That note was certainly there, and Pusey could write to Keble in 1844, when he asked Keble to hear his confession, in the darkest terms.

My dear wife's illness first brought to me, what has since been deepened by the review of my past life, how, amid special mercies and guardianship of God, I am scarred all over and seamed with sin, so that I am a monster to myself; I loathe myself; I can feel of myself only like one covered with leprosy from head to foot; guarded as I have been, there is no one with whom I do not compare myself, and find myself worse than they; and yet, thus wounded and full of sores, I am so shocked at myself that I dare not lay my wounds bare to any one . . . ; and so I go on, having no such comfort as in good Bp. Andrewes' words, to confess myself 'an unclean work, a dead dog, a putrid corpse,' and pray Him to heal my leprosy as He did on earth, and to raise me from the dead: to give me sight, and to forgive me the 10,000 talents. . . .[30]

The strict rule that Pusey proposed for himself in 1846 was marked by the same sense of his own unworthiness, and although Keble expressed his admiration for Pusey's example of humility, he also chided him gently: 'for my sake, and for all our sakes, be not hard upon yourself—remember what is said about "often infirmities".'[31]

Liddon defended Pusey by pointing out the extent to which Pusey's language can be paralleled in that of many renowned for their holiness of life: Augustine, Francis, Vincent de Paul; Francis de Sales; Bunyan and Wesley; Philip Neri and Charles Simeon. The over-whelming sense of the awe and majesty of God and the wonder of his condescension to us in love must indeed bring home the sense of utter unworthiness, that such grace is entirely unmerited. Taken out of context Pusey's expressions may appear simply masochistic, but this is in no way the over-all character of his understanding of the Christian life, of sin and grace, as we find it in his sermons. Penitence is not punishment, it is at its heart an expression of love, a response to the greatness of the love of God, in creation, redemption, and sanctification. The reality of that grace, the reality of the penitence which it calls forth, and the reality of the salvation God offers are the true themes of Pusey's teaching. In his sermons, as in his more technically theological writings, he protested strongly against views which would reduce in any way the living power of the Gospel.

In the Preface to the *Parochial Sermons* Pusey stated that the very heart of his preaching was 'the inculcation of the Great Mystery, expressed in the words to be "*in* Christ", to be "Members of Christ", "Temples of the Holy Ghost"; that Christ doth dwell really and truly in the hearts of the faithful'.[32] One of the dangers of Hampden's teaching was, Pusey suggested, that it undermined this central reality of faith by suggesting that the doctrine of our participation in the Divine Nature was Pantheistic. It was nothing of the kind, Pusey argued: 'so far from being consistent with Pantheism [it] contradicts it, for it implies personal existence', and quoted with approval W. H. Mill's comment that 'the sacred and mysterious doctrine of the Trinity in Unity, has ever been the surest safeguard against Pantheism in the Christian Church'—a statement strongly reminiscent of Coleridge's dictum that 'Pantheism is but a painted Atheism and that the Doctrine of the Trinity is the great and only sure Bulwark against it'.[33]

Pusey's sermons are shot through with a sense of awe, reverence, and wonder before the grace, mercy, and holiness of God. The adoration of the contemplative before the mystery of the God who, coming down to the lowest part of our need, takes us to himself, and exalts us in Christ to the heavenly places—that is the temper and disposition which he sought to share. He begins, more often than not, powerfully and directly, as in a sermon for Christmas Eve.

The Grace of God at all times awaits, forecomes, accompanies, follows, encompasses us. It is within us, and without us. It comes to us through ordinances, and without them. It never fails us, if we never fail It. It is every where, for It is the Holy Spirit, Who is every where, since He is God. . . .

Although He comes to all alike who look for Him, He doth not come alike to all. He filleth all; but all do not alike contain Him. He, the Same, dwelleth in the Seraphim, on fire with love, and close around His Throne, and in the poorest, weakest, penitent; but not in the same way. . . . The wider the mouth of the soul is opened by our thirsting desire for God, the more largely will He fill it. Our capacity to receive Him, is our longing for Him.[34]

The 'intensity' of the Christmas mystery is 'God with us':

To retrace His Image upon us, He, Who is the Co-Eternal Image of the Father, took us into Himself, and stamped again His Likeness upon us, by taking the likeness of our sinfulness; that us, who were aforetime alienated from God, He made to be at one with God, by Himself becoming one of us, and giving us of His Oneness with the Father; us, who were a blot in the Creation of God, outcasts from His Sight, He has brought back into the harmony and order of His obedient creatures, uniting us to the Father in Himself; replacing our deadness by Himself, Who is Life; our darkness by Himself, Who is Light; our blindness by Himself, Who is Wisdom; our corruption by His Incorruption; our sinfulness by His Holiness; our emptiness by His Fulness, enlarging our finiteness to receive God, Who is Infinite.

Where shall be the bound or measure of His Mercies or of our praise? Our nature in itself the last, made, so to say, the Union between God and His

creatures! For in Him Who is the Mediator between God and man, being
Very God and Very Man, shall all things, 'both which are in Heaven and
which are in earth,' be gathered together and summed up in one; Angels and
Saints shall together be in-oned, being together in-dwelt by the Ever-Blessed
Trinity, in 'the Church, which is His Body, the fulness of Him that filleth all
in all.'[35]

Christ took our nature into himself so that 'in Him it is In-Godded,
Deitate'—the Greek theology of *theosis* is thus powerfully emphasized.

The mystery of the Incarnation prepares us for the mystery of the
Eucharistic presence, but the discernment of that presence is linked
inseparably with the response of love to Christ's poor. Theology and
practice are conjoined; living the life is a condition of knowing the
doctrine.

If we would see Him in His Sacraments, we must see Him also, wherever He
has declared Himself to be, and especially in His poor. . . Real love to Christ
must issue in love to all who are Christ's, and real love to Christ's poor must
issue in self-denying acts of love towards them. Casual alms-giving is not
Christian charity. . . the poor, rich in faith, have been the converters of the
world; and we . . . , if we are wise, must seek to be like them, to empty
ourselves, at least, of our abundance; to empty ourselves, rather of our
self-conceit, our notions of station, our costliness of dress, our jewelry, our
luxuries, our self-love, even as He . . . emptied Himself of the glory which He
had with the Father, the Brightness of His Majesty, the worship of the Hosts
of Heaven, and made Himself poor, to make us rich.[36]

The Incarnation is 'a depth of mystery unsearchable'. 'We must
shrink with awe', Pusey writes, 'when we pronounce it'. 'That God
. . . should take into Himself what is not God; one must stand
speechless with awe at so amazing a mystery.'[37]

The descent of the Incarnation is fulfilled in the ascent of the
Lord's exaltation and the outpouring of the Holy Spirit, and again
we find Pusey moved to adoration in his sermons for Ascension Day
and Pentecost. 'We are in Heaven in Him, He on earth in us.' 'This
then is the great blessedness of this our citizenship, as of every other
Gift of Grace or Glory, that we have it not in ourselves, but of, and in
Christ.'

All in us, which is of Heaven, is of His Spirit in us. His Holy Spirit, the Bond of the Oneness of the Father and the Son, Which encircleth all things, taketh us up into Himself. . . .

This, again, is the very Mystery and Blessedness of the Sacraments; that by the one, Christ knit us into Himself; by the other, He descendeth to us, that He may become 'One with us, and we with Him.' This is the force of prayer, that it is a calling down of God into ourselves, a going forth of ourselves to God.[38]

'Whit Sunday', Pusey tells us, 'is the filling up of the Ascension'. 'The wondrous exchange was half made on the Ascension, when Man in God was taken up into Heaven, and sat on His Father's Throne; the day of Pentecost fulfilled the Promise of the Father, and as man now dwelt in God, so God, in a New and Ineffable Way, dwelt thenceforth in man.'

Such is the Wondrous Goodness of God, such His Overflowing Love towards us, His Divine Joy in imparting Himself to us His most fallen creatures, if we will but receive Him, that this His Divine Work in us, He worketh in a way wholly Divine. It is not enough for His Love, to give us any or all the Gifts of His Grace; not enough to give us His Love, and 'Righteousness, and Sanctification, and Redemption;' but He is Himself all these and all besides to us. His Gifts are the Fruits of the Spirit, not without us, but within us. His Gifts stream forth from His Gift, Himself. His Gift is Himself. . . . His Gift is the Very Fountain of His Love. . . . He, by His Presence, will so enlarge the soul, that, like the garden of Eden, He should . . . walk in it, and it shall be His pleasure to dwell there. . . . He would give us All that He is. He asks of us in return the nothingness we are.[39]

Pusey follows Irenaeus in his stress on man as made in the image of God and formed to receive the divine likeness. Adam in Eden as created by God 'reflected His Maker's Will, as clear water gives back the face of Heaven, or a mirror flashes back the brightness of the earthly sun which shines upon it'.[40] In heaven, made perfect in the likeness of God, 'glory shall fill the Elect above the brightness of the sun, shall make them transparent with light, all-bright, all-pure; and that, with the imparted light of God'. Then, 'when faith is turned into sight and hope into its substance . . . then shall we love with the love of God, shall love God as God loveth Himself, even through His love cleaving unto His love, ever borne to God, uplifted, filled, overflowing, receiving, giving back so as again to receive, the unutterable love of God, and by His love changed into His own unchangeableness.' 'How can we ever cease to love, when we love unceasing Love with His own Love?'[41] So, drawing on Ruysbroek and Bernard, Augustine, Chrysostom, and Gregory Nazianzen, Pusey grounded his understanding of salvation as participation in the Divine Nature in the character of that Nature as love, which in giving to the uttermost transforms entirely into its likeness.

'In Thy Light shall we see Light.' It shall be we who see that Light which is God, yet in His light, the light of Glory wherewith the souls and bodies of the Blessed shall be filled. Even here, where what we love or gaze on, is created, yet as long as we can gaze, our minds are filled the more, the more we gaze. Even in deep human love, the longer the soul dwelleth on that which reflects Heaven in the object of its love, the intenser and more entrancing is its love. . . . (There) we shall not cease to be; but God being All things in us, we shall be other selves, and, as St. John says, 'like Him.'

Oh what shall it be to range freely within that boundless bliss, to be admitted into its very depths, or . . . 'to be translated into the glory of God;' to move, to think, to see, within God; in Himself and by Himself to see Himself. . . . The love which melteth us shall sustain us. And because no created heart can contain such love, we shall joy in the bliss of others, as our own.[42]

The Christian is called by prayer and penitence to live towards this vision of glory. The Cross is borne both for us and in us. 'Our life', Pusey tells us, 'from Baptism to our death should be a practice of the Cross, a learning to be crucified, a crucifixion of our passions, appetites, desires, wills, until, one by one, they be all nailed, and we have no will, but the will of our Father which is in Heaven'.[43] Fasting and self-denial are ways by which we take the Cross; the acceptance of the suffering which comes to us unsought is the way by which we bear it. Like Justin Martyr, Pusey saw the Cross engraved on the very fabric of the natural order.

It is the commonest form in art and nature; it is impressed everywhere, from the courses of the heavenly bodies to some of the stones upon your shore, or the flowers of the field; it is presented to us by the very birds as they soar heavenwards; 'the birds of the air and the fishes of the sea' float, as it were, upheld by it; the despised animal, which bare our Lord, bears on its shoulders the memorial of His Cross; the human countenance, 'the image of God' is moulded upon it; it is raised aloft upon our ships; it is formed involuntarily . . . on our doors, our windows, our streets, our roads, on dress, on furniture, on ornaments, on the soldier's sword and spear, on the very mills which prepare our 'daily bread', that we may at all times think on it, and regard nothing common which God has cleansed and sanctified, as in Christ he hath our world, and all which it contains.[44]

In his introduction to Surin's *Foundations of the Spiritual Life* he speaks of the wounds of Christ as having 'the capacity of His Godhead'; they are the gate of Paradise.[45] The Passion of Christ is God's love displayed without; the Spirit is the fire of love within. Both lead to the way of redemptive suffering, of compassion.

It were a dream . . . to think that we could love the Passion of Christ and not engrave it on our lives; that we could be melted by His sorrows . . . and ourselves not sorrow or suffer with Him. . . . The Sufferings of Christ cannot be real to him who never suffers.[46]

To be moved to love by the Cross of Christ is not an automatic response; we may remain 'ice-cold under His very Cross, unless He Himself kindle our hearts with His piercing look of love'. Christ is 'the Hidden Magnet, Who, having no Form or Beauty when He died for us, draws mightily to Himself all who have that which can be drawn, and drawing, holds them to Himself, imparting to them of the Virtue which goeth forth from Him, and thereby transforming them into Himself'. In the Passion of the Lord 'are hidden the treasures of His Divinity'. The Cross 'is the measure of the depth of our misery whence It raises us, and of the Infinite love of God, to which It draws us, and Whose treasures it lays open to us.'

Yet not the doctrine of the Cross alone, nor its preaching, nor gazing on it, nor bearing it, but He Himself Who for us hung thereon must impart Its virtue to us; Himself, Who bore the Cross to atone for us, applying Its saving efficacy to our souls; Himself, our living Pattern, tracing His own Divine Image on all who 'look to' Him.[47]

The first-fruit of the Cross is the cleansing of the soul in penitence; a deep awareness of the diseased self-centredness of sin. That first stage of penitence is tinged with joy, for it is an experience of forgiveness and liberation. This is given, said Pusey, as 'an earnest of His endless love, a ray of light which comes from His Divine Presence, which may shine to us in all our darkness, and guide us on to the perfect Day'. Yet, as we are led in the deeper ways of the Cross there will come 'seasons of darkness, dreariness, disquiet through evil thoughts'. By them Christ teaches us 'to abide patiently on our little crosses by His Side, beholding the end of His and the glory which should follow'.[48]

The holiness which is the Christian calling is a summons to an ever-deepening life of prayer. Like the great spiritual writers of the Orthodox tradition Pusey took seriously the command that we should pray without ceasing. 'The one plain rule', he insisted, 'is to set about doing it', and in that very attempt the difficulties become less intractable. The distractions of business or pleasure, which are often pleaded as the reason for the impossibility of such total praying, are in reality a prayer, an expression of dependence upon other gods. The hours of public prayer may be counted, but private prayer may be at any time: 'when in company, as well as when alone; amid conversation, as when silent; . . . in the midst of business and employment, as when unoccupied; in short intervals when for the moment thou seemest to have nothing else to do, or when most employed'. The divisions of the day and its varied tasks are all to be marked with prayer and so consecrated to God.[49] Pusey lists five points which, he holds, are conditions of acceptable prayer: a right faith ('in My Name'); a right life ('if My words abide in you'); that we be members of His body ('if ye abide in Me'); confidence as to the subject of prayer ('believing that ye shall have them'); and perseverance. The confession of our emptiness, our nothingness before God, is the very condition of our being filled. Prayer is prayer in the Church, in the communion of the Body of Christ, yet the Church is disunited and so prayer suffers.

It is too likely that all our privileges are impaired by these rents, that the stream of grace no longer runs so richly through all the branches, which are thus torn, though not wholly severed. We have all the more reason to pray for the peace and unity of the Church, as suffering ourselves from its disunion. As we are not saved by ourselves, are not members of our Lord by ourselves, but in His Church and the Communion of Saints, so our privileges and the helps to our salvation are, in a mysterious way, wrapped up in the well-being of the Church.[50]

Pusey is clear that life and prayer run together, and that it is primarily the infrequency of our praying which makes prayer so difficult. Prayer, again, may be thought of as a breathing to and in God, and there are ways in which this may be enabled: recollection; a concern for reverence; and avoidance of haste; the use of brief petitions.[51] 'Prayer to God', Pusey wrote, 'asks for Himself, to be the soul's own', and, although 'man cannot be God' and 'cannot be a god unto himself', he may be 'a partaker of the Divine Nature'. And so prayer is 'the ascent of the soul to God', and our restless heart, which issues in prayer, is a sign that nothing can satisfy us except the fulness of the love of God. Those who so pray will find that their last prayer on earth in the Name of Jesus will 'melt into the first Halleluiah in heaven, where too doubtless prayer shall never cease, but the soul shall endlessly desire of God, what God shall unintermittingly supply, more and yet more of the exhaustless, ever-filling fulness of Divine Beauty and Wisdom and Love, yea of Himself Who is Love'.[52]

Pusey could indeed be ecstatic, as this exploration of his sermons has shown. He could also be controversial, and in particular his sacramental teaching in his university sermons of 1843 and 1846 and 1853 on the Eucharist and on sacramental Confession was so regarded. J. B. Mozley commented that Pusey's deepening of the idea of Baptism brought with it the consequence of magnifying post-baptismal sin, which was no less than a falling away from a new life, the undoing of a new nature, and the defiling of the temple of the Holy Spirit.[53] Pusey was aware that he was criticized for rigorism, and his sermon of 1843 was in part a response to that criticism. He could have chosen the theme of confession and absolution, which followed later in 1846, but he judged that eucharistic doctrine was less controversial. The 1843 sermon, 'The Holy Eucharist a Comfort to the Penitent', followed closely the phraseology of the Fathers, emphasizing that the life bestowed in the Eucharist 'is greater than any gift, since it is life in Christ, life through His indwelling, Himself Who is Life'. He spoke of 'that bread which is His Flesh' and of 'touching with our very lips that cleansing Blood'. The words of institution spoke of the body broken and the blood shed for the remission of sins, and so the Eucharist is both the means of union with God and the source of grace removing the barriers of sin to that union. So Pusey urged the need for more frequent celebrations of the Eucharist than the monthly pattern that was then prevalent in Christ Church Cathedral. 'We cannot know the Gift of God', he pleaded, 'if we forfeit it; we must cease mostly even to long for what we forego. We lose the very sense to understand it.'[54] Ten years later Pusey stated that his wish had been to impress on the souls of hearers, 'the actualness and closeness of the union of man's soul with its

Redeemer, and in Him with God . . . to show how, through the Holy
Eucharist, we have life from our living and loving Lord Himself,
re-creation in Him, and the earnest of endless joy and bliss in Him'.[55]
The patristic quotations were intended to serve that end, and Pusey
stated that Cyril of Alexandria was the Father he had endeavoured to
follow most carefully. He expressly repudiated the doctrine of transubstantiation.[56] Nonetheless his sermon was called into question by
the university authorities, and, after proceedings of questionable
judicial fairness, Pusey was suspended from preaching before the
university for two years, on the grounds that he taught in his sermon
doctrine contrary to that of the Church of England.

In 1853 Pusey returned to the theme of eucharistic doctrine in a
sermon before the university. He began with a vigorous statement.

The Holy Eucharist is plainly the closest union of man with God. Through
the Incarnation God took our nature, took the Manhood into God. But
although we had that unspeakable nearness to Himself . . . this was a gift to
our whole race. It was a gift which, by its very nature, must overflow to us
individually; yet still it required a further act of God's condescension fully to
apply it to each one of us. . . .

    We could not be united to Him, save by His communicating Himself to us.
This He willed to do by indwelling in us through His Spirit; by making us,
through the Sacrament of Baptism, members of His Son; by giving us,
through the Holy Eucharist, not in any carnal way, but really and spiritually,
the Flesh and Blood of the Incarnate Son, whereby 'He dwelleth in us, and we
in Him; He is one with us, and we with him.' Through these, He imparteth to
us the life which He Himself gives us. He, the Life of the world, maketh those
alive, in whom He is. This is the comfort of the penitent, the joy of the
faithful, the Paradise of the holy, the Heaven of those whose conversation is
in Heaven, the purity of those who long to be partakers of His holiness, the
strengthening of man's heart, the renewal of the inward man, the fervour of
Divine love, spiritual peace, kindled hope, assured faith, burning thankful-
ness,—that our Lord Jesus Christ, not in figure, but in reality, although in
spiritual reality, does give Himself to us, does come to be in us.[57]

Pusey went on to reject not only transubstantiation, but also the
doctrine of consubstantiation commonly ascribed to the Lutherans.
Not only is this a false ascription, but such a doctrine would, as much
as transubstantiation be accounted a physical explanation. Pusey
stressed that the words 'This is My Body' are not to be taken in
isolation from other parts of Scripture, and are not to be treated as

the kind of definition which belongs to the 'laboured statements' of systematic theology. The sacramental Presence, Pusey wrote, has been termed 'sacramental, supernatural, mystical, ineffable, as opposed *not* to what is real, but to what is natural'.

The word has been chosen to express, not our knowledge, but our ignorance; or that unknowing knowledge of faith, which we have of things Divine, surpassing knowledge. . . . But it is a Presence without us, not within us only; a Presence by virtue of our Lord's words, although to us it becomes a saving Presence, received to our salvation, through our faith.[58]

Pusey cited with approval St. John Damascene's stress on the eucharistic Presence being as inseparably linked to the epiclesis of the Spirit as was the Incarnation itself. 'It is true', he went on, 'that the outward elements are, as some of the Fathers call them, figures, types, symbols, images of His Body.' 'But who authorized men to add, "of his absent Body?"'[59] Pusey picked up again the themes of type and symbol that he had expounded in his 1836 Lectures.

Abstract terms go but a little way in declaring to us the ways of God. He mirrors Himself in the works of His Hands. He stamps in the book of His Word the meaning of the book of His works. . . . All is one great picture-language, to make present to our sense and minds what is invisible, intangible, inconceivable.

Whether then our Lord be called a Lion, a Lamb, a Rock, a Hiding Place . . . these are but different letters of the one great alphabet of that condescending language in which God reveals Himself to man.[60]

There followed a lengthy and valuable catena from the Fathers on the Presence of Christ in the Eucharist, concluding with a moving appeal, particularly to his younger hearers, to receive the eucharistic gift of Christ Himself with faith and repentance. Citing the Homilies, which say of the Eucharist that it is 'the salve of immortality and sovereign preservative against death, a deifical Communion' and 'the defence of faith', Pusey urged them to receive the Eucharist as a foretaste of the life of heaven.

Then shall all truth be open to you, all love shall fill you; soul and body shall be satisfied with His likeness; they shall rest in His love; they shall have all they long for, and long for all they have. All you long for, shall be for ever yours; for the All-Holy Trinity shall be for ever yours. . . . (The Lord will fill you) with His Grace, fill you with Himself, the Author of Grace.[61]

Once again the patristic theme of salvation understood as participation in the Divine Nature is stressed.

The theme of penitence which Pusey linked with the Eucharist in his 1843 sermon was picked up again in his sermon of 1846, *Entire Absolution of the Penitent.* In the December of that year he was to make his own confession to John Keble, and in this sermon he pressed the use of sacramental Confession, having previously discussed with John Keble the form the sermon would take. As the first sermon Pusey preached before the University following the lifting of the sentence of suspension, and considering the subject was calculated to arouse anti-Catholic fears and suspicions (particularly when Newman had been received into the Church of Rome only some three months previously), it is not surprising that the sermon attracted considerable attention. Liddon wrote, citing an eye-witness account:

The choir . . . was crowded from end to end: the organ-loft looked as though it might give way, such was the mass of Undergraduates who had got into it; even the triforium had been invaded by eager listeners. Every inch on the floor of the church was occupied. Dr Pusey . . . had to move slowly through the dense mass on his way to the corner of the Cathedral where the Vice-Chancellor and Doctors assemble . . . his perfectly pallid, furrowed, mortified face looking almost like jagged marble, immovably serene withal, and with eyes fixed in deep humility on the ground.[62]

Pusey spoke, with his characteristic intense restraint, of the way in which sacramental words and forms do not point to the Church and the Christian Ministry supplanting Christ, but rather to their being made the instruments of Christ. It is no more impossible for God to use the forms of absolution to bestow the grace of his forgiveness than for him to use the water of Baptism to wash away sin. The form of confession and absolution in the Prayer Book order for the Visitation of the Sick is no more than an intensification and a sharp personalizing of the confession and absolution in Morning and Evening Prayer and in Holy Communion. At ordination, Pusey reminds his hearers, priests are commissioned to absolve. That sacramental absolution is a work of healing, and the personal relationship which it involves is of a piece with God's approach to man in the Incarnation.

It may be one of the fruits of the Incarnation, and a part of the dignity thereby conferred upon our nature, that God would rather work His miracles of grace through man, than immediately by Himself. It may be part of the Mystery of the Passion, that God would rather bestow Its fruits, through those who can suffer with us, through toil and suffering, than without them. It may be part of the purpose of His Love, that love should increase while one member suffers with another, and relieves another.[63]

Pusey was well aware that sacramental Confession was suspect because it was thought to be an easy and mechanical process by which sin was treated lightly, a view he believed to be gravely mistaken.

Deep sins after Baptism are forgiven, but upon deep contrition which God giveth; and deep contrition is, for the most part, slowly and gradually worked into the soul, deepening with deepening grace, sorrowing still more, as, by God's grace, it more deeply loves; grieved the more, the more it knows Him Whom it once grieved, and through that grief and love inwrought in it by God, the more forgiven. So then, by the very order of God with the soul, (except when He leads it in some special way, and by the Cross, and His own overflowing love blots out the very traces of past sin and its very memory,) continued sorrow is not only the condition of continued pardon, but the very channel of new graces and of the renewed life of the soul.[64]

The Church aimed, he argued, 'not to diminish sorrow for past sin, but to make it joyous'; it was, as the early Fathers witnessed, 'a Baptism of tears'.[65]

Concern for holiness, for a faith which took seriously the transfiguring grace of God, came to mean for Pusey and for the other Tractarian leaders that sacramental Confession should be seen to be more and more central in the pastor's care of his people and in his own spiritual discipline. Manning could write to Samuel Wilberforce in 1849 that the lack of any real systematic theology in Anglicanism was mirrored in the piecemeal character of Anglican moral, spiritual, and ascetical theology. 'We were drawn off to controversy, and . . . the practice of confession was neglected.'

The Puritans . . . retained the tradition of spiritual direction but when separated from Confession and the Priesthood, it became fanatical. The same we see among Dissenters. What we call enthusiasm, and fanaticism, and experience, is the disembodied soul of Confession. . . . And I suppose that while the spirit of the Confessional went to the Puritans, the Formality remained as a Theory in the Church, so that while they became fanatical, we became lifeless—a miserable divorce which drives one side into unspiritual-ity and the other into unbelief.[66]

Pusey concurred. 'I am more and more convinced that nothing except an extensive system of confession can remedy our evils.'[67]

The same concern for holiness was the central impulse in Pusey's long concern with the revival of the religious life in the Church of England. Following the death of his wife in 1839, and fortified by what he had read in the Fathers of the consecrated single life, Pusey believed that he himself was henceforth called by God not to re-marry. He encouraged his daughter Lucy in her early thoughts of a call to a single life. He saw also the part which might be played by sisterhoods in both breaking out of the restrictions of the un-reformed parochial system and in offering opportunities to dedi-cated women to serve the Church. In December 1839 he told Keble that Newman and he had independently 'come to think it necessary to have some "Sœurs de Charité" in the Anglo-Catholic (Church)' and 'that might begin by regular employment as nurses, in hospitals and lunatic asylums, in which last Christian nursing is so sadly missed'.[68] He corresponded on the same topic with Dr Hook, the Vicar of Leeds, whose own sister was drawn to such a life. Hook was aware of the suspicion that such sisterhoods might arouse and warned of opposition 'from those "Evangelical" ladies who at present control the visiting societies, and employ the clergy as their agents'.[69] Four years later Samuel Wilberforce echoed Hook's advice to start by practical action rather than by promoting anything which Protestant detractors might accuse of resembling a Catholic religious order.

The strange doctrines and the startling practices of the party, whom for shortness I will call the 'Tract-writer-party' have brought many most un-objectionable things under a just suspicion, and we have no right to endanger great attempts by letting them come before the Church in any suspicious garb. On this account it will be, I am sure, essential to our success, first, to begin with small and unobserved steps; to let all we do *grow* as much as possible out of what we have in the Church around us, and secondly, not only to be ourselves heartily attached to the doctrine, and discipline, and spirit of our own Reformed Church, but to secure as our first co-operators persons of the like temper; and to let this true affection to our own Commu-nion, its articles, formularies, and temper, speak itself freely out in our arrangements, and never be cloaked under ambiguous disguises. If it should please God ever to bring such a scheme to perfection, we might then hope to show that a life of great devotion, and self-denial and charity, was not necessarily a copying of the blurred characters of exalted human merit, or of formal or self-righteous asceticism. But we must not disguise from ourselves the difficulty of establishing clearly this difference between ourselves and 'Solitaries' or 'Nuns,' and we must, therefore, walk with the utmost circumspection.[70]

This meant for Wilberforce that all such undertakings ought to have the full sanction of the Bishop, and that ventures should be begun by groups of ladies working through the parochial system by offering assistance with the parochial school. Pusey felt that religious orders demanded a much greater autonomy, particularly after his experience of the early sisterhood experiment at Park Village linked with William Dodsworth's parish of Christ Church, Albany Street. Thus he wrote to Arthur Stanton in 1865—when there was a possibility of Stanton going to St. Saviour's, Leeds, where Stanton would have hoped to have formed and directed his own sisterhood—that he had seen 'the cramping effect of Mr Dodsworth's plan of making the Sisterhood at Park Village a sort of district visiting society'. If sisters were under the direction of the parish priest, they would be living 'like the Scythians in their wagons, and, like gypsies, be ready to remove, on the warning of the Parish Priest, as the gypsies do at that of the parish constable'.[71] Autonomy was necessary to provide appropriate stability.

In 1841 Marian Rebecca Hughes became the first woman to make a religious profession in the Church of England, although there was then no society of which she could be a member. Miss Hughes, the daughter of a Gloucestershire priest and the cousin of the Revd Thomas Chamberlain, Vicar of St. Thomas the Martyr, Oxford, made her profession before Dr Pusey who used the service for the Consecration of a Virgin in the Roman Pontifical. Following that service she attended Communion, celebrated by Newman at St. Mary's.[72] The same year Pusey visited Roman Catholic communities in Ireland, having already received information from France about the constitutions of the Augustinian sisters and those of St. Vincent de Paul, a reminder of the influence of French seventeenth-century orders on the revival of the religious life in Anglicanism.

In 1843 the death of the poet Robert Southey, who had urged the revival of sisters of charity in the Church of England, led to a proposal by Lord John Manners that a house of such sisters would be the best memorial to Southey. This was the origin of the Park Village Sisterhood whose aims were to include: visiting the poor or the sick in their own homes, visiting hospitals, workhouses, or prisons; feeding, clothing, and instructing destitute children; and assistance in the burial of the dead. Pusey was much involved in the drawing up of the Rule, consulting with Beresford-Hope, Dodsworth and Keble, and mindful that it would have to have Bishop Blomfield's approval.

We naturally went by experience. Lord John Manners procured us the Rules of the Sisters of (Mercy) at Birmingham. I had some rules by me, used by different bodies in England and on the continent. We took as our basis St. Augustine's Rule, as extant in an Epistle of his to some "Sanctimoniales" whom he had brought together; thinking it most in accordance with our Church to take Rules from one of the Fathers of the Church. On this we engrafted others, always bearing in mind the character of English Church-women.[73]

By 1850 the small community was following the pattern of life described by a novice in the following terms:

The Sisters rose at five. . . . The service called Lauds was at six a.m., said in the Oratory . . . at a quarter to seven the Sisters assembled in the same room and Prime was said. . . . Breakfast followed, which was taken in silence; indeed silence was observed all day, except at the hours appointed for recreation. After that meal we said Terce and then went to hear Morning Prayers read in the church. . . . The Sisters who taught in the poor school went to their duties. . . . The school lasted till twelve, when we went home and said Sext. We had dinner at twenty minutes to one, still in silence. The food was plain, good, and sufficient. After dinner we talked together in the Common Room. At three we said None. . . . The school was dismissed for the day at half-past four. At five there were three quarters of an hour for spiritual reading, then Vespers. Supper followed at six o'clock, and after it a few moments' . . . relaxation. We then prepared for church: . . . those who could not go after the fatigues of the day read the service at home. On our return from church at eight o'clock Compline was said, and the Sisters remained in the Oratory after its conclusion for private devotion till twenty minutes past nine, when Mattins was said.[74]

The seven hours of the Breviary said by the sisters were translated and altered by Pusey, so that legendary material, invocation of ˌ

saints, and other controversial devotions were omitted. 'There is no passage read from a Father', Pusey told Beresford-Hope, 'which I could not myself preach in a sermon before the Bishop, nor any prayer which the Bishop himself might not use.'[75]

Although Pusey was so closely involved with the Park Village Sisterhood, the course of its development did not run smoothly. There were problems with the first Superior, Emma Langston, and difficulties springing from ill-health in the community, from time to time exacerbated by a demanding Rule framed by those without the benefit of experience of community life. There was divergence of view between Pusey and Dodsworth, since the latter was sensitive to his position in relation to Bishop Blomfield. With Miss Sellon and her Devonport sisterhood it was a somewhat different matter, partly because of the strong backing of Bishop Philpotts of Exeter. Pusey regarded Miss Sellon as 'the restorer after three centuries of the Religious Life in the English Church', and there can be little doubt that what lay behind this was both Miss Sellon's organizing genius and the trust that grew between her and Pusey through difficult years.[76] In A. M. Allchin's judgement both Pusey and Lydia Sellon had a deeper grasp of the meaning of monasticism than some other founders. 'At a time when others were thinking primarily in terms of activity, Pusey had already grasped the contemplative inner reality of the monastic life', and 'as early as 1850 Mother Lydia was making plans for the inclusion of an order of contemplative nuns within the Society of the Holy Trinity'.[77] In 1856, after the amalgamation of the Society of the Holy Cross (the Park Village Sisterhood) and Miss Sellon's Devonport Society to form the Society of the Most Holy Trinity, the Rule of the Sisters of the Second Order laid down that the sisters were to offer 'day and night throughout the four and twenty hours . . . the voice of mourning for sin, of interceding for grace, of adoration of the Majesty of the Divine Trinity and of the Love of Jesus', praying especially for the charitable work of the first and third orders.[78] Pusey's influence can be seen here, as it can also in the theology and spirituality of Richard Meux Benson, the founder of the Cowley Fathers.[79]

That there was a defensive side to Pusey cannot be doubted. He came to consider his early work on the theology of Germany to have been misguided, and in his will forbade its republication. He stood out against the endeavours of the University Commission to alter the Anglican exclusiveness of Oxford. He kept up a dogged resistance to what he saw as the destructive results of the new critical study of the Bible. Yet in a sermon preached only four years before his death, *Un-Science, not Science, adverse to Faith*, he could ask sharp and pertinent questions about the limits and character of scientific investigation and conclusions and give positive appreciation as a theologian to scientific theory: 'theology places no limits on the modes of [God's] working, Who works all things in all', for 'the workings in nature are to Theology only the workings of God'.[80] After Newman became a Roman Catholic, Pusey remained concerned with the unity of the Church, striving in the *Eirenicons* that he published in the 1860s to reconcile theological differences. In his opposition to the liberalism of *Essays and Reviews* and his dry response to F. W. Farrar's universalism he continued the defence of orthodoxy, which was an important strand in the Oxford Movement.

The defensive, even obscurantist, side of Pusey would not suffice to account for his influence. Colin Matthew has suggested that, 'although spiritually he enlarged the boundaries of Anglican devotionalism, intellectually and theologically he led Anglo-Catholicism ... into a dead end'.[81] If devotion and intellect, theology and spirituality, are kept in separate compartments then there may be some justification for such a judgement, and it would be wrong to deny the need for theological adjustment recognized at the time of Pusey's death in 1882 by Gore, Scott Holland, and the men of a younger generation. But the genius of the Oxford Movement and the secret of its influence was in its rediscovery of the wholeness of patristic theology, of the reality of sacramental grace, and a refusal, similar to that of Kierkegaard, to confine theology to the domain of the speculative. The 'Great Mystery' of transforming grace, of the Divine Indwelling and participation in the Divine Nature, which Pusey saw as central to the life of the Church in the first four centuries, he made central to his own teaching. This was what made 'real' and not 'nominal' Christians, this distinguished a living theology rooted in worship from rationalist, academic speculation. The scholar must advance in holiness and that in the end was what made Pusey attractive and drew the streams of penitents to his lodgings in Christ Church.

Tuckwell wrote that, when he first saw Pusey close, two things impressed him: 'his exceeding slovenliness of person; buttonless boots, necktie limp, *intonsum mentum*, unbrushed coat collar, grey hair "all too ruffled"; and the almost artificial sweetness of his smile, contrasting as it did with the sombre gloom of his face when in repose'.[82] Another, anonymous, writer has left us the following account of his visit to Pusey in old age, in 1877.

The hall-door is opened by no smart butler or trim waiting-maid; everything is plain, simple, severe. The janitress is a middle-aged woman in a plain print dress; the only covering which the floor of the hall and passages knows is a thin strip of cocoa-nut matting. The whole air of the place is rather that of a country vicarage, whose vicar is in reduced circumstances. . . .

There is nothing in the exterior or in the raiment of the short, stoutish little gentleman who rises to greet you, to say certainly that he is a clergyman. . . . The coat is buttoned close up to the neck, with a very narrow interspace of white visible; the massive and powerful head, with its copious growth of gray hair, is surmounted with a skull-cap of somewhat loose and ill-constructed fit. But the two most remarkable features about Dr. Pusey are his eyes and mouth. The latter is mobile with every kind of expression; the former are a deep blue, perfectly clear, free from the aqueous film of age, varying, as the mouth does, with the thought which animates the mind or proceeds in language from the lips. Never could there be a more speaking face, never a face into which there was concentrated more of the blended sentiments or capacities of earnestness, humour, solemn intensity, subtle satire. It is impossible not to be impressed by the perfect breeding, the true patrician ease, the masterly *savoir-faire*, which make up Dr. Pusey's manner. He has about him that indefinable air of superiority which stamps him at once as a man born to be what he has been, a leader of men; and it is easy still to recognize the presence and possession of those qualities which made Newman . . . greet him as 'the great'. . . . The general aspect of his face is one of keenness and benevolence combined. It is the face of a man whom you could not mistake to be other than both good and great.[83]

V. John Mason Neale: Symbolism and Sisterhoods

THE CONTRIBUTION of John Mason Neale to the Catholic revival was fourfold. First, through his part in the founding of the Cambridge Camden Society, he laid down principles of church architecture and church furnishing which were widely influential. Secondly his liturgical interests and capacity for translating the riches of ancient and medieval hymnody gave him a significant role in the transformation of Anglican worship and in the communication of patristic tradition and sacramental doctrine to ordinary congregations. Closely linked with this were his ecumenical concerns, and in particular his study of the history of Eastern Christianity, which counterbalanced the enthusiasm of others for contemporary ultramontane Catholicism. Finally his founding of the Society of St. Margaret was an important element in the revival of the religious life in the Church of England.

Neale was born in 1818, the son of the Revd Cornelius Neale, a pious Evangelical who had taken Holy Orders at the age of 33, only to die a year later, when his son was only 5. After a varied education at schools and with private tutors Neale went up to Trinity College, Cambridge in 1836. With his friends Benjamin Webb and Edward Jacob Boyce, he founded the Cambridge Camden Society in 1839, having already developed an ardent interest in medieval church architecture and a concern for the restoration and building of churches on medieval liturgical principles. In 1841 he was made deacon, serving for brief periods as chaplain of Downing College, Cambridge, and curate of St. Nicholas, Guildford. In 1842 he was ordained priest and was offered the living of Crawley in Sussex. Although he began work there, his delicate health meant that he suffered a breakdown before he could be instituted, and he was sent off, with his newly acquired wife, Sarah Webster, to Madeira, where he resided for the best part of three years. Returning in 1846 he was offered the wardenship of Sackville College in East Grinstead, an ancient almshouse with a private chapel, and here he remained for twenty years until his death in 1866. The College provided him with a small community to which to minister, and an opportunity for study and writing. It also left him free to travel each summer, visiting continental churches, observing architecture and liturgical customs, and collecting material from ancient service-books for his translations of medieval hymns and sequences. His relations with Bishop Gilbert of Chichester were never easy, and for a considerable time he was inhibited by the Bishop, despite the claim that Sackville College Chapel was strictly extra-diocesan.

A contemporary description speaks of Neale as 'a tall, angular, rather loosely-limbed man, dressed in the old-fashioned way that Pusey, and Keble, and Isaac Williams used to dress, in swallow-tailed coats, tall hats and white ties'.

> He was sallow in complexion, with dark and not very tidily brushed hair, short-sighted, wore spectacles, and had a distraught and dreamy look, as though his thoughts were far away. . . . Within the College precincts, and at the Sisterhood, he always dressed in his cassock, with a trencher cap on his head, and a pair of bands under his chin.[1]

Neale was a scholar and a brilliant linguist. He could be animated and full of enthusiasm and conversation in a small group, or when with congenial companions, but could be silent and gauche in larger gatherings. A story is recorded of an occasion when he had been invited to Lavington to meet Bishop Samuel Wilberforce, and when he did not appear at dinner it was discovered that he had gone to bed as the only defence for his shyness.[2] In his preaching he drew heavily on the symbolic and mystical interpretations of Scripture of the medieval commentators, of which he had an unrivalled knowledge. If not an original poet his facility for versifying made him the winner of the Seatonian Prize Poem for eleven years in succession from 1845, and his skill as a translator of hymns showed itself particularly in his capacity to reproduce the rhythm and metre of the original so that the ancient plainsong melodies could be used for his English versions. He had a romantic imagination, delighted in wonders, was intrigued by spiritualism when it first made its appearance in England in the 1850s, and used his imaginative gifts to good effect in a number of novels and tales. The earliest of these, and certainly one of the most significant, was *Ayton Priory, or the Restored Monastery*, published in 1843, which anticipates some of Neale's later concern with the restoration of the religious life. His literary output was very considerable, some 130 items (books, translations, and tracts) published during his lifetime, and a further thirty which appeared posthumously. Of these it is his carols and hymns which have ensured that his name has not been forgotten.

Neale was fascinated by the mystical interpretation of Scripture. Like Keble, Pusey, and Newman he believed that the believer lived in a world of image and symbol; that the natural order comprised a hidden language which spoke of the unseen world of the spirit; that the Old Testament prefigured the New, not only in a general but in a detailed way. As he became more and more steeped in the medieval commentators so he looked for numerological significance in Scripture. In many ways Neale pushed mystical and symbolic interpretation to extremes. Preaching in the 1860s to the East Grinstead sisters, he maintained that 'everywhere, first, last, and middle . . . our dear Lord is the whole aim of the Bible'. 'Just as there is no parable in the gospel which may not have been also a literal fact, so, in the Old Testament, there is no fact which may not be a parable.'[3] Thus in a Michaelmas sermon he could take a verse from Ezekiel—'every precious stone was thy covering, the sardius, topaz, and the diamond, the beryl, the onyx, and the jasper, the sapphire, the emerald, and the carbuncle and gold'—and expound its hidden meaning.

Now notice: the sardius here stands first; in the foundations of the Holy City, as given in the Revelation, it comes sixth: the sardius, with its spotted red, is the Passion of CHRIST; fitly either first, because He is the foundation of all, or sixth, because those precious blood-drops were shed at the sixth hour of the sixth day. The topaz is said to glow or to fade as the sun shines out or is hidden in a cloud: and therefore is the very type of a true Sister's soul, reflecting in every moment the light of the Sun of Righteousness, her Bridegroom. The diamond, the hardest of all precious stones: that well sets forth what ought to be your inflexible firmness in resisting temptation; and notice, this stone is not found in the catalogue of Revelation, for there is no temptation to be resisted in that happy country. The beryl, the higher graces of the HOLY GHOST; those, I mean, that lead to the adoption of the Evangelical counsels of perfection, such as poverty, obedience and chastity. It is well placed fourth here, as being the highest sum and substance of the four Gospels: equally well it occupies the eighth place in the Apocalypse, as having to do with the octave of perfection.[4]

Preaching on the Name of Jesus he points out how medieval craftsmen would incorporate the IHS even into humble items of domestic furniture: 'Go . . . into many of the farms round here, and notice the fire-dogs that stand in the yawning chimney: how they are wrought at the sides into those most blessed of all letters, the *I.H.C.*, by which our dear LORD is set forth.' In the same sermon he indicated how, 'not content with seeing the same Name in Joshua, the leader of his people to the Land of Canaan, in Joshua the son of Josedech, the noble High Priest, the man "wondered at" of the Jewish Restoration, they saw it also in deeper and more recondite mysteries'.

In the three hundred and eighteen servants of the Father of the faithful, they saw the three letters, *I.E.S.*, which make up the monogram of our LORD's Name. They took those letters in their later form, *I.H.C.*, or *I.H.S.*, . . . and in *I.H.S.* some saw the initials of JESUS *Hominum Salvator*: JESUS the Saviour of men: others some of *In Hoc Signo*, by this sign: in *I.H.C.*, some saw JESUS *Hominum Consolator*: JESUS the Comforter of men: some JESUS *Hominum Conservator*: JESUS the Preserver of men.[5]

The same delight in typology and symbolism that we find in Neale's sermons and hymns, also characterized his architectural concerns. In common with his fellow-enthusiasts in the Cambridge Camden Society Neale was concerned to forward the cause of 'Ecclesiology'. By 'Ecclesiology' the Camdenians meant 'the principles which, it was supposed, guided mediaeval builders'. A writer in the *Ecclesiologist* put it thus: 'Given that there exists a certain general idea of church-building and church-arrangement in which we have a right to share; Ecclesiology is the science of rightly using this privilege, of investigating, expanding and practically exhibiting this idea.'[6] Gothic architecture was not to be viewed simply aesthetically, as supplying an appropriate ornamentation for churches. It was itself the outworking of liturgical and theological principle, an architectural medium which proclaimed a theological message. To restore a medieval church, clearing away box pews and the three-decker pulpit, refurbishing the chancel and sanctuary, reinstating the font, and uncovering ancient sedilia, aumbries, and piscinas, was to provide a sacramental expression of the church catholic and its worship. To build a new church according to strict ecclesiological principles was to affirm the difference between a sacramentally worshipping church and a meeting-house or preaching conventicle. The destruction of pews not only served this theological purpose, it was also a protest against the Erastian encroachments of the wealthy, whose rented pews, sometimes fitted up with Brussels carpets and 'somniferous sofas', banished the poor to benches at the back of the church. The attack on 'pues' and the similar attack on funeral vaults were an affirmation that secular hierarchies ought not to intrude on the divine order.

To forward their cause the Camdenians issued tracts and pamphlets. *Hints for the Practical Study of Ecclesiastical Antiquities*; *A Few Words to Church Builders*; *A Few Words to Church-Wardens on Churches and Church Ornaments*; and *Twenty-three Reasons for Getting Rid of Church Pues* were amongst the earliest. Later, in 1847 and 1856, when the Cambridge Camden Society had become metamorphosed into the Ecclesiological Society, the two volumes of *Instrumenta Ecclesiastica* were published, providing approved designs for lecterns, candlesticks, altar-crosses, reading-desks, hearses, tomb-stones, chalices, patens, and every conceivable item of church furnishing. The architect William Butterfield was a notable contributor to the series, which was widely influential, not least in the colonial church.

It was in 1843 that Neale in collaboration with his friend, Benjamin Webb, produced a translation of the *Rationale Divinorum Officiorum*, written by William Durandus, the thirteenth-century Bishop of Mende, prefixed by a long introductory essay. Both in the work of Durandus himself and in the essay by Neale and Webb the sacramental principles of church architecture are discussed in great detail. The character of the argument is typically summarized by Basil Clarke:

Regeneration is symbolized by octagonal fonts; the Atonement by a cruciform plan and by gable crosses; and the Communion of Saints by monuments and lady chapel. Windows symbolize the Light of the World; a circle above a triple window typifies the crown of the King of Kings; a hood mould above all three lancets means the unity of the Godhead. A two-light window symbolizes the two Natures of Christ, or the mission of the disciples two by two. . . .[7]

Nothing in a medieval church is without symbolical purpose, and of that purpose the text of Durandus provided the ecclesiologists with a wealth of explanation. For example:

The glass windows in a church are Holy Scriptures, which expel the wind and the rain, that is all things hurtful, but transmit the light of the true Sun, that is,

God, into the hearts of the faithful. These are wider within than without, because the mystical sense is the more ample, and precedeth the literal meaning.

The piers of the church are bishops and doctors: who specially sustain the Church of God by their doctrine ... the bases of the columns are the apostolic bishops, who support the frame of the whole church. The capitals of the piers are the opinions of the bishops and doctors. ... The ornaments of the capitals are the words of Sacred Scripture, to the meditation and observance of which we are bound. ...

The tiles of the roof which keep off the rain are the soldiers, who preserve the Church from paynim, and from enemies. ...

Bells do signify preachers. ... Also the cavity of the bell denoteth the mouth of the preacher. ... The hardness of the metal signifieth fortitude in the mind of the preacher. ... The clapper or iron, which by striking on either side maketh the sound, doth denote the tongue of the preacher. ... The wood of the frame upon which the bell hangeth doth signify the wood of our Lord's Cross. The rope hanging from this, by which the bell is struck, is humility, or the life of the preacher.[8]

Only when such symbolic principles were understood by church restorers and church architects would, so Neale and his fellow ecclesiologists believed, truly Christian churches result.

Detailed canons were laid down. Decorated was considered as the acme of Gothic architecture and was therefore the most appropriate style for new church building. Perpendicular was disparaged as a turning aside from the vertical, God-ward dimension to a horizontal man-ward perspective. Chancels and sanctuaries were elaborated as peculiarly marking the distinction between churches and meeting-houses. Altars were restored to prominence, and indeed it was con-troversy surrounding the attempt by the Camdenians to provide a stone altar for the restoration of the Round Church in Cambridge which led to the withdrawal of many of their most prominent supporters, earning them the accusations of Evangelicals and others that their activities were no less than the surreptitious attempt to introduce popery into the Church of England. There were further campaigns by the Camden Society against the installation of hideous stoves in churches without regard for architecture or aesthetics, and against the wanton destruction of antiquities in church restoration, though their rigid principles meant the Camdenians were not always guiltless in this respect where the antiquities in question were not those of the period they held in the highest regard. Stained-glass, tiles, flowers, frescoes, mosaics were all part of the Ecclesiologists' programme for new and restored churches. Neale wrote in *Church Enlargement and Church Arrangement*:

A Church is not as it should be, till *every* window is filled with stained glass, till every inch of floor is covered with encaustic tiles, till there is a Roodscreen glowing with the brightest tints and with gold, nay, if we would arrive at perfection, the roof and walls must be painted and frescoed. For it may safely be asserted that ancient churches in general were so adorned.[9]

In an age of church building, such as was the mid-nineteenth century, there can be no doubt of the influence of the ecclesiologists' principles, and to their ardent belief in an archetypal symbolism of church architecture we owe the common conceptions of what a proper church building ought to be. Of all the Victorian Church architects it was William Butterfield whom the Ecclesiologists most favoured, and in the building of All Saints', Margaret Street, in London, they hailed a church 'in which the embodiment and the success of our principles find their best illustrations. If . . . not in all respects that "model-church" which was one of our earliest anticipations, it is at least the nearest approach to that ideal which the ecclesiological movement has yet produced.'[10]

Church architecture spoke sacramentally of a Catholic theology. In looking to the Middle Ages Neale and his friends affirmed the continuity of the Church of England. They wanted decency and order in worship; vestments, and gesture, and colour. To take medieval Gothic churches as the model setting for contemporary worship was inevitably to influence that worship. If churches were to be not so much auditories for hearing sermons as windows into heaven, then glorious chancels should speak of God's majesty, and the liturgy celebrated there should reflect the mystery of the heavenly places. If ordinary worshippers were taught to claim the architectural heritage of medieval Christendom as their own, then Neale was determined that English worship should be enriched by the treasures of Christian hymnody from both the Greek and Latin churches, and even from further afield. There can be little doubt that his work of translation of hymns which became, and remain, well-loved parts of Anglican worship did more to teach the great doctrines of the Creed and sacramental theology than did many tracts and theological treatises.

In his concern for English hymns Neale differed from his friend,

Benjamin Webb. Writing at a time when hymn-singing was all but unknown in the Church of England, and particularly amongst High Churchmen, Webb argued that the ancient Latin hymns should be introduced in the original. He worried lest new compositions should be more like subjective, pious effusions than the theologically objective hymns of the Ancient Church. He wrote to Neale in 1849:

I am more and more convinced that the age of hymns has passed. Happy those who can use the ancient Latin ones; with our vernacular we have lost our privilege. It is the same throughout; the translation into English reduced everything to common sense—the curse or glory (as you choose) of our present ritual. . . . I doubt, in short, the possibility for the language of common life, in such an age as this, being fit for this sort of composition.[11]

Neale was unconvinced—so much so that his *Collected Hymns*, both translations and original compositions, runs to a volume of some 450 pages. In the end he succeeded in persuading Webb of the validity and importance of English hymns and they collaborated together in the production of the *Hymnal Noted*, the first part of which appeared in 1851.

Neale was not the first translator of the ancient Latin hymns. Some earlier attempts had been made by William Copeland, Bishop Mant, Newman, and Edward Caswall, and a collection of these and other translations had appeared in 1847. Neale regarded it as very unsatisfactory. He had already produced *Hymns for Children* (1842) and *Hymns for the Sick* (1843). The first of these, intended for use in village schools, follows the pattern of *The Christian Year* in providing hymns suitable for all the Church's seasons and holy days, a few of which have found a permanent place in hymn-books. Neale deplored the loss of the ancient hymns at the time of the Reformation, noting that only the *Veni Creator Spiritus* appeared in the Prayer Book in the Ordination service. In his contribution to the *Hymnal Noted* he endeavoured to rectify the omission, translating mainly from the hymns of the Sarum rite, of which forty appeared in the first part of the hymnal. In the same year, 1851, he produced *Mediaeval Hymns and Sequences*, a collection consisting of translations of Latin hymns which were not office hymns. To glance through this collection is to appreciate just how many of Neale's translations have become part of the heritage not only of Anglican, but of all worship in England. There are the great hymns of Venantius Fortunatus, 'The

Royal banners forward go', and 'Sing, my tongue, the glorious battle'; the eighth-century *Urbs beata Jerusalem*, 'Blessed City, Heavenly Salem', of which the second part, 'Christ is made the sure Foundation' is now perhaps more widely known. There is the translation of the Palm Sunday hymn of St. Theodulph of Orleans (d.821), 'All glory, laud and honour', which contains the quaint verse not included in modern hymnals:

> Be Thou, O Lord, the Rider,
> And we the little ass;
> That to GOD's Holy City
> Together we may pass.

The Michaelmas hymn of St. Hrabanus Maurus, 'Thee, O Christ, the Father's splendour', appears, as do the Easter sequences of Adam of St. Victor, whom Neale regarded as the greatest of the medieval Latin hymn-writers. Even so these sequences have not found a permanent place amongst English hymns, though the twelfth-century Easter sequence, *O Filii et Filiae*, 'O sons and daughters of the King', has done. Neale's translations of *Finita iam sunt proelia*, *Veni, veni, Emmanuel*, and *Adoro Te devote* have not become the preferred ones, but 'Of the glorious Body telling'; 'Alleluia, song of sweetness'; 'To the Name that brings Salvation'; 'O what their joy and their glory must be'; 'Come Thou Redeemer of the earth'; 'The Word of God proceeding forth'; 'Ye choirs of New Jerusalem!'; 'The Lamb's high banquet we await'; 'Eternal Monarch, King most high'; 'Come, Thou Holy Paraclete'; 'Light's abode, celestial Salem' are all well established. Likewise 'Jerusalem the Golden', which is part of Neale's translation of Bernard of Morlaix's *Hora Novissima*, has found its way into many collections. The influence of his hymns can be gauged by a comment by Neale's daughter that 'in one of the editions of *Hymns Ancient and Modern*, not less than one eighth of the hymns and translations—61 out of 473—came from his pen', whilst in the *English Hymnal* more than one-tenth are his: 72 out of 656.[12]

One of the notable features of these hymns is what might be called their heavenly reference. Time and again the hymns which Neale chose to translate were hymns which pointed the worshipper to the glory and adoration of heaven. This is particularly true of the *Hora novissima*, of which Neale said that its 'description of the peace and glory of heaven' is 'of such rare beauty as not easily to be matched by any mediaeval composition on the same subject'.[13] This echoes his understanding of Christian worship, expressed both in his ecclesiological concerns, and in many of his published sermons. It is a feature likewise of the other major collection of translated hymns, the *Hymns of the Eastern Church* published in 1862. Many, though not all, of these are Easter hymns, and again they have become widely known: 'The day is past and over'; 'A great and mighty wonder!'; 'The Day of Resurrection'; 'Thou hallowed chosen morn of praise'; 'Come, ye faithful, raise the strain'; 'Stars of the morning, so gloriously bright'; 'Jesus, Name all names above'; 'O happy band of pilgrims'. As Neale noted in his preface, whereas there had been some attempts at translations of the Latin breviary hymns, the hymns of the Greek Church were *terra incognita*. He found it incomprehensible that this rich vein of Christian hymnody should have remained for so long untapped; it was, he said, 'a glorious mass of theology'.[14]

Neale had long been interested in the Eastern Church. During the time that he was in Madeira for the sake of his health he conceived the idea of writing a history of Eastern Christianity. It was at the same time that he was avidly investigating the Portuguese Church in Madeira, and making the acquaintance of Montalembert, the French Catholic writer, who was also resident on the island. The ultramontane views of Montalambert did not find favour with Neale, who found them at variance with his study of the development of the Church of Alexandria. He wrote to his friend Webb in January 1844:

I know you are afraid that I shall take an Oriental view, i.e. I suppose so Oriental that it will cease to be Catholick. I hope not. At the same time, without becoming a shade more Anglican, I do see more and more clearly that the High Papal theory is quite untenable. . . . I cannot make, as Montalambert does, visible union, or . . . the desire for visible union with the Chair of Peter, the key-stone, as it were, of the Church, at least not in the sense in which the Western Church has sometimes done. We *Orientals* take a more general view. The Rock on which the Church is built is St. Peter, but it is a triple Rock, Antioch where he sat, Alexandria which he superintended, Rome where he suffered.[15]

Webb wrote back:

I *do* fear your Orientalizing. For my own part, I cannot see any strong objections to what you call the High Papal theory. . . . Let me earnestly warn you against the Orientalism of books. I have lately heard not a little of *real* Orientation, and, believe me, it is nearly as bad as Anglicanism.[16]

Webb was writing in the context of intense speculation in the English church about Newman's probable secession and the troubles over W. G. Ward's *Ideal of the Christian Church*, with its presentation of the Roman Church as the model for every church concerned to enable men and women to grow in holiness. Neale, removed from immediate ecclesiastical excitements, and living amongst Catholics who had always asserted a certain independence from Rome, could allow his views to be shaped by a longer and broader historical perspective.

It may well be that part of Neale's motivation in writing the history of the Eastern Church was the bearing of the iconoclast controversy on his theories of symbolism. He noted in an early letter to Webb about the project that he was rather startled by the thought that he would be 'the first Anglican of Catholic principles who has touched the iconoclast controversy'.[17] He later commented on that same dispute that 'no controversy has been more grossly misapprehended'.

Till Calvinism, and its daughter Rationalism, showed the ultimate develop-ment of Iconoclast principles, it must have been well nigh impossible to realize the depth of feeling on the side of the Church, or the greatness of the interests attacked by her opponents. We may, perhaps, doubt whether even the Saints of that day fully understood the character of the battle; whether they did not give up ease, honour, possessions, life itself, rather from an intuitive perception that their cause was the cause of the Catholic faith, than from a logical appreciation of the results to which the Image-destroyers were tending. Just as in the early part of the Nestorian controversy, many and many a simple soul must have felt intuitively that the title of *Theotocos* was to be defended, without seeing the full consequences to which its denial would subsequently lead. The supporters of Icons, by universal consent, numbered amongst their ranks all that was pious and venerable in the Eastern Church. The Iconoclasts seem to have been a legitimate outbreak of that secret creeping Manichaeism, which . . . so long devastated CHRIST's fold.[18]

Significant as this may have been for Neale, his interests ranged wider, and his work as a whole must be seen as yet another instance of the remarkable influence of the Greek Fathers on Anglican theo-logy.

Neale's original scheme was to write the history of each Eastern patriarchate separately, though this was not in the end realized. The history of the Church of Alexandria was published in two volumes in 1847. The general introduction, which had grown to another two volumes, was published four years later in 1851. He then began work on the patriarchate of Antioch, with typical thoroughness learning Armenian for the purpose. Other concerns, however, intervened, and the unfinished work was completed after Neale's death by the Revd George Williams. Williams, along with William Palmer of Magdalen College, Oxford, was one of a small group of English churchmen who, along with Neale, had a deep interest in Eastern Christianity. Palmer indeed, had the advantage over Neale in that he had personal contact with the Russian Church, whereas Neale, although he corresponded with Eastern bishops, both in Russia and in the Middle East, had only the briefest direct acquaintance with Orthodoxy in the course of a journey he undertook with Dr Oldknow in 1860 when he visited Dalmatia and Montenegro. He maintained a close contact with Father Eugene Popoff, the chaplain of the Russian Embassy, who advised him on many matters connected with his work on the Eastern Church, and who was present, together with an Archimandrite, at the laying of the foundation stone of St. Margaret's Convent in 1865.

Neale's concern with the Eastern Church was not simply antiquarian. He wished to make the theological and liturgical heritage of the East more widely accessible, and to place the contemporary debates with Rome in a broader perspective. His work he saw as an ecumenical endeavour. It is interesting to note that in his consideration of the *Filioque* controversy he came down firmly on the Greek side, commenting that the insertion of the clause into the Creed was an 'utterly unjustifiable' act. 'No true union', he wrote, 'can take place between the Churches, till the *Filioque* be omitted from the Creed, even if a truly Oecumenical Synod should afterwards proclaim the truth of the doctrine.' He cited Bishop Pearson in support of this position.[19] He told Webb in 1851, 'I suppose that Blackmore, Palmer, and I are the only men in the English Church who are thoroughly convinced that the Latin doctrine is grievously erroneous, suspected of heresy, and, even if logically carried out, heretical. Half our men would never "alter the creed" as they would call it.'[20] His mind on this point seems to have been decisively shaped through reading the Russian theologian, Zoernikov in 1849, after he had acquired enough Russian to do so.[21]

It might be expected that Neale's interest in, and devotion to, the

Eastern Church would appear more frequently than it does in his sermons. Although much of the typology which he employs is patristic in origin and is characteristic of the Eastern tradition, his direct allusions to Christian writers are overwhelmingly to those of the West. There can be no doubt that Neale was astonishingly widely read in the spiritual and devotional writings of the Latin Church and we find casual reference to and illuminating quotation from an extraordinary variety of writers: Jerome and Augustine; the medieval commentator, Rupert of Deutz; the Cistercian, Guerric of Igny; Teresa of Avila and Luis of Granada from Spain; Angela of Foligni; Jean-Baptiste de la Salle; Francis de Sales and Jeanne de Chantal; Tomé de Jesus, a Portuguese Augustinian; Thomas of Villanova; St. Bernard; and many others.

1855 saw the flowering of another major contribution which Neale made to the life of the Church of England, the founding of the Society of St. Margaret. It was on Trinity Sunday, 1841 that Marion Hughes had taken the three vows of religion privately before Dr Pusey, and in 1845 that the first Anglican sisterhood had come into being at Park Village West. Since that time other communities had been founded, the Community of St. Mary the Virgin at Wantage in 1848 under the influence of W. J. Butler, and Priscilla Lydia Sellon's society of the Most Holy Trinity at Devonport in the same year. In 1851 Harriet Monsell became the Superior of the Community of St. John the Baptist at Clewer, which devoted itself to penitentiary work amongst prostitutes under the guidance of T. T. Carter, the incumbent of Clewer. Neale's community was not, therefore, the first Anglican sisterhood, but it was undoubtedly significant. In his novel, *Ayton Priory*, Neale had lamented the dissolution of the monasteries at the Reformation. The foundation of his sisterhood had, however, as much to do with the social needs of the area around East Grinstead as with a concern for the restoration of the religious life in the Church of England. The condition of the industrial towns in nineteenth-century England can sometimes lead us to forget the extent and nature of rural poverty and deprivation. Neale was well aware of the distress and squalor of poor families in the isolated cottages and hamlets of Ashdown Forest, and of the challenges that this presented to the Church. The work of Florence Nightingale's nurses in the Crimean War, some of whom had had links with the nascent Anglican communities, gave another impetus to the founding of a community to meet this particular need. He told

his friend Webb how he saw evangelism and service going hand in
hand.

You know that . . . it was a favourite speculation of mine, how it would be
possible ever to get at the scattered collections of houses in our great Sussex
parishes, so as positively to evangelize them as you might do a heathen
country, for they are heathen to all intents and purposes. Some three or four
years ago Fowler had an idea that by nurses trained physically and religiously, something might be done.[22]

Ann Gream, the daughter of the neighbouring rector of Rother-
field was to become the first Superior of the community which Neale
founded in 1855. He consulted Carter and Harriet Monsell at
Clewer and Butler at Wantage about details of the Rule, but owed
much to his own investigations in France. Just as Anglo-Catholic
parochial missions were to owe much to French and Belgian Catholic
practice, so too was there a significant influence on these early
Anglican communities from French sources. In January 1855, Neale
and four Sisters visited the Sisters of St. Vincent de Paul, the Little
Sisters of the Poor, the Blue Sisters, and the Beguines, to seek advice
and guidance about the founding of his community. When he came
to draw up the Rule he based it on the original rule of St. Francis de
Sales for his Visitation Sisters, but incorporated features deriving
from the Sisters of Charity of St. Vincent de Paul. Neale's biographer
cites St. Vincent de Paul's words about his Sisters as part of Neale's
own inspiration:

Instead of a convent they have only the dwellings of the sick; for a cell, some
poor chamber, often a hired one; for a chapel, the parish church; for a
cloister, the streets of a town; for enclosure, obedience; for a gate, the fear of
God; for a veil, holy modesty.[23]

Neale told Webb that he disliked the 'pseudo-asceticism' he thought
that he detected in Miss Sellon's sisterhood, but had gained much
positive and balanced help from Harriet Monsell at Clewer. His
scheme, he continued, had resolved itself into a plan for a 'central
house . . . in which we may have a community of trained Sisters,
ready to be sent out at the superior's discretion *gratuitously* to any
Parish Priest within a circuit of (say) twenty-five miles, that may need
their services in nursing any of his people'. He succeeded in making
an arrangement with the Westminster Hospital for the training of the

Sisters as nurses.[24] Neale's biographer records some early instances of how Neale's vision was translated into reality.

Application was made for a Sister in a case of diphtheria. She went instantly. It was of a most malignant kind—spread through the household, and in five days she had, in that one household, attended four deathbeds. Again, yesterday afternoon, a message that Mr Whyte had sent for a Sister for the most malignant case of scarlet fever he ever saw at Ashurst Wood, we agreed that Sister K. should go. I went up to the cottage first. The mother, a widow out of her sense (with anxiety, not disease); a boy, and two girls, wildly delirious, only kept alive by port and brandy; all the cases Mr Whyte thought desperate. I back to town, ordered a fly, and Sister K. was off in half-an-hour. The woman in one of her lucid intervals said, 'I will not have any ladies that worship images in my house.' However, Mr Whyte talked very reasonably to her, and finally she consented.[25]

Conditions in the cottage were hard:

There was no proper grate or range, only a couple of stones to make even the household fire on. The Sister . . . had to go into the forest to get wood and then that had to be dried; and when she thought a little stock was provided for the day's use, as likely as not the children burnt it up while she was out of their way. The difficulty of lighting or keeping a fire at all under such circumstances was extreme, and every expedient was resorted to to avoid it. The Sisters, for instance, would wrap up an egg in damp paper, and put it in hot ashes to cook. . . .[26]

The Sisters nursed many suffering from diphtheria, typhus, and scarlet fever, all at considerable risk to themselves.

In his study of the sociology of Anglican religious communities in the nineteenth century, Dr Michael Hill points out how the sisterhoods both won acceptance by their charitable, and in particular nursing, work, and how in turn their involvement in nursing was a significant factor in the development of the nursing profession and in changing conceptions of women's work. Hill cites both a contribution to an 1878 Convocation debate and a reviewer of works on nursing in support of his thesis. Archdeacon Ffoulkes maintained that 'the names of Miss Nightingale, and Miss Sellon, and of the East Grinstead Sisters' would 'long be remembered as having taught the people of this country the true character of women's work'. The reviewer wished that all Hospital Nurses could be organized in the same way as sisterhoods, 'having a lady who would work for pure love's sake' at their head, 'and who would infuse into the staff that would be under her management and control some of her own spirit and principle', thus counteracting the tendency of nurses to be 'too much of the hireling order'.[27]

Two years after the community began there was trouble when a Sister [Amy Scobell] died, leaving a sum of money to the community. Her father, an Evangelical clergyman, accused Neale and the sisterhood of putting pressure on his daughter to make the bequest and then engineering her death. At the funeral at Lewes there was an ugly riot in which Neale and the sisters attending were attacked. Despite this incident, with all that it reveals of both Victorian family conflict and 'no-popery' prejudice, the community grew. Neale drew on his wide knowledge of Christian spirituality and the monastic tradition, expounding the Scriptures and the life of prayer in the small oratory in the sisters' house. Mother Kate, one of the original sisters, recalled these early days, remembering Neale's 'wonderful Bible-classes on the mystical interpretation of Holy Scripture'.

I can recall it all so vividly, the narrow dark little Oratory, with three plain wooden arches shutting in the Sanctuary, where the red lamp flickered in the semi-darkness, and the tall figure of the Founder stood before the altar, speaking words of comfort, encouragement, and, where he deemed it necessary, of the very sharpest reproof. . . . We always had the example of the Saints and Martyrs put before us: the Gates of Gold and the City of the Lamb were always glittering before our eyes. . . . There was a consciousness of God's Saints actually round and about us, which moved and inspired us to do and to dare anything and everything.[28]

Neale's sense of the glory of God and the joy and wonder of heaven, which is apparent in so many of the hymns which he chose to translate, was undoubtedly one of the themes which came across most powerfully in the addresses he gave to the sisterhood. In 1864, in a sermon entitled '*Deus Meus et Omnia*', Neale comments:

There is something wonderfully solemn, as well as wonderfully comforting, in the way in which the early and mediaeval Saints speak of (the Beatific Vision). How the whole heavenliness of Heaven is summed up in that, and well nigh in that alone. I know nothing that so shows the declension of the last three or four centuries, as the little prominence, (comparatively speaking) that, in every part of the Church, the holiest writers give to that. No one would say that either primitive or mediaeval doctors failed in reverence to, in longing to be near, in realizing their communion with, the Saints. But find them preaching or writing of heaven, and the one great thought swallows up the rest. Infinitely beyond, infinitely above all things, it is that Beatific Vision to which they point.[29]

It was that glory, and the grace which God gives to bring men and women to that glory, which Neale saw as the reality of every anti-phon, psalm, and reading of the offices and liturgy. Time and again in his sermons he would dwell on the way in which a common text, a seasonal antiphon for instance, could become a focus of meditation, and meditation was not by rules but by love.[30] And again in that 1864 sermon he spoke of the Beatific Vision as the fulfilment of that love.

What the Beatific Vision is, we can only fancy by knowing what it is not. And keeping all this in view, small regret shall we have in 'I saw no Temple therein', when that Beatific Vision itself will be our Temple. It is that GOD who is Love, filling His happy servants with the outpouring of that love: it is the GOD who is Light, satisfying them the perfect brilliancy of that Light. And always remember, that into that height of glory our Human Nature has entered: that there in its fullest blaze, a Man is seated at the Right Hand of the FATHER: that eyes, in every point fashioned as our eyes, behold Him there, Whose Face, however afar off, we could not see and live.[31]

In the liturgical ordering of his sisterhood Neale went consider-ably beyond the pattern of the earlier Tractarians. Prayer Book Matins and Evensong were only said on Sundays, on other days translations of the Hours from the Sarum Breviary were used. The Society of St. Margaret was the first Anglican sisterhood to produce a translation of the Night Office. The centre of the society's devo-tional life was the Eucharist, and Neale instituted a daily celebration in July 1856. At the end of the following year permanent reservation of the Sacrament was commenced, for the first time in the Church of England. The Community Diary records: 'Mr Neale went to London and brought home a Pix and a Tabernacle', and the next day 'the Tabernacle was fixed in the Oratory'.[32] He told the Sisters that he hoped henceforth 'that each one of you will no more think of omitting her visit to the Blessed Sacrament, than she would her daily prayers'.

Here, daily, you must shut the doors of your hearts from everything else, to be alone with the Beloved. Here, daily, you must try, long, strive, yearn, after that nearness to Him, which His Sacramental Presence can give His people here.[33]

In 1859 Neale began Benediction, and it would also seem, from an undated Maundy Thursday sermon, that the Maundy Thursday watch before the Sacrament was part of the liturgical pattern of Holy Week.[34]

Neale's sacramental and eucharistic practice might suggest that he looked more to the Church of Rome than to the Church of England. It would be truer to say that he wished the Church of England to lay claim to the whole Catholic heritage that was rightfully hers. The devotional treasures of both East and West were part of that inheritance. Of contemporary ultramontane Catholicism Neale was in fact quite critical. If England ever became a Catholic country, he believed, it would be through the Church of England not the Church of Rome. He told his sisters that he could teach them directly from medieval and patristic commentators in a way in which contemporary Roman Catholic priests could not. He gave as an instance the doctrine of the Immaculate Conception, which had been repudiated by St. Bernard, and popular devotions concerning the pains of purgatory compared with the traditional prayers for the departed of East and West. Likewise the withholding of the chalice from the laity and certain features of Marian devotion were strongly criticized, as well as the growing infallibilist claims of the Papacy.[35]

Neale was one who welcomed John Keble's advice to eschew originality, but only because he believed that the Christian tradition itself contained so many riches that had been widely neglected. This concern lay behind his *Commentary on the Psalms*, on which he was aided by R. F. Littledale, who eventually completed the work after Neale's death in 1866. Of this work Neale wrote, 'I claim nothing but the poor thread on which the pearls are strung', the pearls of the spiritual meaning of the Psalms which could, for instance, by taking all reference to God's Word in the Psalms as having a hidden reference to the Incarnate Word, transfigure the 119th Psalm 'into a beauty which cannot exist for those that reject Mysticism'.[36] It was perhaps appropriate that the day of Neale's death was the Feast of the Transfiguration in 1866, just a little over a year after the foundation stone was laid of the great convent for his sisterhood at East Grinstead.

VI. Pioneers in the parish: Ritualism in the slums

THE CATHOLIC Revival began in the University of Oxford. The Tractarian fathers were clerical dons, concerned with theological issues in an academic as well as a pastoral and devotional way. They were learned men and part of their achievement was to draw on the inheritance of patristic theology and devotion which had for many years been neglected in Anglicanism. They were also pastors, to their pupils, and to the many who subsequently came to them for advice. But the setting of their own immediate pastoral work was the university, or, in the case of John Keble, the country parish. College parishes and old pupils in orders gave them contact outside the university environment, and the vision of church, ministry, and sacraments which they had imparted through sermons, tracts, and the work of spiritual direction took root amongst clergy in very different situations.

If the Church of England was ill adapted in its organization and government to respond to the increasingly rapid changes in nineteenth-century society, nowhere was this more evident than in the expanding urban areas. Vested interests, the rights of patrons, ancient endowments, and the medieval parochial system all hampered the ease with which the Church could provide new pastors and places of worship to meet the needs of the towns, and particularly the needs of the urban poor. The story of the slum priests of the Catholic revival is in part a story of pioneering work in response to these difficulties. If the Oxford Movement may be said to have changed the pattern of Anglican worship it was in these urban parishes that the changes both began and were pressed to extremes. Decorous restraint and academic discourse were alike out of place in the slums. Mystery and movement, colour and ceremonial were more powerful. The sacramental sign could speak more strongly than the written word. But if these were the characteristics of worship in the town parishes influenced by the Oxford Movement, that worship impressed through the devotion and holiness of life and pastoral concern of the priests who led that worship. The legend of the Anglo-Catholic slum priest is not without foundation, as a consideration of some of the leading figures of the revival will make clear. Time and again in their battles with bishops and ecclesiastical lawyers and 'no-popery' agitators they maintained that the richness of Eucharistic worship was not only the legitimate heritage of the Church of England, but that which embodied as nothing else could the sense of the reality of Divine grace in a way which could be grasped by the poor and unlettered.

The deprivation and squalor of many of these urban areas was extreme. Robert Linklater, a priest who worked for eleven years in the East End parish of St Peter's-in-the-East, wrote of 'the murky atmosphere of fog and dust' pervading the narrow courts and alleys, half-naked children playing in the gutter, 'many of them stunted, half-witted and deformed, and all wan and sickly looking'. He described the living conditions of one poor woman as being typical of many:

We come to a garret where a poor woman lies dying on the floor, huddled into a corner on a bag of straw, covered for the sake of warmth with all the rags which constituted the property of the place. One is half stifled with the intolerable smell. At a glance we take in the awful poverty, for literally there is not a stick of furniture, save a crazy-looking table and one broken chair. The children—well, I have seen them quite naked like savages. Perhaps even in the depth of winter no fire in the grate. Of the horrors of vermin one cannot speak. We are told, and we could have guessed it from their faces, that they have not tasted food that day.[1]

At the end of a series of sermons on the needs of the London poor, delivered in the 1860s before the University of Oxford by Robert Gregory, later to be Dean of St. Paul's, a number of similar examples are collected. The Medical Poor-Law Officer of the Isle of Dogs wrote in 1867:

I visited a family the day before yesterday, one of whom was in a fever. Three or four shillings would have purchased all they possessed in the world. They were lying on a little straw, and the mother's thin shawl was the only night-covering for the whole family.[2]

Another medical man reported:

I went to see a family, who, I heard, were ill. After climbing up four pairs of stairs I found them in a terrible place: on the bedstead lay a dead baby, with the mother crying over it, having died through starvation; two shivering, dirty skeletons of children in the corner, quite naked; a third with some rags on: all crying with hunger: and the father with ulcers on his legs, and having had no work for a year.[3]

Under-nourishment and starvation was the lot of many families attempting to exist on inadequate poor relief, the amount paid being little more than that required for a diet of bread only. Theft and prostitution flourished under such circumstances. When the Revd John Slatter took charge of a district in Leeds he was given a list of brothels in the area by the police, and was 'horrified to find that, in a circle of one hundred yards of which my room was the centre, there were no less than *thirteen* of such dens'.[4] In Wapping, Charles Lowder noted the close liaison between public houses and brothels, and the terrible conditions in which many children grew up, with drunken parents and only one room for accommodation.[5]

The Church made little impact in such areas. Efforts to provide new churches did not do more than touch one small aspect of the problem. Gregory reminded his Oxford congregation in 1867 that in South London not 1 in 50 working-men ever entered a place of worship.[6] He noted the ignorance of religion amongst children revealed in the evidence given to the 1862 Children's Employment Commission:

Joseph Jobbins, age 9, of Bethnal Green. Has never been to school anywhere, day or week. Has never been inside church or chapel. Heard somebody preach out of doors last Sunday. He preached about Jesus. Never heard of Him before then. Never heard about God. Never heard father or mother speak about Him or heaven. . . . Father or mother never go to church or such place.

Or another example, of a child in Newcastle:

Learned to read and write, but cannot read and write now. G-O-D spells 'be'. Does not know about Him. Has heard say that He was 'kaind' and lived up there, (pointing). They said He was a nice man and was 'kaind to us'. He was the first man.[7]

Gregory believed that where there had been religious influence of any kind it had tended to leave the impression that the hearing of sermons was the purpose of church-going, and that religion was essentially a private matter. Sacramental worship had been neglected in England, and so religious practice had never taken root amongst the mass of the population in the same way that it had done in Catholic countries.[8]

The slum priests were determined that sacramental worship should be the centre of the Church's ministry in the areas of urban deprivation. The foundation of churches such as St. Saviour's, Leeds, St. Alban's, Holborn, and St. Peter's, London Docks, and the work of men like Alexander Heriot Mackonochie, Charles Lowder, George Rundle Prynne, and Robert Dolling provide outstanding examples of such heroic attempts. Not surprisingly there were links between such priests and between such parishes. Pusey pressed Prynne to join the community of celibate priests that he hoped to establish at St. Saviour's, Leeds.[9] Mackonochie was a friend of Prynne's, and worked with Lowder in the St. George's-in-the-East Mission between 1858 and 1862. Dolling, of a younger generation, made his first confession to Bishop Forbes of Brechin—who had for a short time been associated with St. Saviour's, Leeds—and, as a young Irish layman in London, worshipped at St. Alban's, Holborn and was a key figure in the St. Martin's League for Postmen founded by the curate of St. Alban's, A. H. Stanton.[10] The Society of the Holy Cross, founded by Lowder and others in 1855, was also a significant link between priests who shared Catholic convictions. The list of priests linked with the Society is a notable one, including Pusey, Liddon, R. M. Benson (the founder of the Cowley Fathers), Stanton, Prynne, Le Geyt, C. C. Grafton (later Bishop of Fond du Lac), George Body (a notable missioner), Bodington, Linklater, R. W. Enraght and J. Bell Cox (both imprisoned during the ritualist prosecutions), R. J. Wilson (later Warden of Keble College, Oxford), W. J. E. Bennett, Archdeacon Denison, and Arthur Tooth, as well as a number of other prominent parish priests.[11] Part of Lowder's inspiration in the founding of the Society of the Holy Cross was the work of St. Vincent de Paul in seventeenth-century France. St. Vincent had also partly supplied the inspiration behind John Mason Neale's East Grinstead Sisterhood, and Florence Nightingale commented with approval on the training given to women by the Order of St. Vincent, lamenting its absence in the Church of England.[12] Allchin perceptively comments that, although Victorian England tended to stress the 'medievalism' of the Tractarians, 'it would be almost impossible to underestimate the debt the Tractarians owed in the formation of their spiritual ideals to seventeenth-century French models'.[13]

Lowder had discovered the life of St. Vincent de Paul in the seminary at Yvetôt, near Rouen, in 1854. The superior, Abbé Labbé, had experience of England from the time when his father was a refugee from the French Revolution. He noted Lowder's interest in St. Vincent and made him a present of the saint's biography. Lowder commented on the deep impression made on him by 'the sad condition of the French Church and nation in the sixteenth century, and the wonderful influence of the institutions founded by St. Vincent in reforming abuses and rekindling the zeal of the priesthood'.

The heart must be dull indeed which is not stirred with emotion at the self-denial and energy with which the saint gave himself to the work to which he was called. . . . The deep wisdom which sought out the root of so much evil, in the unspiritual lives of the clergy, and provided means for its redress . . . was well calculated to impress those who seriously reflected on the state of our own Church and people, and honestly sought for some remedy. The spiritual condition of the masses of our population, the appalling vices which prevail in our large towns, and especially in the teeming districts of the metropolis, the increasing tendency of the people to mass together, multiplying and intensifying the evil, and the unsatisfactory character of the attempts hitherto made to meet it, were enough to make men gladly profit by the experience of those who had successfully struggled against similar difficulties.[14]

In the foundation of the Society of the Holy Cross Lowder attempted to give substance to St. Vincent's ideals in an English context. The objects of the Society were 'to defend and strengthen the spiritual life of the clergy, to defend the faith of the Church, and to carry on and aid Mission work both at home and abroad'.

The members of this society, meeting together as they did in prayer and conference, were deeply impressed with the evils existing in the Church, and saw also, in the remedies adopted by St. Vincent de Paul, the hope of lessening them. They all felt that the ordinary parochial equipment of a rector and curate, or perhaps a solitary incumbent, provided for thousands of perishing souls, was most sadly inadequate; that in the presence of such utter destitution, it was simply childish to act as if the Church were recognized as the mother of the people. She must assume a missionary character, and, by religious association and a new adaptation of Catholic practice to the altered circumstances of the nineteenth century and the peculiar wants of the

John Keble (*above left*) (1792–1886).
A photograph in old age.

John Henry Newman (*above right*) (1801–90).
An engraving from the 1840s.

Edward Bouverie Pusey (*left*) (1800–82). An
engraving from the Oxford Movement period.

'The Oriel Fathers': Manning, Pusey, Newman, and Keble.

Altar plate designed by William Butterfield, which was displayed at the
1851 Exhibition.

John Mason Neale (*left*)
(1818–66) in Eucharistic
vestments.

The restoration of liturgical
dress (*below*): one of a series
of Reformation/Deformation
cartoons.

Pusey preaching in St. Mary's. In this scene from the 1870s notable Oxford figures are portrayed, including John Ruskin, Edward King, H. P. Liddon, E. S. Talbot, and W. E. Gladstone.

The last celebration of the Feast of the Epiphany at the Margaret Chapel, 1850. Water-colour by Thomas S. Boys.

George Rundle Prynne (1818–1903), Vicar of St. Peter's, Plymouth.

Richard Meux Benson (1824–1915), Founder of the Society of St. John the Evangelist.

John Coleridge Patteson (1827–71), Bishop of Melanesia.

Robert Gray (1809–72), Bishop of Cape Town.

Henry Scott Holland (1847–1918), Canon of St. Paul's and Regius Professor of Divinity at Oxford.

Edward King (1829–1910), Bishop of Lincoln.

Reaction to *Lux Mundi* (*above*): Gore's espousal of biblical criticism seen as destructive of the Church.

Charles Gore (*left*) (1853–1932) as Bishop of Worcester.

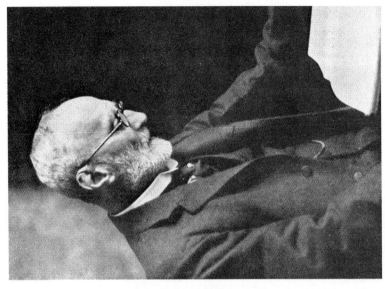

Viscount Halifax (1839–1934).

Frederick George Lee (1832–1902). 'Dr Lee of Lambeth', one of the founders of the Association for Promoting the Reunion of Christendom.

English character, endeavour, with fresh life and energy, to stem the pre-vailing tide of sin and indifference.[15]

From the Society sprang the work of the St. George's Mission, with which Lowder was to be especially associated. Before embark-ing on this work he and some seventeen other priests went to spend a week in devotional exercises under the guidance of Dr Pusey. It was, said Lowder, 'an attempt to revive a kind of Retreat for Clergy', though, as Liddon notes, there was no rule of silence. Those attend-ing met at 6.30 a.m. to say Prime and to prepare for Communion; then to Communion, remaining for prayer afterwards, followed by corporate Thanksgiving and Terce. A book of meditations was read at breakfast, which was followed by Morning Prayer at the Cathedral. After Sext there was a conference on themes such as conversion or confession, then a late dinner, Nones and Evening Prayer at the Cathedral, followed by a second conference and then Compline.[16] This first move towards retreats for clergy in the Church of England was followed in 1858 by a retreat with rules of silence which the Society of the Holy Cross organized at the Revd F. H. Murray's Rectory at Chislehurst. This was conducted by Father Benson, the retreat the following year being led by T. T. Carter of Clewer.[17] Such were the beginnings of retreats in the Church of England.

The ideals of the Society of the Holy Cross, or SSC as it was commonly known, as they relate to the missionary situation of the Church in the mid-nineteenth century, are set out in an essay by one of its members, the Revd James Edward Vaux, in the 1868 collection of essays, *The Church and the World*. Vaux had led the first retreat for women in the Church of England at the chapel of the Sisters of Bethany in Lloyd Square in 1862.[18] Vaux argued for the importance of missions and mission priests as necessary adjuncts of the parochial system. He cited the example of St. Vincent de Paul and acknow-ledged his influence on new ventures in the Church of England. He urged his readers that more attention should be given to Catholic missions of revival and renewal, and that Anglican clergy should learn from the preaching orders of the Catholic Church, especially the Dominicans, the Passionists, and the Redemptorists. He was critical of the 'hum-drum' character of Anglican worship.

Without laying ourselves open to the charge of a morbid craving after unhealthy excitement, we may venture an opinion that the repetition of 'Dearly Beloved Brethren', at the least seven hundred and thirty times each year, is calculated to become a little wearisome by the time that we have reached mid-life. The 'soberness' of the Prayer Book services, of which we have all heard so much at various times, past and present, may not unfairly be regarded as a convertible term with dullness; and, unless I am mistaken, has had not a little to do with the Church's loss of influence with the masses. It is that very 'soberness' which makes our Services so uninteresting and unattractive.[19]

New considerations have replaced the 'reserve' of the Tractarians. Vaux argued that the Church should not shy away from colourful services or dramatic preaching through fear of the charge of sensationalism. 'The duty of the Church is to deal with men, not as they ought to be, but as they are; to take notice of their varying pecularities, and even of their foibles; and to do her best to turn them to account for their soul's health.'[20] There was an urgent need for more popular evening services, and for services more closely related to seasonal themes, and for occasions such as harvest festivals. Sermons needed to be less literary and polished and more pungent and direct.

Underlying the work of particular missions and mission services, Vaux suggested, was the need for an order of mission priests. 'What we really want, is a Religious Order, or rather a "Congregation", in the Roman sense of the term, composed of Priests who really know how to *preach*, *i.e.* who can do something more than "deliver a Sermon"; and who should live in Community and under rule, being ready to go to any parish to which they were invited, and to hold a Mission.'[21] Vaux acknowledged that a start had already been made in Benson's Cowley Fathers, who taking the name of the Society of St. John the Evangelist, characterized themselves as Mission Priests. Nonetheless, he suggested, 'the thing to be aimed at is a Society with a large central House—say in London—and as large a body of Priests suited for the work as could be brought together, who . . . should live strictly under rule whilst at home, but who should be free to go, two or three together, to any parish where a Mission was desired'. Such a mixture of the active and contemplative life afforded, he thought, exactly what the times demanded. Such an idea, he continued, had been mulled over for some time. Were such a community to come into existence there would be other advantages: a retreat house; a centre for spiritual direction; a place which would complement theological colleges in offering a distinct training in spirituality and experience of mission work.[22]

If we look at the notable parishes of the Catholic revival we find that in a surprisingly large number of instances this community dimension was present as supplying an important element of the new patterns of ministry. St. Saviour's, Leeds, built anonymously by Dr Pusey, was initially the setting of an informal community. J. S. Cazenove, who was one of the original group, describes their pattern of worship.

Our day was arranged as follows. Prime at seven A.M. morning; Prayer in Church at half past seven; Breakfast at eight; Sext at one P.M. then dinner. Afternoon Service in Church at four P.M.; Tea at half-past five; Vespers at six; Evening Office in Church at half-past seven, a light Supper at nine; Compline at ten; after which we were at liberty to retire.[23]

Visiting occupied about three hours each day. The Eucharist was celebrated on Sundays after Morning Prayer, and on Holy Days after the half-past seven service. Edward Jackson, another member of the group, who had once visited Newman's community at Littlemore with the intention of joining them, wrote of how they had lived together 'for the sake of both economy and Christian fellowship and support'. Any money not needed for their frugal living was required for the relief of the sick and the poor. He noted the work in the school, and the numerous baptisms, churchings, marriages, and burials.[24] The departure of Richard Ward, the first Vicar, following both dissensions with Hook, the Vicar of Leeds, and secessions to Rome, allowed this pattern to continue only from 1845 to 1847, but it was more or less resumed when Thomas Minster succeeded to the living in 1848. Again the day began with Prime, but at 6 a.m., and the day was marked by times of prayer and the observance of the lesser Hours. After a choral Evensong at 7.30 p.m. there were classes for those under instruction and also time set aside for hearing confessions. The classes consisted of an exposition of Scripture, the singing of an evening hymn, and certain collects. During Lent dietary rules were observed: no meat except on Sundays, Tuesdays, and Thursdays; butter only allowed at tea; on Wednesdays and Fridays only a piece of bread at breakfast, with coffee without milk or sugar. Dinner was eaten in silence whilst a portion of one of the lives of the saints was read.[25]

Ten years later, in 1857, Lowder and Mackonochie took up residence in the Mission House in Wellclose Square, following the kind of semi-monastic community life of which Lowder had dreamed when he was a curate at St. Barnabas, Pimlico. The pattern followed was similar to that at St. Saviour's, Leeds.

The first bell for rising was rung at 6.30; we said Prime in the oratory at 7; Matins was said at St. Peter's and St. Saviour's at 7.30; the celebration of the Holy Eucharist followed. After breakfast, followed by Terce, the clergy and teachers went to their respective work—some in school, some in the study or district. Sext was said at 12.45, immediately before dinner, when the household were again assembled; and on Fridays and fast days some book, such as the 'Lives of the Saints' or Ecclesiastical History, was read at table. After dinner, rest, letters, visiting or school work, as the case might be, and then tea at 5.30 p.m. After tea, choir practice, classes, reading, or visiting again until Evensong at 8 p.m. After service the clergy were often engaged in classes, hearing confessions, or attending to special cases. Supper at 9.15, followed by Compline, when those who had finished their work retired to their rooms. It was desired that all should be in bed at 11 p.m., when the gas was put out; but, of course, in the case of the clergy, much of whose work was late in the evening with those who could not come to them at any other time, it was impossible absolutely to observe this rule. In an active community the rules of the house must yield to the necessities of spiritual duties.[26]

Lowder and his fellow mission-priests, being thus rooted in a corporate spiritual life and discipline, had as the prime concern of their ministry the conversion and sanctification of those to whom they ministered. Lowder warned his younger brother against allowing even the diligent use of the sacraments to take the place of such deep renewal of life, and was insistent that all social activities fostered by the Church were ancillary to that central concern. So he could write of their ministry:

We believed that though it were a much more difficult work to win souls to Christ in the sorrowful ways of true repentance, and in the fruits of penitential discipline—to build them up and train them in the whole faith of the Catholic Church, and in the duties of the Christian life; yet that thus only were we fulfilling our special obligations as missionary priests of the Church.[27]

It was hard work and the numbers were not great, as we can see, for example, from a note in Mackonochie's diary for Easter Day, 1859.

A most happy day. All the communicants whom I had reason to think could come communicated. They numbered 31. The congregations were Matins—

Men 15, Women 13, choir 12. Evening—Men 21, Women 60, choir 19. In the afternoon we admitted five choristers, churched two women, baptized 34 children. The order of service was—Procession before and after each service —choral celebration. Psalms and Litany chanted. The rest as usual. DEO GRATIAS.[28]

Mission-house life was ascetic. One of Lowder's assistants wrote that 'certain dinners meant sick headaches and agonies untold'. Pea-soup fog in the winter and the stench from the river in the summer meant additional discomfort.

In Plymouth George Rundle Prynne, who had declined Pusey's invitation to join the community of priests at St. Saviour's, Leeds, as he was already all but engaged to be married, had nonetheless close links with a community, in this case Miss Sellon's Society of Sisters of Mercy at Devonport. Prynne had only been in charge of the new district of St. Peter's—a dockland area of great poverty and many problems—for a year when, in July 1849, the cholera broke out. Miss Sellon's small band, established the previous year and engaged in work with orphans, teaching, and in the care of the sick, asked Prynne if they might assist in the emergency. After an initial hesitation as to whether it was fitting for ladies to be exposed to the squalor and the danger of infection, Prynne welcomed their help. The conditions were appalling, Prynne and his curate on one occasion finding an overcrowded tenement house with all its inmates dead. An eyewitness described the suffering of the poor, Irish community:

The crowding, the hustling, the shouting, the screaming were fearful. Sometimes people would seize the medical officer and carry him bodily . . . into the miserable den where young and old were stretched in agony on the floor, and he, literally, had to step over the bodies of the dead to attend to the living.[29]

Prynne wrote that 'for three months we seemed to be living amongst the dying and the dead'. A temporary hospital was erected in the parish, with an altar set up in the largest ward, 'in order that everything might be ready for communicating the dying'. The sisters asked to be allowed to receive communion daily to strengthen them in their work, and so, for the first time in the Church of England since the Reformation, a daily Eucharist was begun.[30]

The crowded conditions in Leeds also led to an outbreak of

epidemic disease. In 1846–7 the Irish refugees from the potato famine, living in overcrowded squalor, were the victims of typhus. Edward Jackson castigated the Poor Law authorities for refusing to provide any kind of reception facilities for the Irish on the grounds that they were not chargeable to the town. He remembered on one afternoon finding twenty-three bodies awaiting burial in the church.

The low howls of the women were terrible. They sat at the grave sides, crouching in their peculiar way, and rocking themselves to and fro, as they looked down into the dark cavities where the dead were lowered, five and six deep, one upon another.[31]

Jackson and his fellow curates at Leeds parish church opened soup kitchens and pressed the authorities for additional relief. Monck, a newly ordained curate of 25, had charge of one of the worst areas, as Jackson describes:

In this district, which was one of an especially Irish character, it was simply horrible. Every place above ground, and underground, was crammed with miserable, famished wretches, scarcely looking like human beings. In one cellar we counted thirty-one men, women and children, all lying on the damp, filthy floor, with only a few handfuls of straw under them; while the frightened neighbours, who would not venture into the pestiliential depth, were lowering water in buckets to allay the intolerable thirst of the miserable people. Our young curate . . . himself would go down to them in their cellars, or climb up into their close choking chamber, raise their heads, put fresh straw under them, give them the gruel with their own hands, and though they wanted not his religious ministrations, having their own priests, who, to their honour never shrank from their duty, and of whom several laid down their lives in the performance of it, yet his heart was continually going out in labours and benedictions for the wretched sufferers.[32]

Monck himself fell a victim to typhus and died in July 1847. The following year massive unemployment meant that 15,000 were receiving relief from the public soup kitchen, as their average weekly earnings did not reach 10d. a head.[33]

In 1849 the cholera spread north to Leeds. In St. Saviour's parish they burnt tar fires in the streets. The death-rate in the parish crept to ten or more a day from the disease. As in Plymouth a daily celebration of the Eucharist was begun. The clergy carried calomel, and cayenne pepper, and spirit of camphor with them, often acting as unofficial doctors. The medicine they used was placed on the altar at the morning Eucharist. They would be called to dying bedsides for spiritual ministrations, and then would often have to return to lay out the body and disinfect the house. They began to visit in their cassocks around the parish. The cries of the sufferers echoed through the streets at night. The St. Saviour's clergy, in a parish where one in twenty was to die from the cholera, spoke of the need for reserving the Sacrament so that the sick and dying might be communicated when there was neither time nor opportunity for individual celebrations of the Eucharist in the sick room.[34]

The pastoral ministry of clergy and sisters during the 1849 cholera won respect, if not approval, for their Catholic inspiration. The demands of the situation also led to the more rapid emergence of the daily Eucharist than might otherwise have been the case. In a similar way the need to prepare the victims of cholera for imminent death led to a stress on confession as central to the church's ministry to the individual.

Confession was to become one of the major points of contention between the slum priests, bishops, and the popular Protestantism of the majority of the country. The other centre of controversy was the increasing ceremonial which was used in worship, and particularly in the eucharistic worship which was at the heart of the catholic revival. The third quarter of the nineteenth century in particular saw an outburst of 'ritual' prosecutions, and many of those prosecutions were directed against clergy in the slum parishes. The Tractarian leaders had been concerned with the identity and catholic continuity of the Church of England. They had stressed the need as they saw it for a better observance of the rubrics and pattern of worship of the Prayer Book. They had taught a doctrine of reserve which reflected their sense of the majesty and mystery of God. They believed in the catholicity of the Church of England, but did not seek to reintroduce either the medieval ritual of the Sarum service-books or contemporary Catholic ceremonial, though they held many Catholic devotional books, and the Breviary in particular, to be valuable. Pusey was not alone in feeling that the awe and reverence of worship needed to be linked with penitence and sobriety rather than with colour and ceremony. Nonetheless, when they were concerned with building churches they were concerned with their order and symbolism, and the slightly later impetus given by the Ecclesiologists meant that Tractarian churches became appropriate settings for the growth of a more worthy and elaborate ritual. The ritualist slum priests, working in what they rightly saw to be missionary situations, were conscious both of the need for greater imagination in worship, and of the importance of proclaiming the Catholic faith in a visible and striking way. Their concerns were not the conventions and legal forms of the Establishment, as bishops found to their cost, but sacramental spirituality and missionary zeal. Certainly antiquarian elements had their influence on anglo-catholic liturgy, but that for which the slum priests at their best were contending was more than medievalism or copying of Roman Catholic practice simply because it was Roman Catholic. The needs of the new religious communities, small at first, but growing, also played their part in the enriching of Anglican worship.

In the mid-nineteenth century accusations of ritualism were provoked by the introduction of practices which would now be considered as bearing no particular party label, whether within the Church of England or outside it. For instance, Bishop Blomfield in 1854 demanded that the services at St. Barnabas, Pimlico, where Charles Lowder was at that time a curate, should be said and not sung. He requested that there should be no procession of clergy and choir from the vestry, no reverencing of the altar on entering and leaving the sanctuary, no eastward-facing position in the celebration of the Eucharist, and no coloured coverings proper to the season on the altar. There was to be a collect and not the invocation before the sermon, and no cross behind the altar.[35] At St. Saviour's, Leeds, Bishop Longley of Ripon took exception to a wooden cross on top of the chancel screen, and to prayers being led facing east.[36]

At St. Saviour's, Pollen noted, a book of hymns, mainly consisting of translations of medieval hymns, was introduced, and in Advent the Advent antiphons were sung. In 1849 there was a Midnight Eucharist at Christmas, the church was decorated, and the choir processed to a version of 'O come, all ye faithful'. The celebrant and two assistants wore white stoles. In Holy Week the Eucharist was celebrated after Evensong on Maundy Thursday; then the altars were stripped, and there was no singing until the first Evensong of Easter on Holy Saturday, when the choir processed to the hymn, 'Jesus Christ is risen today!' There was a midnight Eucharist that evening just as at Christmas. Through office hymns, antiphons, and the observance of saints' days and seasons St. Saviour's endeavoured to create an awareness of both the mystery of redemption and the communion of saints. Baptism was surrounded by symbols to emphasize its importance, the choir processing to the font and standing in a circle around it accompanied by lights. At Christmas there was a feast in the large school with a great Christmas tree 'fifteen feet high, all covered with lights, and hung with pictures, lolly-pops, "spaice whistles," [i.e. barley sugar whistles], &c.' This was cited as a ritualist practice to the Bishop, as was a picture of the Nativity surrounded with greenery. This was thought, according to Pollen, to indicate worship of either 'Adam and Eve' or else 'Cain and Abel'![37]

At St. Peter's, Plymouth, at the same time Prynne used a much more restrained ceremonial; even the choristers' surplices were little more than pinafores made of rough towelling.[38] Rather later, in the room over the costermonger's fish-shop in Baldwin's Gardens, which preceded the church of St. Alban's, Holborn, Mackonochie celebrated the Eucharist with lighted candles on the altar and wearing an alb and chasuble of white linen, with a black stole and maniple.[39] After the church was consecrated in 1863 Mackonochie introduced coloured vestments (in 1865) and incense (at Epiphany 1866). In 1864 St. Alban's became the first Anglican parish to introduce the Three Hours devotion on Good Friday. Lord Shaftesbury, who attended St. Alban's in 1866, recorded his horror at the ceremonial in suitably purple prose.

In outward form and ritual, it is the worship of Jupiter and Juno. . . . In a few minutes, the organ, the choristers, abundant officials, and three priests in green silk robes, the middle priest having on his back a cross embroidered as long as his body. This was the beginning of the sacramental service. . . . Then ensued such a scene of theatrical gymnastics, and singing, screaming, genuflections, such a series of strange movements of the priests, their back almost always to the people, as I never saw before even in a Romish Temple. Clouds upon clouds of incense, the censer frequently refreshed by the High Priest, who kissed the spoon as he dug out the sacred powder, and swung it about at the end of a silver chain. . . . The Communicants went up to the tune of soft music, as though it had been a melodrama, and one was astonished, at the close, that there was no fall of the curtain.[40]

Shaftesbury, an Evangelical, asked his readers whether such worship would lead men to Christ or to Baal. On the Tractarian side Beresford Hope, the chief benefactor of All Saints, Margaret Street, was at pains to emphasize the transformation of Anglican worship as a consequence of the Oxford Movement. In his defence of the dignified and unfussy ceremonial he saw as characteristic of the Catholic revival in Anglicanism he reminded his readers of the kind of service he had known as a child in Surrey in the reign of George IV. In the church the chancel was partitioned off, the eastern ends of the aisles were appropriated as family pews or private boxes, from which the local magnates would nod recognition to each other across the nave.

The portion of the Communion Office, preceding the sermon, was Sunday after Sunday, read from the desk, separated from the Litany on the one side, and from the sermon on the other, by such a rendering of Tate and Brady as the unruly gang of volunteers, with fiddles and wind instruments, in the gallery, pleased to contribute. The clerk, a wizened old fellow, in a brown Welsh wig, repeated the responses in a nasal twang ... while the local rendering of 'briefs, citations, and excommunications,' included announcements by this worthy, after the Nicene Creed, of meetings at the town inn of the 'executors' of a deceased Duke. Two hopeful cubs of the clerk sprawled behind him in the desk, and the back-handers, occasionally intended to reduce them to order, were apt to resound against the impassive boards. During the sermon this zealous servant of the sanctuary would take up his broom and sweep out the middle alley, in order to save himself the fatigue of a week-day visit.[41]

The changes in worship promoted by the 'Ritualists', as they came to be popularly known, provoked strong reactions. A mixture of 'no-popery' prejudice and genuine concern for the Reformation heritage of the Church of England produced both disturbances and prosecutions. The riots at St. George's-in-the-East in 1859 were the most publicized of the disturbances and focused particularly around the appointment of a strongly Protestant clergyman, the Revd Hugh Allen, as lecturer of the parish, of which the rector, the Revd Bryan King, was a staunch Tractarian. Charles Lowder and his fellow priests had begun their mission work in the parish three years earlier. One of the teachers in Lowder's small community observed that violence and disorder were characteristic of the area, and suggested that it was partly for this reason that the authorities were reluctant to restore order. One of his night school pupils doubted whether theological concerns had much to do with the rioting:

'It's all a question of beer, sir, and what else they can get. We know them. They are blackguards like ourselves here. Religion ain't anything more to them than it is to us. They gets paid for what they do, and they do it like they'd do any other job.'[42]

There are graphic descriptions of the rioting, which lasted several months.

> The mob took possession of the seats occupied by the choir, and turned the clergy and choir out of their places in church; they shouted the responses aloud in the most indecent and outrageous manner, sometimes even into the ear of the officiating minister; they tried to stop the prayers, lessons, and sermon by continued coughing and hissing, stamping of feet, whistling, and slamming of pew doors. They turned dogs, howling from the effects of drugs purposely administered to them, into the church on one occasion, and on other occasions crackers were let off and musical instruments used in the church to disturb the service.[43]

In January 1860 *The Times* reported that the conduct of the congregation was 'devilish'. At least three thousand were present, a third of them boys bent on mischief:

> There was cat-calling, cock-crowing, yelling, howling, hissing, shouting, of the most violent kind, snatches of popular songs were sung, loud cries of 'Bravo' and 'Order' came from every part of the church, caps, hats and bonnets were thrown from the galleries into the body of the church and back again, while pew doors were slammed, lucifer matches struck, and attempts more than once made to put out the gas. . . . A considerable amount of church furniture has been destroyed, the cushions in the galleries were torn up and thrown into the body of the church, Bibles and Prayer-books flew about in all directions, and many of the altar decorations have been injured.[44]

Tait, the Bishop of London, who held King's use of vestments to be a 'childish mimicry of antiquated garments', tried in vain to bring order to the parish, but without success until King was persuaded to take a year's leave in July 1860. He did not return to the parish, and the peace which Tait somewhat uncertainly secured was only at the expense of a complete capitulation to the mob, and the Dissenting members of the parish Vestry who played a large part in fomenting the dissension. It is interesting to note that Lowder believed that, on the whole, the riots had tended to consolidate the work of the Mission.

> The very dregs of the people were taught to think about religion. Many were brought to church through the unhappy notoriety which he had gained; and some who came to scoff remained to worship.[45]

The various attempts to control Ritualism are to be found in the Ritual Commission of 1867–70, the Public Worship Regulation Act of 1874, and the various legal actions brought both before and under that Act against ritualist clergy. None were successful. The Ritual Commission's reports, although containing lengthy examinations of ritualist clergy, did not make enough concessions and the Commission was too divided. The Public Worship Regulation Act was too clearly intended to put down ritualism, and the court which administered it was in the end made ineffective because of the refusal of the priests prosecuted to acknowledge its Erastian jurisdiction. When priests such as Arthur Tooth at Hatcham and Sidney Faithorn Green at Miles Platting were prepared to go to prison rather than obey the monitions of Lord Penzance, the former Divorce Court judge who presided over the court created by the 1874 Act, a scandalous situation had been created. Much later, when Archbishop Davidson gave evidence before the Royal Commission on Ecclesiastical Discipline set up by the Prime Minister, Arthur Balfour, in 1904, he stated his belief that it was the imprisonment of four clergy under the Public Worship Regulation Act that 'did more than any single thing that has occurred in the ritual controversy to change public opinion upon the whole question of litigation of this sort'.[46] He also cited a charge of Bishop Thirlwall of St. Davids in 1866 warning of the doctrinal innovation of the ritualists.

Its partizans seem to vie with one another in the introduction of more and more startling novelties, both of theory and practice. The adoration of the consecrated wafer, reserved for that purpose, which is one of the most characteristic Roman rites, and a legitimate consequence of the Romish Eucharistic doctrine, is contemplated, if it has not already been adopted, in some of our churches, and the Romish festival of the *Corpus Christi* instituted for the conspicuous exercise of that adoration has, it appears, actually begun to be observed by clergymen of our church. Already public honours are paid to the Virgin Mary, and language applied to her which can only be considered as marking the first stage of a development to which no limit short of the full Romish worship can be probably assigned.[47]

When the 1904 Royal Commission reported in 1906 it listed a number of breaches of the current law that it regarded as particularly grave, including interpolation in the Eucharist of prayers from the Canon of the Roman Mass, adoration of the reserved Sacrament, Benediction, non-communicating Eucharists, invocation of saints, and the veneration of images and roods. But it also concluded that 'the law of public worship in the Church of England is too narrow for the religious life of the present generation'.

It needlessly condemns much which a great section of Church people, including many of her most devoted members, value; and modern thought and feeling are characterised by a care for ceremonial, a sense of dignity in worship, and an appreciation of the continuity of the Church, which were not similarly felt when the law took its present shape.[48]

A consequence of the Commission was the eventual issuing of Letters of Business to the Convocations, which began the process of liturgical revision leading to the 1927–8 Prayer Book and, more remotely, to the Alternative Service Book of 1980.

Those first described as Ritualists had as their prime concerns the centrality of Eucharistic worship, the doctrine of the Real Presence, and missionary motivation. Linklater said of Lowder that 'he was not a Ritualist at all in the modern sense of the word, after the gushing, effeminate, sentimental manner of young shop-boys, or those who simply ape the ways of Rome'.

He had glorious ritual in his church because he thought the service of God could not be too magnifical. He considered that it was as much his duty as parish priest to put before the eyes of his people the pattern of the worship in Heaven, as it was his duty to preach the Gospel. He felt that he had no more right to alter the features of the heavenly worship, as represented in the earthly service, than he had to alter the faith once delivered to the saints. He understood that those features are made known to us by our Lord's command. 'Do this,' by the revelation of heavenly worship to St. John, and by the testimony of the unbroken custom of the Christian Church.[49]

In an article on the missionary aspect of ritualism R. F. Littledale argued that ritualism was the 'Object Lesson' of religion, which communicated religious truth to the illiterate and to women and children. As such it was superior to the sermonizing of Evangelicalism and the aridity of Broad Church liberalism. 'It is not easy', wrote Littledale, 'to conceive the idea of a Broad-Church lady.'[50] Ritualism, he argued, was the natural complement of a written liturgy. 'What an oratorio would be without instrumentation; what jewels uncut and unset are; what a handsome house in the country is without hangings, curtains, carpets, mirrors, or pictures, that, and worse than that, is the Prayer Book without ritual.'[51] The restoration of ritual in worship would enable those of the poor to whom the churches were now more accessible as a result of the abolition of pew-rents and private seating to be drawn to an appreciation of Christian truth. Later on, at the end of the century, Robert Dolling in Portsmouth was another exponent of a ritualism that was not in the least antiquarian or fastidious but intended to serve a missionary purpose. His friend and fellow-Irishman, the Catholic Modernist, George Tyrell, noted how it was a matter of indifference to Dolling whether his methods were borrowed from Rome or from the Salvation Army. Believing that at the heart of Christianity was not the example of Christ but the sacramental gift of the life of Christ as the reality which could alone transform sinful human life, he urged that 'what we have got to do in the Church of England is to put the Mass into its proper place.' He encouraged congregational singing and extempore prayer. He maintained that two kinds of worship were necessary—'one very dignified and ornate', speaking of the majesty of God; one very simple and familiar, pointing to God as a loving Father. In his dispute with Davidson, then Bishop of Winchester, he wrote:

We condemn as a fundamental error the idea that men were created for the sake of the Sacraments. We believe that the Sacraments were created for the sake of men. But it seems that, by this new theory, men were created for the sake of the rubrics of the Book of Common Prayer.[52]

The missionary concern of many of the ritualists was shown particularly in their involvement in the promotion of the Mission to London in 1869. R. M. Benson, S. W. O'Neill, Charles Lowder, A. H. Mackonochie, and W. J. E. Bennett were all involved, as well as George Howard Wilkinson, later Bishop of Truro and subsequently of St. Andrews. Although the meeting to plan the pattern of the Mission was only held in September, one hundred and twenty churches are said to have taken part in the Mission two months later. At St. Alban's, where O'Neill was the missioner, the Mission ended with the renewal of baptismal vows, and the distribution of lighted candles, a pattern which, Professor Kent suggests, may have been derived from French Catholic missions in the years following the Bourbon Restoration.[53] The Evangelical *Record* viewed with alarm the place given to Confession in the Mission, commenting that 'the attempt seems to be one which grafts the earnestness of revival preaching on the sacerdotal errors of Romanism, and associates the call to repentance with the deadly poison of the Confessional.'[54] Although the Mission had left freedom to individual parishes and missioners as to how to proceed, the planning conference had given Confession special consideration, and it figured significantly in the appeals and addresses of some of the missioners. At St. Alban's, Holborn, one of the consequences of the 1869 Mission was the abandonment of the earlier practice of hearing confessions by appointment in the vestry.

It was notified that the Clergy would hear confessions in church at fixed hours, and each chose a station where he could be found. There were no 'Confessional-boxes', if by that term are meant the solid structures seen in Roman Catholic churches; but only a seat for the Priest set crosswise in the open sittings with a curtain to screen the penitent from curious on-lookers. . . . The alteration marked a stage in the history of the Catholic revival. It is one thing to slink into a dismal vestry, like an intending criminal bent on some unlawful act. It is altogether different, and vastly easier, to take one's place among one's fellows in the aisle of a well-lighted church, and then, when one's turn comes, to do one's business without fuss or mystification.[55]

The dark, vestry setting for hearing confessions, and the prurient questions which it was thought confessors asked, particularly of women penitents, were a favourite theme of Protestant opponents of the confessional. Dr Elisabeth Jay gives a good example from the pages of the *Christian Observer*.

It was, then, on a Friday, at four o'clock, in the autumn, when light was dim in London, and in the vestry of St. Barnabas there was almost total darkness, that this young dissolute woman called by appointment on Mr Poole. She called on him at the Parsonage; she was taken into the vestry. The vestry, which looks into a gloomy court, is even in sunlight obscure; at such a season and such an hour, it was nearly dark. It is, however as Mr. Poole naïvely says, *the place where confessions are wont to be made*. The door was locked, or, as Mr. Poole puts it, was secured, and then proceeded the ceremonial.[56]

It is ironic that, according to Pollen, at St. Saviour's, Leeds, in the late 1840s Confessions were heard in the clergy-house or sacristy after the Bishop had forbidden them to be heard in church.[57]

The London Mission of 1874 again brought the subject of Confession to the fore. An accusation was made that at the mission addresses, 'when the gas was lowered, the clergy went about and urged the people who remained to go to Confession', and such was the sensitivity of the subject that G. H. Wilkinson, at whom the charge had been particularly aimed, felt it necessary to defend himself in two sermons on the themes of Confession and Absolution.[58] The previous year, a petition from the Society of the Holy Cross, requesting Convocation to make provision for 'the education, selection and licensing of duly qualified confessors in accordance with the provisions of Canon Law', had led Lord Shaftesbury, in a speech at Exeter Hall, to ask why the bishops had resorted to an inquiry instead of saying 'Away with this foul rag—this pollution of the red one of Babylon?'[59] A month later, Bishop Samuel Wilberforce, only four days before his death, addressed a warning to his rural deans on the subject of Confession, which is a good indication of the way in which a Tractarian sympathizer and believer in the use of Confession in particular cases of spiritual need, could nonetheless react strongly to the teaching of habitual Confession as something 'almost necessary for the leading of the higher Christian life'.

This system of Confession is one of the worst developments of Popery. In the first place, as regards *the Penitent*, it is a system of unnatural excitement, a sort of spiritual dram-drinking. . . . It is the substitution of Confession to Man for the opening of the heart to GOD. . . .

Then, in *Families* it introduces untold mischief. It supersedes God's appointment of intimacy between husband and wife, father and children; substituting another influence for that which ought to be the nearest and closest, and producing reserve and estrangement where there ought to be perfect freedom and openness. Lastly, as regards *the Priest* to whom Confession is made, it brings in a wretched system of casuistry. But, far worse than this, it necessitates the terrible evil of familiar dealing with Sin, specially with the sins of uncleanness; thereby sometimes even tending to their growth, by making horrible particulars known to those who have hitherto been innocent of such fatal knowledge, and so poisoning the mind of priest and people alike.[60]

It was after Wilberforce's death that a further controversy arose over Confession, when Lord Redesdale drew the attention of the House of Lords in 1877 to a manual for confessors, *The Priest in Absolution,* compiled by the Revd J. C. Chambers, and circulated privately by the Society of the Holy Cross.

The Catholic associations of Confession and the suspicion of sacerdotalism and the improper exercise of priestly power lay behind much of the opposition to confession. It is worth noting, however, as Dr Anthony Russell has pointed out, that in some respects the growth of the practice of sacramental Confession was but one aspect of a general development of the counselling role of the clergy which was characteristic of all traditions in the Church of England in the nineteenth century. As general visiting became impossible in large parishes, counselling a few parishioners in depth became the pattern of pastoral ministry. As the old agricultural community fragmented, concern shifted from communities to individuals. As private life developed in an urbanized, industrial society, so tensions and problems came to the fore which had not previously existed, and so 'the clergyman's activity in counselling became a system of personal therapy for the people, who were deprived of the solidarity of the traditional village and the extended family'. To some extent this was forwarded by Evangelical emphases on the individual and his responsibilities. Russell cites Monro's view that 'men must be worked upon individually; it is impossible to operate very efficiently on the mass; whether in a town population or an agricultural'.[61]

In his book *Catholic Evangelicalism* the German scholar, Dieter Voll, suggested that what we see in the ritualist priests is the convergence of Catholic and Evangelical traditions, and that nowhere is this more evident than in the mission work. Newman had been suspicious of playing on excited feelings; the ritualists felt this to be necessary for the work of conversion. Professor Kent has criticized Voll's thesis for ignoring the sharp polarization of Anglo-Catholics and Evangelicals which was certainly evident over such central matters as Confession, and for failing to discern the influence of Roman Catholic mission preaching on the ritualists. He suspects twentieth-century ecumenical concerns of having led Voll to blur differences.[62] Kent has a point but has perhaps over-reacted, and not given sufficient recognition to the common concern of Anglo-Catholics and Evangelicals for a vital rather than a formal religion, and the need for a greater preaching of conversion in contexts where there was next to no folk-religion or conventional religious practice to give support. Certainly sermons such as those of Arthur Stanton, or of Joseph Leycester Lyne (Father Ignatius) in the West London Mission of 1885, centre strongly on the need for conversion in Evangelical terms, sometimes with an explicitly Evangelical reference. Thus Ignatius can ask, 'what is the use of the Sacraments to a people who have not received the Spiritual life that the Evangelical movement brought?' 'Unless I have first obtained the blessings of the Evangelical movement, the Tractarian movement will be to me a curse instead of a blessing. I do not believe in Sacraments unless the person who participates in them has a personal belief in a personal Saviour.'[63] So he appealed directly in his mission addresses:

It is Jesus Christ, in His fulness, offered *now* to you, His righteousness, His love, His peace, His salvation; God's gift to you *now*, and NOW, you can take hold of it with childlike faith. . . .

If you say to me: 'You ask me to give up my sin,' I answer: NO, I do not. All I ask of you is to receive Christ and to trust in Jesus. Directly you trust in Him His love fills you, and you will not care for sin.[64]

And Stanton could speak in one of his last sermons of the cleansing Blood of Christ, personal faith in a Saviour, and of the Mass as expressing both of these:

Never be ashamed of the Blood of Christ. I know it is not the popular religion of the day, They will call it mediaevalism, but you know as well as possible that the whole Bible from cover to cover is incarminated, reddened, with the Blood of Christ. Never you be ashamed of the Blood of Christ. You are Blood-bought Christians. . . . The uniform we Christians wear is scarlet. . . .

And the second thing is this: Let us remember that our religion is the religion of a personal Saviour. It is not a system of ethics, it is not a scheme of philosophy, it is not a conclusion of science, but it is personal love to a personal living Saviour—that is our religion! Why, you can hear the voice of Christ off the altar to-day at Mass, 'Do this in remembrance of Me'. '*You*' and '*Me*'.[65]

In Portsmouth, Dolling maintained that the 'frigid simplicity' of the unadorned Prayer Book services would never have converting power in the slum, and it was no surprise that people had preferred 'the warm, loving and personal worship' of the Nonconformist chapel. 'Is it so long ago', he asked, 'since many dignified clergymen believed that the chapel was really more suitable for common people?'[66] So Dolling was not afraid to be thought vulgar in order that a living faith might be communicated. His congregations could kneel in silent prayer before the Blessed Sacrament, and also sing 'I need Thee precious Jesu' to the tune of 'Home, sweet Home'.[67] Like many slum priests it was not only the worship which was important to him, but a whole range of other activities which met community needs: communicants' guilds, a boys' gymnasium, work amongst sailors, rescue work for alcoholics and prostitutes, and battles for causes such as reasonable hours for shop-girls. His social involvement brought him, as it brought other ritualist priests, under the condemnation of the Establishment. After Stewart Headlam, the founder of the Guild of St. Matthew, had delivered a lecture on Christian Socialism in Dolling's parish, in which he had advocated land reform, Bishop Harold Browne of Winchester wrote that 'this so-called Christian Socialism . . . appears to me to strike at the very root of Christianity'. The Warden of Winchester College, whose Missioner Dolling was, was equally outraged: 'With your ultra High-Church proclivities on the one hand, and your Socialist teaching on the other, no sober-minded and loyal citizen can be expected to support the mission, my connection with which must now be severed so long as you continue to be the head of it.'[68]

It is hard to measure the 'success' of the Anglo-Catholic slum priests, but the influence of the popular, sacramental worship which they pioneered on the one hand, and of their devotion and care on the other cannot be doubted. This stubbornness in fighting for what they believed to be right, and their refusal to accept the limits laid down by bishops, church courts, or Privy Council, resulted in an extension of the boundaries of Anglican practice and to some extent theology. In his survey of religious influences in London at the turn of the century Charles Booth cited a number of opinions concerning the attitude of working-class people to Anglo-Catholic priests and churches. Some asserted that 'very High lines are understood and liked best', others indicated that 'as to High Church doings people like brightness, but ignore doctrinal meanings'. Another maintained that 'the poor do not believe in church-going because they do not believe in church-goers. They see the church-going class spending huge sums on all kinds of luxury, and look upon their religion as humbug.' Or again: 'among working men a kind of sublimated trades' unionism is the most prevalent gospel: a vague bias towards that which is believed to be good for one's fellow man'. Booth himself concluded that in parishes in which the poor outnumbered all the rest, 'the High Church section is more successful than any other. They bring to their work a greater force of religious enthusiasm', and their 'evidently self-denying lives appeal ... to the imagination of the people.' Nonetheless, 'the churches themselves' were 'largely filled by people from other districts and of higher class, attracted by the stir of religious life'.[69] 'To live a life of voluntary poverty', he wrote, 'seems to be the only road to the confidence of the people'.[70]

VII.   Edward King's 'Bishopric of Love'

WHEN EDWARD King was appointed to succeed Christopher Wordsworth as Bishop of Lincoln in 1885, Henry Scott Holland wrote with characteristic enthusiasm that his would be 'a Bishopric of Love'.[1] At King's consecration Liddon suggested that his 'great grace of sympathy' pointed to an episcopate which would rank him with bishops such as Lancelot Andrewes, Thomas Ken, and Thomas Wilson of Sodor and Man, as a true father in God.[2] That promise may be said to have been in large measure fulfilled, and Edward King is rightly revered as an outstanding example of pastoral care and holiness of life rooted in a deeply sacramental faith.

Edward King was born in 1829, the son of a clergyman who was later to be Archdeacon of Rochester. He was educated at home and with a private tutor and in 1848, three years after Newman had joined the Church of Rome, he came up to Oriel College, Oxford. There he came under the influence of R. W. Church, later Dean of St. Paul's, and Charles Marriott, Newman's successor as Vicar of St. Mary's. Marriott's example was particularly significant. His concern for the poor, his availability, his capacity to draw out the awkward and the shy, combined with a donnish eccentricity and a capacity for academic work which bore its chief fruit in his large share in the editing and translating of *The Library of the Fathers*, made a profound impact on Edward King. He said of Marriott that he was 'the most Gospel-like man I have ever met'.[3] At a time when the character of Oxford was changing from what it had been in the hey-day of the Oxford Movement, King allied himself with the Church party and was assiduous in his religious duties. At the end of his first term he earned a sardonic comment from Provost Hawkins: 'I observe, Mr King, that you have never missed a single chapel morning or evening, during the whole term. I must warn you, Mr King, that even too regular attendance at chapel may degenerate into formalism'.[4] Like Hurrell Froude in earlier years King was scrupulous in observing the rules of fasting and abstinence. Academically he was not outstanding, reading only for a pass degree, but developing a particular interest in the works of Bishop Butler as well as Plato's *Republic* and Aristotle's *Ethics*. When in later years he was appointed as a Canon Professor of Christ Church his lack of public academic distinction was a cause of some concern to him, and his friends and biographers endeavoured to point out that this in no way indicated an absence of intellectual power. It was rather that in Edward King the Tractarian emphasis on the priority of moral attitude over intellectual virtuosity was particularly exemplified.

In 1854 King was ordained to the curacy of Wheatley, a village to the east of Oxford, by Bishop Samuel Wilberforce. In this small parish he first showed his remarkable pastoral gifts, and he continued to correspond with some of those he had known as young parishioners there until the end of his life. He remained at Wheatley for four years and was then invited by Wilberforce to be Chaplain of the theological college Wilberforce had founded opposite his episcopal residence at Cuddesdon. In 1854, the year of Edward King's ordination, Henry Parry Liddon had been appointed as Vice-Principal of Cuddesdon. This appointment had been made by Wilberforce with some misgivings because of his suspicion that Liddon was too much under the influence of Pusey, whose teaching on the Eucharist and on sacramental Confession Wilberforce distrusted. But he took the risk because of Liddon's manifest spirituality and high ideals of Christian ministry, once Liddon had assured him that he would only recommend sacramental Confession to the Cuddesdon students in certain instances, and had also agreed to take Keble rather than Pusey for his confessor. It was Liddon, the Vice-Principal, rather than Alfred Pott, the Principal, who framed the pattern of Cuddesdon with a disciplined spirituality centred on the daily offices and systematic meditation, with celebrations of the Eucharist on Sundays and holy days, as well as regularly on Thursdays and daily during the Ember weeks. The chapel was ornamented, and a moderate ceremonial and Gregorian chant characterized the services.

Such things, however aroused suspicion, and the suspicion was fermented by the propaganda of C. P. Golightly, a stout opponent of liturgical innovation. In 1857 Wilberforce imposed a number of changes. There was to be no eastward position by the celebrant at the Eucharist; the altar cross was to be removed; the altar was no longer to be adorned with a frontal and hangings. Liddon reluctantly accepted Wilberforce's rulings. With Cuddesdon becoming a focus of attention for the opponents of ritualism and suspected Romanizing, Wilberforce was anxious to make changes in the staff, though at the same time he was reluctant to lose Liddon, whose force and drive were so clearly an inspiration as well as being in another way at the root of the hostility the College was attracting. It was in these circumstances that Wilberforce appointed Edward King to the College staff.

King had not been in Cuddesdon for ten days when the bishop pressed him for his immediate reaction to the situation he found in the College. With considerable twinges of conscience King wrote in reply: 'I think the cause of the wrong will be found in the dear Vice-Principal. I know he is the very soul of the College.' But, King continued, Liddon's view of the Real Presence of Christ in the Eucharist was, although not the Roman doctrine of transubstantia-tion, nonetheless 'different from your Lordship's as I know it, and I may humbly add different from my own'. The difficulty lay, he said, in Liddon's strong will, which led to 'a determination to fit the Cuddesdon shoe on every foot', in inessentials as well as essentials. Perhaps it was the memory of Liddon's attitude in these days that led King much later to advise Edward Talbot, the first Warden of Keble College, not to try to 'Talbotize' his men. So he told Wilberforce with reference to Liddon, 'this pertinacity in doubtful things appears to be most hurtful to a strong and healthy judgement.'[5]

In 1859 Liddon resigned as Vice-Principal. H. H. Swinny was appointed Principal in place of Pott. King resisted Wilberforce's pressure to make him Vice-Principal, but when, three years later, Swinny died, King yielded to a further invitation from Wilberforce to take charge of the College.

For ten years Edward King served as Principal of Cuddesdon, bringing stability to the College, and a strong and gentle pastoral sense—his favourite text was from the Psalms: 'thy gentleness hath made me great'. Scott Holland said of him, in a vivid phrase, that 'he could draw love out of a stone', and it was this quality of surpassing pastoral sympathy which was King's outstanding quality. Taken apart from all else that we know of Edward King, accounts of his time as Principal of Cuddesdon can sound idealized, but the testi-mony to his pastoral gifts and the quality of the common life that he inspired at Cuddesdon is so consistent that we have no real reason to question the testimony of those on whom he left so marked an impress. Scott Holland tried to capture something of the impact that he made simply by his presence and his total lack of affectation.

It was light that he carried with him—light that shone through him—light that flowed from him. The room was lit into which he entered. It was as if we had fallen under a streak of sunlight, that flickered, and danced, and laughed, and turned all to colour and to gold. Those eyes of his were an illumination....

Was there ever such a face, so gracious, so winning, so benignant, so tender? Its beauty was utterly natural and native.... It seemed to say 'This is what a face is meant to be. This is the face that a man would have, if he were, really, himself. This is the face that love would normally wear.'....

The whole place was alive with him. His look, his voice, his gaiety, his beauty, his charm, his holiness, filled it and possessed it. There was an air about it, a tone in it, a quality, a delicacy, a depth, which were his creation.... There was nothing of the forcing-house, of the seminarist pose, as was popularly supposed. All was human, natural, free.[6]

As Professor Chadwick comments, King had discovered 'that the right method of training ordinands was not to drive them by exhortation along preconceived tram-lines: It was to live a worshipping life in community and let the Holy Spirit do the rest'.[7]

When King left Cuddesdon in 1873 Liddon preached at the College Festival. He spoke on 'The Moral Groundwork of Clerical Training', reflecting in his sermon the ideals which King had striven to put into practice during his time as Principal. The concern of a theological College was to train the Church's teachers and pastors so that their teaching and pastoral care would be with living power:

If a man would teach the power of religious truth, he must personally have felt the need of it. And this need can only be felt in the secret depths of the moral being, when conscience has been aroused to a sensitiveness which is often and most wholesomely not less than agony; when the strength of habit, old and bad, and the weakness of resolution, good and recent, has been fully appreciated; when men have recognized the simple justice of that solemn sentence of Scripture that the heart—that is the centre-point of moral activity in man—is, when man is left to himself, 'deceitful above all things, and desperately wicked.' Until language such as this is real to a man, expressing not merely what he takes it for granted is conventionally correct, but what he knows and sees to be experimentally true, the Atoning work and eternal Person of Christ our Lord, and all the varied and blessed consequences of these facts in the Church and in the Soul, must belong to the region of phrase and shadow.[8]

This realization of Christian faith demanded, Liddon said, both system and spirit, a pattern of devotional life and 'a moral and religious atmosphere which will justify and interpret its system to those who live in it'. That spirit Liddon recognized abundantly in Edward King. As Basil, Chrysostom, and Augustine 'were centres of moral and spiritual light and force, which constantly escaped from them, even without their meaning it, and which made companionship with them, of itself, a discipline', so a similar gift was to be recognized in King.

It is this which explains that indescribable attraction and power of the place,—it is this which irradiates all else; which redeems everything here from the suspicion of triviality or wearisomeness; which gilds all the habits, all the associations, all the localities . . . with a spiritual and moral beauty, at least in the eyes of those who amid these scenes have first learnt what life, and work, and death, really mean.[9]

Looking back in 1900 King said of his time at Cuddesdon that 'it was here that I learned to realise more than ever I did before the possibility of the reality of the love of God and the love of man'. Or, as he said on another occasion, 'we were brought to love God, and one another in God, in a real and special way, not understood by people unless they themselves knew what it was to be thus free'.[10]

For King the way of Christian love was to be learned in the school of prayer and devotion, a total offering of the self to God. At the 1897 Lambeth Conference he gave the devotional addresses and spoke to his brother bishops of the way in which men like T. H. Green had protested against the narrow reductionism of a positivist science and had reaffirmed the moral and spiritual nature of man. 'We received new assurances to our belief in a personal God—not as a mere intellectual conclusion, but as the outcome of our entire personality acting as a whole—our reason, our affections, our will.' God having 'so distributed the evidences of Himself' to man's whole being, it was man's duty 'to believe in Him to fear Him, and to love Him with all our *heart*, all our *mind*, all our *soul*, all our *strength*'.[11] And he cited the words of his mentor, Charles Marriott, that mediation on Christ, 'prayer to Him, learning of Him, conformity to Him, partaking of Him, are the chief business of the Christian life'.[12]

No man can love without the experience of pain and suffering, which is the very condition of love, and Edward King's greatness as a pastor was inevitably costly. It was because he understood so well the cost of that 'setting love in order', of which St. Augustine speaks, that he could so effectively bring wholeness to individuals and to communities. His spiritual letters, written with great simplicity, perception, and delicacy, reveal the spiritual father who knew the unsearchable riches of the grace of God and the utter dependence of the man of faith. As he told Edward Stuart Talbot on the eve of his consecration: 'I have always regarded the feeling of the slenderness of the thread of Faith to be a warning that one must hold on with the whole being. If I could have got such a hold with my mind I might have trifled with my heart and body—as it is there is nothing for it but an absolute *aufzugeben* (abandonment).'[13] De Caussade would have agreed. So he writes to an ordinand torn at parting from a friend:

I should have written last night, because I felt you must be a little silently sad. But, dearest child, it will be all right. The more we can throw our wills in with the great Will of God, which is being done by good people round us, the stronger our lives become. . . .

And then, do let me assure you that the heart is of such immense capacity if we only give it up to God to discipline, that these woundings are rather prunings for greater beauty and richer fruit. Had you gone with your good friend it might have narrowed the circle of your love, and you would not have had the sense of freedom to love all who may be waiting to be won by you to Him through your real love for them.[14]

Then there are three letters to a young tutor in a church college struggling against choking formality and stiffness, which gives us a glimpse of how King himself felt and acted in his time at Cuddesdon.

I am sorry that things are so needlessly stiff. There must be an immense loss of power. I should aim at absolute *oneness*, all higgledy piggledy. . . . The different social power must be a serious difficulty, and probably you will have to feel your way keeping up old-fashioned social barriers before you can safely trust to their perceiving the necessary order and harmony in a real Christian community. It will want *heaps* of *talk*—MOUNTAINS of talk— with individuals, and you will have to be worn out and out, and done for, and broken-hearted, and miserable, and not understood, and deceived, before you begin to get the right sort of relation which is absolutely necessary for the students' sake *now*, and to enable them to know what to do when they go out, be ordained, and preach, and give meditations: and get them to see that you are heart and soul in earnest to bright them one and all, not to yourself but to the mind of Christ. They they will love you, and you will soon be entangled in helpless love for them, and you will be broken-hearted again, and suffer miseries, and then the life will begin!

I am sorry you are so *squeezed*, but it must be so, more or less. Anyone who has a high ideal and love of perfection must be prepared to suffer.

Only by breaking your poor heart into pieces over and over again can you hope to make them begin to think of believing that there is such a thing as love!

Don't mind, be miserable, but don't stop loving them.[15]

If Edward King knew the cost of pastoral care he also knew very deeply the delight and joy of God. For him as for Thomas Traherne, 'eternity was manifest in the light of day, and something infinite behind everything appeared, which talked with my expectation and moved my desire'. So he can write: 'the more I see of life the more wonderful it is, but it all points to this world being only the little short beginning'. Or again, 'you must not over worry yourself about your advance in the Christian life. It is very simple, the *love of God* and *love of man*. That is perfection! Keep your *heart* with God, and then do the daily duties, and He will take care of you.'[16] He can write of going on his 'simple superficial way', loving flowers and birds and the sunlight on the apples, and the sunset, and thinking with the Psalmist 'With Thee is the well of life, and in Thy light shall we see light.' 'And so again: "Thou openest Thine hand and fillest all things living with plenteousness." The flowers and the birds, and angels and men, all things that are!!'[17] The world is charged with the grandeur of God, and not least in and through the joy of friendship.

It is so good of you to be so true and such a delight! The longer one lives the more one values true friends! I like to think of this world as the place for making friends, and the next for enjoying them! I sometimes am troubled when I think how little I have seen of old Cuddesdon men, but, please God, when we meet in Paradise, it will all come back again, and then go on and on, as Dr Pusey liked to translate the Hebrew word for eternity, 'For *ever*, AND YET!'[18]

We know something of what King taught at Cuddesdon, and subsequently in the years from 1873 to 1885 as Professor of Pastoral Theology at Oxford, when the outhouse at the bottom of his garden, which he called his Bethel, was crowded with undergraduates drawn by his spiritual magnetism. Those who would learn to be pastors were sent to the great writers of Christian history, not to contemporary handbooks and manuals: St. Gregory the Great on pastoral care, the *Moralia* of St. Basil, and the writings of St. Ambrose from the early church; Hugh and Richard of St. Victor from the Middle Ages; and later Pascal, and Pearson, and Bishop Bull. Those who would learn to preach were pointed to representatives of three great ways of preaching: Augustine, Chrysostom, Bernard, and Pusey; Massillon, Lacordaire, and Liddon; Andrewes, Newman, and Keble. In his moral theology King drew much from the German Catholic, Johann Michael Sailer, to whose works he had been introduced by the Old Catholic leader, Döllinger.[19] The lectures, which we know only from notes, are full of pithy phrases and wise discernment. 'If a priest is to be a pattern to others he *must* bear the solitude of greatness.' 'Christ lives in His saints. We know His life in them. St. Paul prayed to know the "*power*" of His Resurrection, though he knew the *fact*.' 'If you are to preach, you must make up your minds that you are sent, and sent by God.' 'Without the gift of love you will never be a preacher.' 'Vanity in a priest is little short of adultery.'[20] The priest in his parish was to pray for his people one by one, he was to go round his parish on his knees. In visiting—and King was addressing himself to a contemporary situation of parishes of some thousand people in rural areas—a pattern was to be worked out that would allow the whole parish to be visited once every two months. Such visits were not to be bound to self-conscious religious talk, but neither was the priest to be no more than a relieving officer. In visiting the sick 'you must make them know that you have more than a mother's tenderness, more than a father's wisdom'. When personal tensions arose caused by envy and jealousy then, King urged, 'take every opportunity of praising the person you envy . . . remember them in your prayers that they may be gifted by God and may use His gifts'. The good-tempered were not to think themselves immune from the sin of anger, for anger could be manifested no less clearly in an ordinate desire for revenging injuries. The laity were to be given the full opportunity for exercising their royal priesthood.[21]

Edward King shared with John Henry Newman the conviction that personal influence was an essential element in the propagation of Christian truth. Newman maintained in his *Lectures and Essays on University Subjects* that 'nothing anonymous will preach; nothing that is dated and gone; nothing even which is of yesterday, however religious in itself and useful'. The preacher 'comes to his auditory with a name and a history, and excites a personal interest, and persuades by what he is, as well as by what he delivers'.[22] This same understanding is emphasized by King in words which must surely have been directly influenced by those of Newman.

Nothing anonymous will ever persuade—the faith and conduct of the preacher give life and power to his message. Thus preaching is different from mere feeling. You may teach mathematics or geography without being fully convinced. But in delivery the Gospel message, if it is to be a living life-giving message, there must be in the preacher a sense of message and the desire to deliver it.[23]

Although King was convinced that he could do nothing better than hand on the teaching of the Tractarians, there was less of that severity which had led Newman to maintain that 'we need the law and not the Gospel in this age'. Those who knew him well said that he was 'less severe, less didactic and dominating, less preoccupied than Liddon, Bright and Church'.[24] In his moral theology, as we have seen, he was particularly influenced by the work of the German Catholic theologian, Sailer, ever since he had encountered his writings on a visit to Döllinger in Germany in 1875. Sailer (1751–1832), who ended his life as Bishop of Regensburg, had seen his theological task as a response to the challenge of the Enlightenment, returning to biblical and patristic roots. The judgement of a recent commentator that Sailer was one of the first 'to again integrate theology with Christian spirituality' indicates his attractiveness for King. His emphasis on the patristic understanding of tradition, his sense of the Church as a spiritual organism whose supernatural life is shared by its members, and his extensive use of biblical examples in his moral theology, were all congenial to one who like King stood in the Tractarian heritage.[25] The influence of Sailer was undoubtedly significant, and is symbolized by the fact that King kept a portrait of Sailer on an easel in his study during the whole of his time as Bishop of Lincoln. This contact with continental thought is a reminder that we ought not to underestimate King's intellectual powers, though he was never an academic in any narrow sense. The contacts he made on his annual holiday travels in Europe, when he would endeavour to meet local Catholic bishops, cannot have been without significance for his own wider understanding of his episcopate.[26]

His episcopate began in 1885 when Gladstone invited him to succeed Bishop Christopher Wordsworth at Lincoln. King accepted, rejoicing that it was the diocese from which John Wesley had come, for he had noted in his pastoral lectures that part of Wesley's power had been his preaching of the doctrine of perfection, a call to sanctity which had touched men's hearts. 'I shall try', wrote King, 'to be the Bishop of the Poor. If I can feel that, I think I shall be happy'.[27]

King delivered his Primary Charge the following year, urging his clergy to have a more thorough acquaintance with the history and tenets of the different forms of Dissent, that they might understand and have a deeper sympathy with the strong chapel life of the diocese. He stressed that ethics and personal morality should always be presented as being 'the vestibule of Politics, the principles of the life of nations'. He looked forward to increased provision of Sunday Schools, and to a growing number of parishes in which the Eucharist was celebrated weekly and on holy days. Under Bishop Jackson in 1864 there had only been twelve parishes in Lincolnshire and Nottinghamshire in which this pattern had obtained. Under Bishop Wordsworth the number had significantly increased, so that by the time of King's Primary Charge 120 parishes followed this pattern; 101 had a fortnightly celebration; 288 a monthly celebration; and 86 less frequently. Nine years later there were 222 parishes in Lincolnshire alone which had a weekly and a holy day celebration. In this same charge King also commented that the laudable desire to provide houses for the clergy had sometimes resulted in generous men of means giving the church houses which were far beyond the resources of the parishes to maintain—an unusually early awareness of the problem of the over-large parsonage house.

'*Through* the villages *to* Jerusalem' was one of the notes of King's Primary Charge, and King was assiduous in visiting the scattered village parishes of his diocese no less than in making provision for new churches in growing towns like Grimsby. The country pursuits which he had enjoyed as a boy and when at Wheatley and Cuddesdon gave him a bond with many of the agricultural poor, as did his knowledge of the vicissitudes of farming life. Part of the King legend is the impact that he made on the young farm-labourers when he went to confirm in the parishes. Two examples may suffice: the words of one recently confirmed boy reported to King by the boy's parish priest:

I was cutting up turnips t'other morning, and they wor that awkward! And I broke out swearing; but then I remembered what t'old Bishop had said when I wor confirmed; so down I plumped on my knees among the turnips, and prayed to be forgiven.

The other is King's response to a worried parish priest who had asked a newly confirmed lad about his preparation for Easter

Communion. The lad had replied 'I's cleaned me boots, and put 'em under the bed'—a preparation which the priest viewed as extremely inadequate. King thought otherwise: 'Well, dear friend, and don't you think the angels would rejoice to see them there?'[28]

The simplicity which so strongly characterized Edward King was not synonymous with weakness. His concern to be a bishop of the poor took him into places where Victorian England considered bishops should not go, such as the death-cells of Lincoln prison. In 1887 a young fisherman from Grimsby, who had killed his sweetheart in a *crime passionel*, was under sentence of death. The chaplain of the prison found the task of ministering to the young man one which was too much for him, and King took his place. Finding him ignorant not only of the Christian faith, but even of much moral awareness, King instructed him, prepared him for Confirmation, heard his confession, and gave him his first Communion. He joined with others in petitioning the Queen for a commutation of the sentence, a petition which was refused. On the night before the execution King celebrated the Eucharist in the young man's cell, taking his hand before the service with the words: 'Let us say a little prayer to consecrate the hand which did the sad deed, before it holds the Body of the Lord.' He accompanied him to the scaffold the next morning praying with him until the end. King wrote to his friend, George Russell a few days later: 'It was a terrible privilege, but I am most thankful that I was allowed to be with the poor dear man. He was most beautiful; and his last (and first) Communion on Sunday morning put me to shame. I felt quite unworthy of him. How little the world knows of the inner life!'[29]

Worship, King once said, consisted in 'the spirit of devotion and self-sacrifice': in heaven the saints cast down their crowns. And so for him it was pride and vanity which were the most destructive manifestations of sin in Christians, and in particular in the Christian ministry. The very continuity of the Church, he believed, rested on the presence of the Lord in the life of its members, and therefore each Christian must be continually Christ-regarding and not self-regarding. In line with what Charles Marriott had taught him, King emphasized that just as the Lord had sanctified himself for the sake of those whom the Father had given him, so the priest was to sanctify himself for the sake of his people. The pride that ran counter to that work of sanctification manifested itself in many ways: in complacency; in the self-centred over-sensitivity of disabling shyness; in extrovert showing off; in the fantasy world of ambition which builds castles in the air; in boasting of achievements, and in hypocrisy. He saw likewise how envy could poison and destroy Christian ministry and Christian love, and so he urged Christians to take 'every opportunity of praising the person you envy', continually remembering them in prayer, 'that they may be gifted by God and use his gifts'. All, he said, 'grows really clear by taking God for our rest and end, with a sense of the reality of love and the need of discipline'.[30]

Edward King's stature as a pastoral bishop and as a known adherent of the Catholic inheritance of the Church of England made him a significant target for the initiators of ritual prosecutions. It was not that King was an 'advanced ritualist' but that the prosecution of a bishop, and that not before the court set up under the Public Worship Regulation Act of 1874, which had signally failed to curb 'Ritualism', but before the Archbishop of the Province, would provide the most public forum for the condemnation of ritual practices, and by a court which it was hoped would command the recognition of those High Churchmen who repudiated the Erastianism of the Judicial Committee of the Privy Council.

The Tractarian fathers, whilst sharing to the full the sacramental sense of the patristic tradition and the recovery of the sense of symbol and imagery in the Romantic movement, were not ritualists. The Prayer Book rubrics were to be observed because they were the guardians of doctrine; churches were to be built and restored as sacramental settings for sacramental worship; but there were doubts and hesitations as to the advisability of promoting elaborations of ritual and ceremonial practice urged by some of the younger adherents of the movement. As late as 1871, when the Judicial Committee of the Privy Council gave judgement against the Revd John Purchas, forbidding the Eucharistic vestments, wafer-bread, the mixed chalice, and the eastward position for celebrating the Eucharist, Pusey could write to Liddon:

I cannot ... personally feel the judgment or opinion of the Judicial Committee as others do; not so much because I cannot, without breach of charity, make myself amenable to it, if ever it shall become law, as because, in celebration of the solemn Sacrament and Sacrifice of the Eucharist, I have not been able to adopt the position which it condemns, except when ministering, accidentally, in churches or private chapels, where it was recognised by the congregation as the natural expression of Eucharistic worship. We, the older Tractarians, acted, you know, on the principle so wonderfully carried out by

St. Cyprian, in times as difficult in their way as our own, first to win the minds of the people.[31]

King, Principal of Cuddesdon at the time, was more concerned. He tried to persuade Samuel Wilberforce to lead a campaign against the ruling, hailing Wilberforce, rather interestingly, as 'the leader, and, under God, the creator of the active results of the Tractarian movement'.[32] He expressed his concern to Liddon that there should be a defence of the judgement of the Court of Arches, overturned by the Judicial Committee, that the Eucharistic vestments were legal.

The service which gave rise to King's own prosecution was a celebration of the Eucharist on 18 December 1887 at the church of St. Peter-at-Gowts in Lincoln. The prosecution was brought by an auctioneer and a solicitor from Cleethorpes, and a foreman and a gardener from St. Peter's parish, backed by the Church Association. King was accused of either using or acquiescing in the use of liturgical ceremonies forbidden by the Book of Common Prayer—lighted candles, mixing water with wine in the chalice, the singing of the *Agnus Dei*, making the sign of the cross at the Absolution and Blessing, and using ceremonial ablutions at the end of the service.

In many ways the importance of the Lincoln prosecution lies not in the liturgical details which were challenged, but in the way in which it illustrates the changing relationship between Church and State in England and marks a significant stage in the emergence of the primatial authority of the Archbishop of Canterbury. When Archbishop Benson was confronted with this ritual prosecution he was concerned neither to assert an authority which other courts might subsequently declare him not to have, nor to deny an authority rightfully possessed. There had only been one post-Reformation case to serve as a precedent, and that had been in 1699 when Bishop Watson of St. Davids had been deprived for simony by Archbishop Tenison. Benson therefore asked the Judicial Committee of the Privy Council for a ruling on the question of jurisdiction. The Committee affirmed that Benson had such jurisdiction over his suffragan bishops, and that that jurisdiction ought to be exercised in person. Randall Davidson, then Dean of Windsor and a confidant of Benson's, welcomed this ruling: 'may we not have gained, by a side-wind, but very really some restitution of a spiritual authority, the area of which might perhaps hereafter be extended?'[33]

The Archbishop was concerned that he should not be confined by earlier legal rulings, and was anxious to draw on wider historical, liturgical, and theological evidence in making his decision. His advisers encouraged him in this approach. He also assumed a personal jurisdiction, even though he appointed episcopal assessors (including the historian, William Stubbs of Oxford, and the liturgical scholar, John Wordsworth of Salisbury). King and his supporters would have preferred that the trial should take place before the Upper House of Convocation as a whole, arguing for collegial rather than primatial authority. They thought this more in accord with patristic precedent, thought it would strengthen the authority of the judgement when given, and were concerned that any admission of primatial authority in this instance would imply that such power had always resided with the archbishop and therefore would have to be regarded as binding in connection with archiepiscopal judgements in the past.[34] A protest from Ely Theological College supported King in his stand against 'the mediaeval and monarchical model of exercising the metropolitan jurisdiction of the see of Canterbury'.[35] Others referred to 'a Canterbury papacy' and to 'a Pope by the Thames being no better than Pope by the Tiber'.[36] G. W. E. Russell, later to be King's biographer, suspected that the trial appealed to a certain theatricality in Benson's character:

The delightful prospect of presiding over an ecclesiastical pageant, with all the attendant 'pomp and circumstance' of legal and religious millinery,— scarlet robes and silver maces and full-bottomed wigs—of sitting in the chair of St. Augustine, surrounded by comprovincial prelates, and solemnly passing judgement on the successor of St. Hugh, proved fatally attractive.[37]

There is a certain irony in the prosecution brought by those concerned to put down Romanism in the Church of England, appealing to a court, which brought accusations from those very 'Romanisers' of the encouragement of an Anglican papacy and Erastian ceremonialism, to which might be added the fact that Benson's special jurisdiction was originally that exercised by the Archbishop before the Reformation in virtue of legatine powers derived from the Pope.

Benson's primatial authority must be seen, however, not only against this distant historical background, but in the context of the growth of the Anglican Communion. In the Church of England metropolitical authority was overshadowed by the complexities of the Establishment. Where Anglican churches were founded overseas it was the Archbishop who came to exercise a semi-patriarchal role towards them. Within those churches the relation of the metropolitan or senior bishop to the rest of the episcopate had to be worked out rather more clearly than in England. At the beginning of the 1860s Bishop Robert Gray of Capetown had been involved in two protracted cases relating to such questions of metropolitical jurisdiction, the most celebrated one being the Colenso case. Gray had found, when he attempted to exercise jurisdiction over Colenso, that the laity of Natal 'knew nothing of the office of Metropolitan and thought that I wished to make myself a Pope'.[38] As the overseas churches of the Anglican Community developed and claimed a degree of autonomy the Archbishop of Canterbury came to be their focus of unity, and communion with the see of Canterbury was as defining for Anglicans as communion with the see of Rome was for Roman Catholics. Bishop John Wordsworth, one of Benson's assessors in the Lincoln trial, is interestingly said to have shared Benson's view 'about the relation of the see of Canterbury to the rest of Anglican Christendom which to many people . . . seemed to go beyond a hegemony of Canterbury and to have a papalising tendency'.[39]

In May 1889 Benson refused King's plea to be tried by the Upper House of Convocation and asserted his jurisdiction. The trial proper commenced on 4 February 1890 and ran for some three weeks, much of the proceedings being occupied with not particularly edifying questioning about the minutiae of liturgical actions at the services for which King had been indicted. Sir Walter Phillimore, King's counsel, brought lengthy historical and liturgiological arguments to bear in King's defence.

The trial having been concluded at the end of February, Benson worked at the judgement over the succeeding months. It was finally delivered on 21 November 1890 in a packed library at Lambeth, Benson sitting on an elevated chair with the metropolitical cross in front of him and surrounded by assessors. A journalist commented that 'many dignitaries . . . distinguished themselves by clambering on tables, scaling the book shelves, and kicking away the oak mouldings of the venerable library in their anxiety to catch a glimpse of the court.'[40] As far as the particular charges were concerned Benson concluded that there should be no mixture of the chalice during the Eucharist; the manual acts prescribed by the rubric during the Prayer of Consecration should be visible to the congregation when 'properly placed'; the sign of the cross at the absolution and blessing were 'an innovation which must be discontinued'; the mixed chalice itself was allowed; ablutions were permitted, and the eastward position, as were the singing of the *Agnus Dei* and altar lights. *The Times* commented on the judgement:

> The Ritualists are to have their way in the chief practices impugned—the other part are diligently assured that there is no such significance as has hitherto been supposed in such practices. The Ritualists . . . are given the shells they have been fighting for, and the Evangelicals are consoled by the gravest assurances that there were no kernels inside them.[41]

There was considerable relief amongst High Churchmen, most especially because of the grounds as well as the particularities of Benson's judgement.

King accepted Benson's ruling, writing to his Sub-Dean at Lincoln of his attitude to rite and ceremony: 'I am not a Ritualist, as you know; but, where the doctrine is sound, I rejoice that our simpler (and, I believe, often better and holier) brethren may have the help which sound and sight may be to true devotion.'[42] It was very much the position which he had stated at the opening of the trial in an informal statement before Benson:

> I. In regard to the externals of worship generally, I believe with Bishop Butler, 'that the form of religion may indeed be where there is little of the thing itself, but the thing itself cannot be preserved without the form'.
> II. The rubric stating that ceremonial should be that allowed as was in use under the first Prayer Book of Edward VI should be taken in its literal and grammatical sense.
> III. This rubric, along with other rubrical directions of the BCP ought to be interpreted:
> (a) On the principle of the continuity of the C. of E., that is to say that omission is not as such equivalent to prohibition, but that intrinsic reasonableness and ancient usage are, on points not expressly determined, the recognised guides of the English Church.
> (b) Absolute uniformity of practice is unattainable and undesirable.
> (c) This liberty must be regulated by 2 principles (1) loyalty to the C. of E.; (2) edification.[43]

By his judgement Benson showed that he largely concurred with this interpretation.

The Lincoln Judgement marks an important staging post in the history of Anglican liturgical change, for it affirmed the continuity of liturgical tradition and gave to those who valued it the liberty to make use of it. It marked new boundaries between ecclesiastical and secular authority and succeeded in bringing to an end the series of ritual prosecutions that had so preoccupied the Victorian church. It accorded a primatial authority to the Archbishop of Canterbury, which, along with other factors enhanced the significance of his office. That Edward King, the most pastorally minded of bishops, should have found the most celebrated event in his life to be a trial for ritual offences is in a way sadly ironic, though as an heir of the Tractarians he was in no doubt that rite and ceremony were the clothing of doctrine, even whilst himself remaining moderate in practice. As an observer commented on a rich and splendid service King attended at Kennington: 'He seemed quite at home amid the florid ritualism of the service, but excepting a coloured stole embroidered with gold and a pectoral cross, he wore none of the "ornaments" proper to his office.'[44]

Significant as the Lincoln Judgement was, it is above all as pastor and teacher and man of prayer that King should be remembered. At Cuddesdon Liddon discerned that it was King who was the channel through whom flowed the spirit that gave life to the system, and prevented that system from becoming a choking law. The same spirit was what made his time at Lincoln a bishopric of love widely remembered, and which marks Edward King as a saint of God. The care and love which he sought, and was sensed, to embody cannot be better expressed than in his own words:

To wish to pardon human failings, and to look to the law-giver not to the law; to the spirit and not to the letter, to the intention not to the act; to the whole and not to the part; to the character of the actor in the long run and not in the present moment; to remember good rather than evil, and good which one has received rather than good that one has done; to bear being injured, to wish to settle a matter by words rather than deeds.[45]

As Archbishop Lang said of him, he was 'the most saintly of men and the most human of saints'.[46]

VIII.   Missionary bishops

THE OXFORD Movement was concerned with Anglican identity, with the apostolic character of the Church and its ministry, and in particular with the succession of the historic episcopate. As British influence spread overseas and churchmen became increasingly conscious of the need both to provide spiritually for colonists from England and to evangelize native peoples, the same questions of identity and continuity were posed in an overseas context.

The question of an overseas episcopate antedated the Oxford Movement by some decades. In 1784 Samuel Seabury received episcopal consecration as bishop in America from the Episcopal Church of Scotland. In 1786 an Act of Parliament was passed empowering the two Archbishops, with the assistance of other bishops, to consecrate bishops for territories outside British jurisdiction. In the next three years three further bishops were consecrated for the American Church, and in 1787 Charles Inglis was consecrated as Bishop of Nova Scotia with jurisdiction over the remaining British dominions in North America. By 1837 there were eight bishops in the British overseas territories: two in Canada; Calcutta, Madras, and Bombay in India; Jamaica and Barbados in the West Indies; and one in Australia.

In May 1840, Bishop Blomfield of London, conscious of the need for an extension of the overseas episcopate, urged that a fund should be established to make this possible. From this sprang the Colonial Bishoprics Fund, which was launched in April 1841. Various potential bishoprics were mooted—New Zealand; one in the Mediterranean to serve English congregations there; New Brunswick in Canada; the Cape; Tasmania; Ceylon; Sierra Leone; British Guiana; South Australia; Melbourne; Western Australia; and Northern and Southern India. In the event, in the seven succeeding years there were new sees created in New Zealand, Antigua, Guiana, Gibraltar, Fredericton (New Brunswick), Ceylon, Cape Town, and three in Australia, together with the controversial Anglo-Prussian bishopric in Jerusalem.

The background to this extension of the Anglican episcopate overseas was, in many instances, already existing congregations formed as a result of missionary work begun by the Church Missionary Society, the Society for the Propagation of the Gospel, and the Society for the Promotion of Christian Knowledge. Inevitably questions arose as to the relation between bishops and missionaries, between episcopal authority and the missionary societies as commissioners of both lay and ordained missionaries, and as the organizations providing financial support. Some were suspicious of the ease with which colonial bishops could act more autocratically than their English counterparts in situations in which there were fewer checks and balances on the exercise of episcopal authority. There were further questions to be considered as to the standing of non-episcopally ordained missionaries, such as the Danish Lutherans employed by the SPCK in India. There were tensions with colonial administrations uncertain as to the extent to which the privileges of establishment should be adhered to in the colonies. The question of episcopal authority and the relation of the overseas bishops to the see of Canterbury on the one hand and to the British Crown on the other became an issue in a number of instances. In 1841, for example, Bishop Broughton of Australia defended his visitation of New Zealand, which was strictly outside the limits of his jurisdiction as set out in the letters patent appointing him, in the following terms:

I had a further reason for complying with that request, to prove to the Romanists by practical evidence that they are guilty of injustice in affirming that we neither have nor can exercise any episcopal powers except such as are derived from our letters and patent under the great seal . . . this, I contend, is the object and effect of letters patent, not to confer spiritual powers, but to define the range within which each prelate shall exercise them. Beyond the limits of British sovereignty (as New Zealand was at the time), I contend that every bishop has an inherent right, in virtue of the powers conferred upon him at the consecration, to officiate, especially wherever the good of the Church may be promoted by his so doing; and where there has been no episcopate previously established upon which he would be an intruder.[1]

A few years later, in correspondence with Joshua Watson, Broughton, whilst welcoming metropolitan jurisdiction in Australia, queried whether the retention of a primacy of honour for the Archbishop of Canterbury sprang from primarily political concerns about the unity of the British Empire, and might lead to such primacy being viewed —erroneously in his opinion—as established *iure divino*.[2]

The Evangelical churchmanship of the CMS viewed the rôle of

bishops somewhat differently from the High Church SPG, and this already existing difference of opinion was sharpened under the influence of the Oxford Movement. It was not that the CMS regarded episcopacy as a thing indifferent, on the contrary there is ample evidence of CMS advocacy of bishops. Josiah Pratt, for instance, as secretary of the CMS, was responsible for a new edition of Bishop Joseph Hall's *Episcopacy by Divine Right*, which affirmed that episcopacy was an order of divine and apostolical institution, though no mention was made of the necessity of apostolic succession or of questions of validity. Nonetheless the CMS did not wish to unchurch non-episcopal churches, and as far as missionary work was concerned the essential prerequisite was personal piety. It was not until sixteen years after its foundation, in 1815, that the CMS enrolled any bishops amongst its members.[3] In India the Evangelical bishop, Daniel Wilson, found himself in conflict with the CMS. The CMS Home Committee stated in 1834, in a manner reminiscent of the claims of independence from episcopal jurisdiction made by religious orders in the Catholic Church, that 'with the Society, as a Society . . . the Bishop, as Bishop, has nothing whatever to do'.[4] The following year difficulties over a Lutheran missionary of the Society, C. T. E. Rhenius, led Wilson to protest against the CMS maintaining 'a system . . . in direct opposition to our Protestant Episcopal Church by the members of which they were sent out'.[5] In 1843 Wilson could defend episcopacy in the following terms:

Our episcopal form of Church government affords us the best means under God of preserving the faith. Had Protestant Germany retained her Episcopacy the Neology of the last hundred years might possibly have been averted. Had Reformed France kept her Episcopacy the Arianism of the Eighteenth century might never have prevailed. Had Geneva preserved the primitive order of church government she might never have apostatised from the principles of her great founder. If the Church of England is to be saved peaceably and in an orderly manner it is her bishops who under God must save her.[6]

Nonetheless it is clear that such an Evangelical endorsement of episcopacy does not reach to the Tractarian position that it was of the *esse* of the Church.

That indeed was also the position of some of the older High Churchmen, who did not in the end go all the way with the Tractarian leaders. William Palmer maintained that '*episcopacy*, or the superiority of one presbyter in each church, was *established by the apostles*; and that is *obligatory on the whole church.*'[7] In India William Hodge Mill, the first Principal of Bishop's College, Calcutta, and later, as a fellow of Trinity College, Cambridge, a friend and supporter of John Mason Neale and Benjamin Webb in the Cambridge Camden Society, could attack the CMS for flouting the principle, 'which appears to us essential to the very existence of an Episcopal Church, it is that of the Apostolical martyr St. Ignatius: *That without the Bishop nothing can be legally done of things pertaining to the Church.*'[8] For Newman one of the strengths of the doctrine of apostolic succession was that it constituted an authority in the Church which Erastian theory had hitherto made part of the law of the land. The apostolic ministry embodied in the episcopate received the fullness of the gifts of Christ to his first apostles.

As well may we doubt whether it is our duty to preach and make proselytes, and prepare men for Heaven, as that His Apostolic Presence is with us, for those purposes. His words then at first sight even go to include *all* the gifts vouchsafed to His first Ministers; far from having a scanty grant of them, so large is the promise, that we are obliged to find out reasons to justify us in considering the Successors of the Apostles in any respects less favoured than themselves.[9]

'If the promises to Christ's Apostles are not fulfilled in the Church for ever after', Newman asks, 'why should the blessing attaching to the Sacraments extend after the first age?'[10] Even in 1842, shaken by the episcopal reaction to Tract XC and troubled by the Jerusalem bishopric affair, Newman could urge obedience to the bishops as standing in the apostolic succession, 'like *de facto* rulers being of the blood royal'.[11]

From this emphasis on the bishop as possessing the fullness of apostolic ministry, from whom all other ministry derived, there emerged the idea of the missionary bishop as the characteristic means by which the mission of the Church should be forwarded. Episcopacy was not a desirable addition to already established churches, but the apostolic foundation-stone. As T. E. Yates has pointed out, the first clear expression of the idea is in a sermon of George Washington Doane, Bishop of New Jersey, in which Doane stated:

This is what is meant by a missionary bishop: a bishop *sent forth* by the Church, not *sought for of* the church; going *before* to organise the church, not waiting till the church has been partially organised; a leader not a follower.[12]

Doane's sermon was preached at the consecration of Jackson Kemper as missionary bishop to Missouri and Indiana in 1835. In 1837 Samuel Wilberforce, then Rector of Brighstone in the Isle of Wight, already beginning work on the history of the Protestant Episcopal Church in America, in which he referred warmly to Doane's sermon, asked Newman his opinion about missionary bishops. Newman gave enthusiastic backing to the idea: 'doubtless the only right way of missionary-izing is by bishops, and the agitation of the question must do good'. He saw such bishops, as might be expected, as a way of freeing the Church from state control: 'One should like to try the powers of at least *colonial* bishops to do without the State.'[13]

Wilberforce pursued the missionary bishop idea in a sermon later that year, which Bishop Sumner of Winchester seems to have regarded as being too tainted with Tractarian ideas. Wilberforce emphasized that his High Church principles did not necessarily mean agreement with the Tractarians. In 1838 he sought the support of Charles Anderson for a memorial to the CMS.

The great object, I am sure, which we ought now to aim at in our missionary exertions is to give them a much more distinct Church character than we have done—to send out *The Church*, and not merely *instructions about religion*. This is the way in which in primitive times the world was converted; and if episcopacy, a native clergy, a visible communion, the due administration of the Sacraments, Confirmation, &c., &c.,—if these things be really important, then how can we expect full success till we send out missionary bishops, *i.e.* bishops and a missionary clergy as a visible Church?[14]

Manning shared Wilberforce's views:

The neglect of (episcopal control) is not only *wrong*, but foolish, and disastrous. I dare not foster any sanguine hope of our success until we grow orderly, teachable and faithful enough to set about God's work in His own way. . . . If there are Bishops sent out, there must be sees and dioceses and a perpetual succession. . . .
Episcopacy is the universal rule of the Church of England both at home, and in the Churches planted by her in our colonial possessions; . . . Episco-

pacy the absolute, indispensable condition to the future communion of the Church of England, and the Churches we may hope with God's blessing to plant among the heathen.[15]

In 1853 Wilberforce, by now Bishop of Oxford, promoted two bills in Parliament, a Colonial Churches Bill and a Missionary Bishoprics Bill. At the same time he was active in measures concerned with the revival of Convocation. Evangelicals viewed both concerns with suspicion, Lord Shaftesbury holding that the revival of Convocation meant the revival of priestly despotism, and suspecting the surreptitious introduction of the confessional.[16] The Colonial Churches Bill was intended to authorize colonial synods of bishops, clergy, and laity to meet to pass ecclesiastical legislation; the occasion of the Missionary Bishoprics Bill was the provision of a bishop for Sir James Brooke's territory of Sarawak. Both bills were viewed as allowing a freedom which might result in Tractarian ideas coming to dominate the Church overseas, and although they passed the Lords they were defeated in the Commons. Sir James Stephen had suggested that the bills' promoters wished 'to establish an English episcopate which should not acknowledge the Queen's supremacy'. Wilberforce replied that he could not allow that the Crown had a power similar to the Papacy 'of Spiritual aggression & of mapping out Dioceses where it has no jurisdiction'.[17] The *Record* stated bluntly:

The Church of England does not stand in need of Bishops with a roving commission, to put down or impede missionary exertions. The Church of England does not believe in the Ultramontane doctrine of Bishop Wilberforce or hold that but for the not very apostolic resident of Cudworth (Cuddesdon) Palace the Church of Christ could not exist in the counties of Berkshire or Oxford.[18]

In 1859 and 1860 the question of missionary bishops was again debated, this time in Convocation. Bishop Tait of London, who was strongly opposed to the weakening of any links with the Crown, expressed his reservations strongly, questioning whether the 'plan of appointing Bishops at the head of merely inchoate churches' was authorized 'by any ancient ecclesiastical usage, whether the system of the Universal Church had not from the earliest times been this— that the Church shall be formed first and the Bishop come afterwards.' In 1861 he returned to the theme, warning of the dangers to the Church if a missionary bishop 'happened to be a man of eccentric modes of proceeding'. The independence of colonial churches could lead to the weakening of their Anglican character, so that a provincial synod might adopt 'so completely . . . a mediaeval view of the Church as to make it very different from that wide and tolerant system which we have inherited from our forefathers'. He urged that no rules should be adopted by colonial churches which would differentiate them from the Church of England 'either on the side of greater exclusiveness or greater reliance on mediaeval traditions'. In somewhat paternalist vein he added:

By all means let us have Missionary Bishops, but all in good time. *Festina lente.* The autonomy of the Colonial Churches is growing fast—too fast; . . . Hurry the matter rashly forward now—in defiance or scorn of State rules and aid—and you will cut these Churches adrift before they are old enough or strong enough to be trusted.[19]

Tait stood by the state connection because it guaranteed the comprehensiveness of the Church and was a bulwark against what he saw as Tractarian narrowness and sacerdotalism. The High Church advocates of missionary bishops and synodical government for colonial churches saw the state's intrusion as unwarranted interference, treating the Church as an aspect of empire. When Bishop Gray of Capetown in 1858 urged missionary bishops for Africa, Wilberforce supported him with a resolution in favour of Gray and his suffragans consecrating bishops 'to head aggressive missions in the parts of South Africa which are exterior to the Queen's dominions', such bishops to be under the metropolitan jurisdiction of the Bishop of Capetown and the supreme jurisdiction of the Archbishop of Canterbury. Tait replied with a strong affirmation of the royal supremacy.

Bishops in Roman Catholic countries were sent by the Pope; in our country Bishops should be sent by the Queen, who stood in the same place as the Pope. The State and our connection with it was our greatest blessing, and there would be great danger to the Church in thus injuring our connection with it.[20]

For Wilberforce this was only to be described as a 'most vicious fallacy'.[21]

Evangelical views, as represented by Henry Venn in particular, continued to follow the line that the episcopate was the coping-stone and not the foundation of the church. 'The office of evangelist necessarily preceded the episcopate.' The idea of a missionary bishop was a romantic, speculative notion, whose counterpart was the apostolic vicariate of the Roman Catholic Church. Native churches should be left to adopt native episcopacies, that, said Venn, was 'the Church principle, though not the High Church principle'.[22]

Throughout Tait's tenure of the see of Canterbury questions concerning the colonial churches continued to press themselves, focusing on the issues of the relation of overseas churches to the Archbishop of Canterbury, state-church relations, and the relations between episcopal and non-episcopal missions. The gradual modification of the quasi-establishment of the Church in many colonial territories altered some of the perspectives, but continued to raise questions about episcopal autocracy. There were difficulties with Madagascar, where Bishop Ryan of Mauritius, with the approval of the CMS, had agreed both to provide episcopal supervision for the coastal mission there and not to intrude upon areas where missionaries of the non-episcopal London Missionary Society were already working. Wilberforce and the SPG refused to recognize Ryan's compact, maintaining that it was 'impossible for the Church of England to look on passively at the growth of a native Christianity which is based upon a system fundamentally wrong because lacking the essential of an Episcopate'.[23] In the end a missionary bishop was consecrated for Madagascar in 1874 by the Scottish bishops. There were also tensions in Ceylon over the constitution of the Church, between the Bishop of Colombo (R. S. Copleston) and the CMS missionaries, who objected to the doctrinal and ritual stance of the bishop.[24]

The influence of Tractarian ideas on the development of the Anglican Communion is undoubted. The questions of Anglican identity raised in England could be posed more sharply and in a different context overseas. Newman had written in *The Lectures on the Prophetical Office of the Church* that it still remained to be tried 'whether what is called Anglo-Catholicism . . . is capable of being professed, acted on, and maintained on a large sphere of action and through a sufficient period'. He acknowledged a call to exhibit principles in action: 'until we can produce diocese, or place of education, or populous town, or colonial department . . . administered on our distinctive principles . . . doubtless we have not as much to urge in our behalf as we might have'.[25] Bishops such as Gray of Capetown, Selwyn of New Zealand, Mackenzie of Central Africa, Patteson of Melanesia, and Weston of Zanzibar, all in their various ways, were concerned not only for the mission of the Church, but to demonstrate the power and reality of true church principles in episcopal authority exercised in independence from the State. The five bishops mentioned above all stood in rather different relationships to the Oxford Movement, but all were significantly and often deeply influenced by it.

Robert Gray, the Bishop of Capetown, who left Oxford two years before Keble's Assize Sermon, first read the *Tracts for the Times* in 1839, and concluded that their principles were 'in the main those of the Church of England'. He noted avidly the sacramental teaching and doctrine of apostolic succession in the seventeenth-century divines republished by the Tractarians, remarking that 'the language is very strong, and sometimes in the sermons on the Eucharist, the expressions border on Consubstantiation.' Reading in the Fathers he endorsed warmly the teaching of Ignatius of Antioch and Cyprian on the church, ministry, and sacraments.[26] In 1845, when he himself became Vicar of Stockton, he was much moved by attending the consecration of St. Saviour's, Leeds, and hearing Pusey preach.

I shall not easily forget the glorious services of that day. . . . The earnest burst of prayer from that whole congregation was such as I never heard before. . . . I have never seen anything so striking as the devotion. . . . Laity of my own age and station sobbing aloud, and engaged for hours in prayer—most of the congregation spending the time before the service (a full hour at times) in reading the Psalms, or kneeling in private devotion, and Pusey's sermons most awakening.[27]

He was already much involved in work for the SPG in the north of England, when he was invited to allow his name to be considered for one of the new colonial bishoprics, either at the Cape or in Australia. Gray was clear that, from his point of view, the state of the Church in either situation left much to be desired.

In each of the Colonies named the Church is *nothing*. Everything has to be done. In both of them every form of religious error is rampant. . . . Then the relations of the Church towards the civil power are, I believe, quite undefined; the laws of the Church unsettled. The foundations of everything have yet to be laid.[28]

It was the Cape that Gray was eventually offered, and in March 1847 he wrote to Archbishop Howley accepting the post of 'a Missionary Bishop at the Cape'.[29] After his consecration and before sailing for Africa, Gray embarked on a preaching tour to raise funds for the Church he was to serve, and also met with a number of the leading High Churchmen of the day—Benjamin Harrison, W. H. Mill, William Dodsworth, Pusey, and Charles Marriott.

Gray's early letters from the Cape reveal his concern to establish church order and discipline in a weak and heterogeneous Church, and his strenuous efforts in travelling the country in difficult conditions. At Capetown he found the only two Anglican clergy belonging to an Evangelical Alliance and failing to observe any distinction between churchmen and dissenters. Lent did not seem to be observed, and Gray made the point by refusing to dine at the first Government dinner at Government House because it was Lent. He fitted up his private chapel 'very ecclesiastically, with proper poppy-headed benches', Communion Table, and prayer desks.

Gray's journal for 1848 records the arduous journey through the Karoo desert.

We rise at 4 A.M., start at 5—I generally walking on, being the first ready. We job on till about 9 or 10, when we outspan, and cook our breakfast at a Boer's, while our poor horses roll and pick bushes or dry grass, or perhaps have a bundle of oat straw for a treat. At 11 we start again under a broiling sun, and, unless there be a sea breeze, a cloud of dust. We outspan again perhaps at 2 P.M., when I walk on. We reach our destination at about 6.30, having generally travelled near fifty miles with a heavy wagon. We read nearly the whole time, and I always, as soon as I decently can, make my escape, write letters and my Journal, and so ends the day.

Calling upon some of the English people, I found one lady who said she had been thirty-eight years in the Colony without seeing any minister of her own Church.

We walked on till near 9 o'clock. . . . I was very tired, and was thankful on arriving at a pool of water to kneel down like the cattle, and drink. . . .

Christian produced an ostrich egg, which he had got from a coloured woman yesterday, and it satisfied the hunger of the whole party. I do not much admire the flavour. . . .[30]

From another journey, in 1850, comes an account of an interpreted conversation with his native guides.

They listened with much attention and apparent interest while I explained to them the Being and Nature of the True God, and told them that He was their Maker and Preserver. They said that in their ignorant state they had some sort of an idea of a Great Preserver, different from and above their gods, who had been their ancestors. I told them God had given us certain commandments, would they like to hear them? They said Yes. I then went through several. This led me to speak of the nature of sin and the punishment of it; of a Redeemer, of repentance, and of faith. They appeared very much struck with God's Attributes of Love and Mercy, so different from anything they knew of or had experienced from men. After speaking to them about praying to God, and asking them if they understood me, they said, 'Yes, it was like going to their chief and asking him to forgive any fault.' They expressed astonishment at being told that God forgave those who were sorry for sin and left off sinning. Very few chiefs ever did this! I spoke to them of the torments of hell, and the happiness of Heaven. . . . Upon telling them that to-day was the holy day of Christians, and that though we prayed to God every day, yet this was our chief day of prayer, and that they must be very quiet while we prayed, they doubled themselves up close beside us, and put their karosses over their faces while I offered the prayers of the Church. In this land of darkness and the shadow of death, cold indeed must he be who prays not fervently and frequently, 'Thy Kingdom come.'[31]

He planned Mission institutions in each of the Government's proposed native locations, hoping to model them on the community ideals he had noted with approval in the Moravian missions, with a priest, schoolmaster, mechanic, and agriculturalist, together with a hospital, farm, and industrial school.[32] He remained concerned about the Erastian bondage of the Church in England and about the constitution of the Church in his own diocese. Writing to his brother in 1850, at the same time as he forwarded a declaration from his diocese to Lambeth in support of the revival of Convocation, he complained that 'the State now almost assumes to be the Church'.

It will soon begin to frame a creed of its own, which it will require the Church to teach. It seems to me that the very Truth of God, and the very existence of the Church, are in danger of being denied, destroyed, by the world. Convocation is the only remedy for you in England. If it does not soon speak, the Church will merge in the State; and the heterogeneous elements of which the British Government is composed will become a new form of Antichrist.[33]

He insisted to another correspondent that 'the House of Commons is not the Church . . . year after year I am also more deeply convinced that the Church of England's position is untenable; that the Royal

Supremacy, as held in these days, is as fatal to the Church's faith as Papal Infallibility.'[34]

Gray was determined to give the Cape Church an appropriate synodical structure and discipline, holding a synod to discuss these issues in 1851. It is a reminder of the difficulties inherent in Gray's situation when we note that one of the archdeacons walked 700 miles in order to attend. In the matter of church discipline Gray read the clergy extracts illustrative of the system of the primitive Church, as well as citing Catholic, Orthodox, and Reformation writers. It was agreed that 'all who were condemned for grievous sins, either in the Civil Courts of the Colony or in a Church Court, should be publicly suspended from communion with the Church, and not be restored until a public acknowledgement had been made, and a public profession of repentance'.[35] Gray invited the Church to consider how a more synodical system of government might be brought about. 'It was necessary', he wrote, 'in an infant missionary Church like ours, that the whole burden and responsibility of what was done should rest upon the Bishop'. Such a pattern was not, however, in accordance either with Anglican principles or with those of 'the Primitive and Apostolic Church'. 'The Presbyters, the Deacons, and the Laity of the Church have each their separate functions, responsibilities, privileges', and Gray was anxious that these should be appropriately exercised, and urged churchmen to consider, during his absence in England, the way in which a synodical structure might be formally brought into being.[36]

In England the bishop renewed his acquaintance with leading High Churchmen and the SPG, visiting Stevens's church and school at Bradfield, and Butler's parish at Wantage, two outstanding examples of Tractarian parochial organization. With Wilberforce he discussed the position of the laity in synods, Wilberforce insisting on a communicant qualification for both delegates and electors. With Pusey, whose language Gray noted 'was full of love and tenderness, and savouring more of Low Churchmanship than of High', he discussed synods and sisterhoods.[37] Division of the diocese was agreed upon and bishops appointed for Grahamstown and Natal, the latter bishop being J. W. Colenso, who was to become the centre of one of the major controversies of the Victorian church. Gray's letters after his return to the Cape indicate that even before Colenso's notorious commentary on the Pentateuch, problems were arising as a result of Colenso's views and what Gray saw as his lack of judgement.

In England again in 1858 Gray took part in the discussions over missionary bishops, lamenting the opposition from 'Lord Shaftesbury's bishops'. He conversed about the same topic with Keble at Hursley, and at East Grinstead with John Mason Neale about an amended Liturgy for African convert congregations, which Neale undertook to draw up. Neale was also consulted about the jurisdiction of metropolitans and about missionary bishops.[38] Gray also spoke in Oxford and Cambridge about the needs of Central Africa, catching the enthusiasm aroused by Livingstone a year earlier. Out of this grew the Central African Mission (later the Universities Mission to Central Africa, UMCA), and the plan to consecrate a missionary bishop for the Zambesi. Charles Frederick Mackenzie, who had been for a time an archdeacon in Natal, was chosen for the work, and, following a great service in Canterbury Cathedral to bid him farewell, at which Samuel Wilberforce preached, he was consecrated by Gray and the bishops of Natal and St. Helena in Capetown.

The ecclesiological principles for which Gray contended were severely tested by the case of a clergyman named Long who refused to obey Gray's monition to attend a synod summoned by Gray, and even more so by the long-drawn-out Colenso affair. In both instances what was at issue was the question of the independence of the Church, the nature and limits of episcopal authority, the relation of the overseas Church to the Church of England, and the limits of state authority, including that of the Crown, in the Church. The Colenso case, in addition, turned on questions of doctrine and interpretation, the discussion in England becoming entangled with the contemporaneous arguments over the theological opinions of the authors of *Essays and Reviews*, which had raised acutely the question of authority in the Church. In maintaining his stance in the Colenso affair Gray had the support of John Keble, who both contributed to his costs and gave friendly advice, applauding Gray's charge as 'a fragment of the fourth century recovered for the use of the nineteenth', but in typical vein reminding him of Bishop Butler's rule that it was better to understate than overstate his case.[39] Gray perceptively noted that most of the difficulties he faced arose from the transition state in which they found themselves, 'the transplanting a branch of the Established Church in England to a country where it is *not* established', and the longer the Colenso case dragged on the more opposed to the notion of establishment the bishop became.

Of course I will never have anything to do with Parliaments. God be thanked that we have escaped almost entirely (and shall soon escape altogether) these fetters forged by States for the bondage of the Church of God. I have long hated the word *Establishment*; I could not endure it as a boy. The chains that hang about us still are light compared with what they were. We shall never rest till we have flung them altogether from us.[40]

The need to obtain appropriate ecclesiastical backing for his action against Colenso led Gray to be a powerful voice in urging the calling of an Anglican Council, a cause he had espoused before the Colenso troubles began. When the first Lambeth Conference did meet in 1867 Gray pressed for the bishops to endorse his sentence on Colenso, and, to the annoyance of Tait and Thirlwall, 56 out of 73 possible signatures were appended to a resolution that Gray's sentence was 'spiritually valid'.[41]

During the time that he was in England for the Lambeth Conference, Gray visited St. Michael's, Shoreditch, where Hannah Skinner, a former parishioner at Stockton, was now the Superior of a small sisterhood, the Community of St. Mary at the Cross, under the guidance of the Revd H. D. Nihill.

I found them [Gray wrote] living in the utmost simplicity and poverty, with beds, furniture, rooms, not better than those of the poor; their only luxury a quiet little oratory. One sister has charge of the school just begun with one hundred children; another of a little shop for the sale of Bibles, Prayer Books, etc., All visit the poor and care for them in sickness.[42]

Gray presided at a Solemn Evensong, which *Punch* caricatured as 'Ritualistic Theatricals in Shoreditch'.[43] The innovations of the ritualists were noted by Gray, who observed that although they might be indiscreet in some things, they often had a firm grasp of the faith. 'My belief is', he wrote, 'that gradually the Church will adopt almost all that these men are contending for'.[44] More importantly Gray visited nearly all the religious communities working in England, and when he returned to South Africa he took with him a small band of women to be the nucleus of the first sisterhood there, dedicated to St. George. Later efforts to encourage the Cowley Fathers to come to work in South Africa were unsuccessful, even though Gray had been in correspondence with their founder, R. M. Benson, for some years. Benson felt that the Society was still too young and small to undertake such work.[45]

In South Africa Robert Gray laid the foundations of an autonomous church. The same pioneering work was done in New Zealand by George Augustus Selwyn. When Selwyn had been appointed Sydney Smith had waggishly commented that it would make quite a revolution in the dinners of New Zealand: '*tête d'Évèque* will be the most *recherché* dish, and your man will add, "And there is *cold clergyman* on the side-table".'[46] Selwyn had been deeply impressed by a speech of Manning's at the opening of the Colonial Bishoprics Fund and told Manning in 1847 that 'it involved no less a consideration than the whole question of my coming to New Zealand'.[47] But although linked with the Tractarians and sympathetic to some of their concerns to the extent that he was suspect in some quarters, Selwyn confessed to not having read any of the Tracts at the time of his appointment in 1841.[48] His view of the episcopal office nonetheless led him to object to the assumption in the Letters Patent by which he was appointed that it was the Crown which conferred on him the authority to ordain. As early as 1844 he summoned a synod of clergy, which admittedly only consisted of three archdeacons, four priests, and two deacons, but it can be reckoned to have been the first formal synodical gathering since the suppression of Convocation.[49] A second Synod was held in 1847, at which Selwyn delivered his Primary Charge. In this, as well as stressing the spiritual character of synodical gatherings, and expressing his vision of New Zealand as a centre of missionary activity for Polynesia, Selwyn set out his relationship to the Oxford Movement in order to allay the suspicions of some of his clergy. He spoke of the Tractarian leaders as 'three men, mighty in the Scriptures, who, when they found us hemmed in with enemies, and thirsting for Catholic unity, went forth to draw water for us from the well of primitive antiquity'. So long as the object of the Movement was 'to develop in all its fullness the actual system of the Anglican Church ... purifying its corruptions, calling forth its latent energies, encouraging its priesthood to higher aims, and to a more holy and self-denying life; exhorting us to fast, and watch, and pray, more frequently and more earnestly; to be more abundant in our almsgiving, more diffusive in our charity', Selwyn felt entirely at one with them. It was only when it seemed to be schism rather than unity to which the Movement was tending, and when it was suggested that there was some essential deficiency in the Anglican Church, that he parted company with them.[50]

In visiting missionaries of other churches Selwyn's rule was to give them every encouragement, though to refrain from taking part in their public services. He considered that the London Missionary Society which did not link native churches into any body in England was easier to deal with than the Wesleyan Missions, to which he objected because of 'the popery of their system, in spreading the name of Wesley, and the authority of their conference over the whole mission field'.[51] Missionary concern was always a foremost one in Selwyn's mind, and was linked closely with his vision of church government, not only in New Zealand itself but in the Western Pacific. In 1851 one of the fruits of the first Synod of the Bishop of Australasia was the setting up of a Board of Missions for work both amongst Australian aboriginal peoples and in the islands of the Western Pacific.[52] In 1853 Selwyn ordained the first Maori deacon, Rota Waitoa. Henry Venn of the CMS had been pressing for some time for Selwyn to relax his high educational requirements for ordinands, especially the knowledge of Greek for those to be admitted to the priesthood, urging that 'fidelity in the long exercise of their missionary duties, and acquaintance with the Native Language may be regarded as sufficient qualifications, where there is competent knowledge of divinity'.[53]

Selwyn travelled indefatigably, both within New Zealand and to the islands of Melanesia. He lived simply, and warned against easy capitulation to 'the gentlemen and lady heresy'. He had a high view of the episcopate, but not a tyrannical one, as he emphasized to his 1847 Synod:

I believe the monarchical idea of the Episcopate to be as foreign to the true mind of the Church as it is adverse to the Gospel doctrine of humility. . . . I would rather resign my office than be reduced to act as a single isolated being. It remains then to define by some general principle the terms of our co-operation. They are simply these; that neither will I act without you, nor can you act without me.[54]

Much later, when back in England as Bishop of Lichfield, Selwyn made a powerful speech in 1873 on the need for division of dioceses in order that episcopacy might function properly. During his time in New Zealand the number of bishops rose from one to seven; he believed that in England there was need for a large extension of the episcopate, even if that meant a reduction in episcopal income.

Something has been said about the necessity of a certain income being essential to the position and influence of a bishop. Now, I deny that altogether.... We ought to be multiplied, so as to be able to become acquainted with every parish, and to spend a day or two each year in each parish.

No bishopric, as a rule, ought to contain more than 500 parishes or more than 500,000 souls. . . . The bishop ought to be able to visit each parish once in three years, and to give a whole day to each for confirmation and inspection of the schools. To know his clergy and be known by them is as much the duty of a bishop as it is the duty of a pastor to know his sheep and be known of them.[55]

He protested that, were he once released from the 'pomp and circumstance' of an English bishopric, he could live down to his own needs instead of up to other people's notions.[56]

Selwyn returned from New Zealand to be Bishop of Lichfield, Robert Gray died in office as Bishop of Capetown. Two other bishops, Charles Frederick Mackenzie and John Coleridge Patteson met with death in their journeyings to preach the Gospel. Mackenzie, chosen as a missionary bishop, sent out from England with high hopes and the commendation of Samuel Wilberforce, consecrated by Gray in Capetown, set out in 1861 in the company of David and Charles Livingstone, two priests, a deacon, a young lay superintendent, a carpenter, a labourer, and a number of Africans, to be 'Bishop of the mission to the tribes dwelling in the neighbourhood of Lake Nyasa and the River Shire'.[57] After a difficult journey by boat up the Shire river, the party set out for the highlands, Mackenzie carrying a crozier in one hand and, after some misgivings, a double-barrelled gun in the other. They released a group of slaves; they found themselves caught up in tribal conflicts; they acquired a group of dependent refugees. When they began a permanent settlement Mackenzie's episcopal residence was said to look like 'a large roughly-built cowhouse, or . . . like an old haystack with the inside eaten out'. The books in his library were the Bible, *The Christian Year*, *The Imitation of Christ*, Trench's study of the parables, and Wordsworth's New Testament commentary, together with a few others. Food was local, goat or chicken meat, yams, beans, peas, 'porridge of ground Indian corn', a loaf once or twice a week. The saying of Prayer Book Mattins was held by some of the Africans to be the practising of magical arts, whereby the white men brewed or imbibed their war-medicine. Tins of preserved meat were thought to be tins of human flesh. There were problems about how and when to impart Christian instruction with an impermanent settlement and a language imperfectly understood. Later there were difficulties when Livingstone, who had left Mackenzie and the group of missionaries, refused to allow his ship, the *Pioneer*, which had brought the party with such difficulty up the Shire, to bring Mackenzie's sister and others in a second party with further supplies. He was only prepared to bring them as far as the mouth of the Ruo some 130 miles overland from the missionaries' settlement. A party sent out to reconnoitre a route was attacked and at first two of the priests were feared captured or killed. The priests, however, made their way back to the settlement, and Mackenzie himself set out with Burrup, another priest who had journeyed alone up the Shire to join him, to meet the ladies at the rendezvous agreed, as well as to impress justice on the hostile tribes. He reached the Ruo to find no sign of Livingstone, and there, as he waited for the party to come, fell ill with fever and died. Burrup, his fellow-priest struggled back to the settlement at Magomero, where he too died of fever a month later.[58]

In Capetown Gray received the news with a heavy heart, noting from Mackenzie's journal, how Mackenzie, a few days before his death, had read to Burrup Keble's poem for the twenty-fifth Sunday after Trinity, with its poignant references to the sorrow and the glory to be known in the death of holy men.[59] He set out for England to find another bishop to succeed Mackenzie. William George Tozer was eventually consecrated in 1863. He followed Mackenzie up the Shire, but within a year had concluded that only from a secure base on or near the coast, with good communications, could missionary work in the interior be safely undertaken, and so moved to Zanzibar. Just after Tozer's resignation in 1873 the Zanzibar slave-market was bought, and on Christmas Day 1877 the first service was held in the Cathedral erected on the site by Steere, Tozer's successor.[60]

In the South Pacific in 1852 Bishop Selwyn visited the Solomon Islands. He noted in his diary that 'the careful superintendence of this multitude of islands will require the services of a missionary bishop, able and willing to devote himself to this work.'[61] In 1841 John Coleridge Patteson, then a boy at Eton, had been deeply moved by Selwyn's farewell sermon, and Selwyn's example was again extolled by the Bishop of Lincoln at Patteson's confirmation. He went up to Oxford, became a fellow of Merton, and in 1853 was ordained deacon to the little village church built by Mr Justice Coleridge to serve the hamlet of Alfrington near Ottery St. Mary, the family home in South Devon. A year later a visit by Selwyn and his wife whilst they were in England led to Patteson joining Selwyn in New Zealand. In 1861 Patteson was consecrated by Selwyn and two other bishops to be missionary bishop in Melanesia. The consecration, like that of Mackenzie in Capetown the same year, was without the Royal mandate. Patteson shared with Selwyn his missionary zeal and his desire for the freeing of the Church overseas from the hampering and irrelevant trammels of the English establishment.

Patteson was an excellent linguist. Like Selwyn, in New Zealand he had learnt Maori. His work in Melanesia, with its multiplicity of languages, called upon all his considerable linguistic skill, so that in the end he was able not only to speak some twenty-three Melanesian languages but had also analysed the structure and set down the basic vocabulary of a good number of them. His linguistic work he described in a letter to the Oxford scholar, Max Müller, in 1866, stressing that the study of the Melanesian languages was always for him subordinate to the communication of the Gospel, and that therefore his prime concern was to elucidate the Melanesian cast of mind. 'These languages', he wrote, 'are very poor in respect of words belonging to civilised and literary and religious life, but exceedingly rich in all that pertains to the needs and habits of men circumstanced as they are.'

I draw naturally this inference, 'Don't be in a hurry to translate, and don't attempt to use words as (assumed) equivalents of abstract ideas. Don't devise modes of expression unknown to the language as at present in use. They can't understand, and therefore don't use words to express definitions. But, as everywhere, our Lord gives us the model. A certain lawyer asked Him for a definition of his neighbour, but He gave no definition, only He spoke a simple and touching parable. So teach, not a technical word, but an actual thing.[62]

He noted that the mode of thought of a South Sea islander closely resembled that of a Semitic man.[63]

Patteson's perception that Melanesian modes of thought were different from English ones also led him to very definite views about the cultural imperialism of missions. He wrote to Miss Mackenzie, the sister of the bishop, who had sent him her brother's copy of *The Imitation of Christ*:

It is easy for us now to say that some of the early English Missions, without thinking at all about it, in all probability, sought to impose an English line of thought and religion on Indians and Africans. Even English dress was thought to be almost essential, and English habits, &c., were regarded as part of the education of persons converted through the agency of English Missions. All this seems to be burdening the message of the Gospel with unnecessary difficulties. The teacher everywhere, in England or out of it, must learn to discriminate between essentials and non-essentials. . . .

There is perhaps no such thing as teaching civilization by word of command, nor religion either. The *sine qua non* for the missionary—religious and moral character assumed to exist—is the living with his scholars as children of his own. And the aim is to lift them up, not by words, but by the daily life, to a sense of their capacity for becoming by God's grace all that we are, and I pray God a great deal more; not as literary men or scholars, but as Christian men and women, better suited than we are for work among their own people. . . . If we treat them as inferiors, they will always remain in that position of inferiority.[64]

He set out his missionary strategy in a letter to a missionary of the London Missionary Society at Lifu. The aim was 'native churches under native pastors', and so the concern must be not to make 'Melanesians English or Scotch Christians, but Christians generally'. Native customs wherever possible ought to be retained. Smoking, for instance, might be undesirable, but was not something which was morally wrong, and any prohibition which put it on the same level as lying, stealing, and fornication would only confuse. Again, it was no use aiming at producing scholars, what was important was tone and spirit.

I am more convinced of the necessity of teaching with exact accuracy the simple statements of Christian Truth in the Creed, the Lord's Prayer, and the Commandments. But I would teach the Commandments *first* in their simplest yet deepest form, as *Love* to God and man; drawing out into detail those particular Commandments which they can most easily comprehend. . . .

I am sure . . . that mere vague hortatory declamations do *very* little good—careful exact teaching is the real thing. We must ascertain with extreme care the meaning that the native school assigns to the words we use, instead of assuming that he understands such words in the same way as we understand them. We ought to take weeks to make even an intelligent islander comprehend what is meant by Repentance, Faith, Prayer. . . .

I don't think it necessary to be in any hurry about printing very large portions of the Bible, even if the knowledge of the language admits of our doing so.

The Gospels of St. Luke and St. John and the Acts of the Apostles contain quite as much as any ordinary person can *really* and *thoroughly* know of the Life of Christ, His Works and Words, His Death and Resurrection, Ascension, the gift of the Spirit, the foundation and extension of the Church.[65]

A further letter to Miss Mackenzie urges the ordination of well-instructed Melanesians to the diaconate, for their work will be not 'to teach theology to educated Christians, but to make known the elements of Gospel truth to ignorant heathen people'. 'If they can state clearly and forcibly the very primary leading fundamental truths of the Gospel, and live as simple-minded humble Christians that is enough indeed.' In the same letter Patteson observes that 'the report of a man going ashore dressed as a Bishop with a Bible in his hand to entice the natives away, assumes islands to be in a state where the conventional man in white tie and black tail-coat preaches to the natives.' Patteson's own costume was 'an old Crimean shirt' and 'a very ancient wide-awake'.[66]

Patteson was, through family connections and personal devotion, close to John Keble, whom he held in special reverence, seeing him theologically as the continuator of the best in Anglican theology. He corresponded with him regularly and Keble responded generously in support of his work, particularly in the provision of the missionary ship, the *Southern Cross*. After he had read with interest Newman's *Apologia* and commented favourably on the good that Newman had done, Patteson wrote that he had never come under Newman's personal guidance, and that, as far as he was concerned, 'his candle goes out altogether by the side of dear Mr Keble's clear, steady flame'.[67] The only theological point on which he differed from Keble was that of the adoration of Christ in the Eucharistic elements, which was not taught by Hooker, whose teaching was, Patteson believed, the truly Catholic doctrine of the Sacrament. He could describe ritualism as a 'great and fundamental error', and was nervous of medievalism replacing the earlier Tractarian appeal to the Church of the Fathers. 'I know very little of the matter', he wrote, 'but I very much question whether, in respect of the truth of Eucharistic doctrine, the Ritualistic development is going in the right direction.'

I don't think . . . the Primitive Church knew, or approved (if in some cases it knew) of the attendance of non-communicants, of the adoration of the Presence localized in the Elements being regarded as the central point of the Eucharistic Service rather than the *koinonia* of the Body and Blood of Christ. The participation in the Death of Christ was at least as important a part of the Eucharistic idea as the adoration of the Living Christ present and glorified in the consecrated Elements.[68]

What he tried to do was to teach his Melanesian communicants 'the actual words of . . . the . . . really ancient Liturgies, and teach them what Christ said, and St. Paul said, and the Church of England says, and bid them acquiesce in the mystery'.[69] Like Keble, Patteson had a strong sense of reverence for the mystery of grace, yet at the same time he felt keenly the frustration of being cut off from the opportunity of theological discussion and debate, which he could only know as reported at second-hand from England. With his reverence for John Keble he longed to have the opportunity of discussing with him the points of Eucharistic doctrine on which he did not feel able, as he understood them, to follow him.

Both in ecclesiology and in his understanding of the mission of the Church in a non-European culture Patteson was remarkably free from the presuppositions of Establishment-minded Anglicans in England and contemporary colonialism. He could write to his sister of the strange confusion of many 'between the real vital principle of union, by which the branches of the English Church ought to be held together, and the peculiar machinery which obtains in England, and in England only'.

If only you can shift your *Stand-punkt*, from that of the member of the Church of England, as it exists in its peculiar relation to the State, to that of the member of Christ's Church in primitive times, and then see also that the reformation of abuses which had corrupted the truth, did not of necessity involve any departure from primitive rules, organisation and government, nor, at all events, entail upon all who were thus reformed, or became, as years went on, descendants from a Church so reformed, whatever peculiar characteristics the peculiar national history of the people in the particular country of England brought with it, then I suppose the question becomes somewhat more clear.[70]

Convinced like Selwyn of the necessity of episcopal government in synod, he was nervous at the seeming clericalism in reports of statements by Pusey and others which seemed to exclude the laity from any effective role in the government of the Church. In Melanesia he worked to create a truly native church.

It was on a missionary journey in Melanesia that he met his death on 20 September 1871, on the island of Nukapu, murdered by islanders, possibly in revenge for five islanders taken to Fiji and thought to have been killed. The bishop's body bore five wounds, interpreted by many as a likeness of the Passion of Christ.

In the month that Patteson died Frank Weston was born, who, as Bishop of Zanzibar, was to represent in a later generation the same self-sacrificing holiness. As a boy he was moved by the life of Father Mackonochie. At Oxford he attended Gore's Bampton Lectures, and was formed in his spirituality by Pusey House and the Cowley Fathers. He joined Stewart Headlam's Guild of St. Matthew, and after Oxford went to the East End to live in the Trinity College Mission. The character of the mission was such as to alarm both College and benefactor with reports that it was teaching both Catholicism and Socialism, and Weston was singled out as the primary cause. During this time, like another great figure of the African Church, Arthur Shearley Cripps, he was much influenced by James Adderley, the founder of the Society of the Divine Compassion.[71]

After the East End followed a curacy at St. Matthew's, Westminster, and from there he went to Zanzibar in 1898, inspired by the lives of bishops Mackenzie and Steere. The particular task he was assigned was the training of ordinands and he set to work to provide both buildings and an appropriate curriculum. It was insufficient to teach doctrine out of a text-book and in European dress. There had to be an inner understanding conveyed in African terms. At Kiungani, where he became Principal of the College, he discovered two colleagues in the school who felt like himself the call to the religious life. They lived for a year under vows, but John Edward Hine, the new bishop refused to recognize them as a community. Weston returned to England on furlough in 1901, and on return found the personnel changed. His biographer comments how at this time he felt himself peculiarly lonely:

The Christ in the loneliness of Gethsemane became the Christ of his adoration; the Christ Whose love was rejected was the Christ Whom he could understand and interpret. Those who listened to his sermons remarked that he never preached without a reference to Gethsemane and the Passion. To suffer and endure became his creed.[72]

It was the Passion which was to be the dedication of the Community of Sisters which he fostered, and which was formerly constituted in 1911. He was deeply aware of the nails of love which are the cost of following Christ. Thus he could write:

So many people go to Communion seeking peace. We go into His Presence, Whose hands are marked with the nails, and we ask for peace; and we get no peace, because we ought rather to ask for that deeper sense of His Presence as He leads us into war. Reach out your hand to receive His Body, and your hand will be marked with the wound. . . . There is always something more in your nature which He wills to mark with the Cross.[73]

In 1908 Frank Weston was consecrated as Bishop of Zanzibar, a position he was to hold until his death in 1924. In his first charge he stressed the need to work so that an African priest could be substituted for a European without disruption, and the importance of planning for flexibility, as well as the over-all primacy of prayer, with every priest of the diocese urged to devote two hours each morning to prayer, including Matins, Mass, and Meditation.

To be an intercessor is the best way to rid ourselves of the unrighteous office of an accuser; and to pray for a brother's work is to make it our own in the sight of God and His angels.
   Prayer is the only known way of bringing to our heathen people the power that is to make the Christians and bring them to heaven: that is to say, it is the supreme secret, the possession of which differentiates us from them.[74]

His own understanding of priesthood was expressed in what he wrote in the flyleaf of the Bible which he took with him to Africa in 1898.

Priests are called to be points of contact between God and the suffering world. Their hands stretched out to heal with soothing touch men's feverish souls, their hearts consecrated to the havens of refuge for the weary and fainting, must alike be pierced. If we can at best reproduce the Crucifix in miniature, let us at least be correct in the details.[75]

Weston believed that it was spiritual warfare in which the Church and every Christian was engaged, and this underlay his passionate concern for the reality of the Incarnation, and the Church, its sacraments, ministry, and unity, as springing from the Incarnation. It is in

this context that we must understand the Kikuyu controversy of
1913, his part in the Appeal to All Christian People of the Lambeth
Conference of 1920, and his speech at the Anglo-Catholic Congress
of 1923. The Kikuyu affair centred on the actions of the Bishops of
Uganda and Mombasa, who, meeting together with Protestant missionaries in the area, had worked out a unity scheme which, whilst
recognizing the importance of not perpetuating English sectarianism
in Africa, seemed to Weston to deny important aspects of the Catholic faith. Episcopacy was not made a condition of ministry; an
undenominational service was agreed upon for common worship;
and on the final day the Bishop of Mombasa celebrated Holy Communion at which representatives of the different groups partici-
pating in the conference communicated. Weston reacted strongly,
and delated the two bishops for propagating heresy and schism to
Archbishop Davidson. Davidson found Weston impetuous, commenting that 'he does not think out his problems before coming to
conclusions.'[76] In his *Case against Kikuyu* Weston maintained that
the neglect of the episcopate in the Kikuyu scheme was a contra-
vention of 'the fundamental principle of Church order, which is, that
every Christian depends for his full membership in the Catholic
Church of Christ upon his loyal fellowship in faith and worship with
his own local Bishop'. 'The local Bishop is the Christ-given centre of
union here on earth, and in the universal College of Bishops is the
permanent bond of union between all members of the Church, of
every nation and tongue, on earth and beyond the veil.'[77] He denied
to non-episcopal churches any *corporate* relation to the Kingdom of
God, though individual Christians were by baptism members of that
kingdom. There is no mediating term, such as the 'ecclesial body'
preserving many of the structural features of the Church that was to
mark the ecumenical thinking of the Second Vatican Council. In
responding to Weston's protest, Davidson, in characteristically
measured vein, argued that the nub of the question was whether the
Church of England had 'laid down a rule which marks all non-Epis-
copalians as *extra Ecclesiam*'. There was no doubt that the Church
of England stood firm by the threefold ministry, but, the Archbishop
suggested, the witness of Caroline High Churchmen, as well as
significant silences in the Anglican formularies, threw 'a grave *onus
probandi* upon those who contend for the rigid and uncompromising
maintenance of the absolutely exclusive rule'. He judged that diocesan bishops had the discretion to invite Christians of other deno-

minations to preach, and to admit communicant Christians not episcopally confirmed to Holy Communion, but that 'serious confusion' would result from an encouragement to Anglicans to receive communion from non-episcopally ordained ministers.[78] Weston was satisfied neither by the Archbishop's judgement nor by the verdict of the consultative committee of bishops, and attempted to make his own position clear in his book, *The Fulness of Christ*. The Church is the divine society, in its essence Christ himself, so that unity is its fundamental characteristic, a unity witnessed to by the reflection of Christ in the diversity of individual Christians, who are nonetheless bound together in one by the apostolic ministry of the episcopate. Through the 'correspondence and intercommunion of the whole college [of bishops] the Catholic faith is preserved intact'. The heart of that faith is the reconciliation of God and man, through the sacrificial offering of love, which is shown forth in the Eucharistic offering. 'The Mass becomes the necessary centre of worship, for it celebrates the central fact of at-one-ment, and communion with our Lord and one another is the pledge of that unity which our Lord died that we might enjoy.'[79]

In retrospect Weston's protest against the Kikuyu events seems shrill and representative of a narrower understanding of Catholic order than is warranted, even though it called forth an impressive theological statement of the relation of church, ministry, and sacraments and their Incarnational grounding. Even at the time a staunch Anglo-Catholic like Lord Halifax could write:

That a pious Nonconformist should wish to come to Communion in any of our churches and should come on his own responsibility is a thing which, it seems to me, need in no way distress us. I can imagine circumstances in which to repel such as one would be the very last thing one would wish to do; rather it might be a thing one would shrink from in horror.[80]

Weston was well aware that 'the Church is always meet to be reformed'. The quest for unity was part of that reformation, as was the defence of the doctrine of the Incarnation against the hedging theology of Modernism, and as was also the needful purging of the institutional church. In 1919 he wrote that he sometimes suffered from 'a kind of institution-sickness'.

Rome and Church of England both seem so disloyal to the Master in respect to the real things of life. I feel sometimes that to breathe Christ-air, I must drop out of institutions, and live the simple life in simple Africa, just taking communion where I may find an altar, at which I am accepted. . . . You know the Church of England and the Church of Rome do *not* represent the Christ truly. They are not revelations of His broken heart. They are as badly infected with *caste*, as Islam in Africa with witchcraft. The problem of to-day is *colour*, which follows on from *caste*: and I'm not sure that the Institutions we name the Church are not playing the traitor.[81]

When he came to the Lambeth Conference in 1920 it would have seemed unlikely from his stand over the Kikuyu scheme that Weston would have been able to play a significant role in the deliberations about unity. Against Hensley Henson's defence of the National Church and denigration of apostolic succession, Weston pleaded for a Catholic church, whose organic life centred in an authority expressed in a college of bishops. A national church was not Catholic. From an African perspective it was bound by race. He put the question to Henson: 'Why am I obliged to take my view of the Church's teaching from the sixteenth and seventeenth centuries when the Church is 1,920 years old?'[82] He was determined that nothing should be done in the cause of unity which put additional barriers against eventual reunion with the Church of Rome, but he wholeheartedly supported Lang in his drafting of 'The Appeal to All Christian People', an Appeal which urged that the Episcopate 'is now and will prove to be in the future the best instrument for maintaining the unity and continuity of the Church'. The Appeal went on to say that 'if the authorities of other Communions should so desire, we are persuaded that, terms of union having been otherwise satisfactorily adjusted, Bishops and Clergy of our Communion would willingly accept from these authorities a form of commission or recognition which would commend our ministry to their congregations, as having its place in the one family life'.[83] Weston's biographer points out that six months before the Lambeth Conference the bishop had set out his own proposals for reunion, which included the acceptance of episcopacy by non-episcopal communions, but went on to say that 'once episcopacy is accepted each "communion" can be left free to reconcile its existing organisation with its newly acquired bishops. We do not want, for example, to abolish the Presbyterial forms of Church government. We want to perfect them.' Moreover, he went on:

We will not inquire, 'Are my orders valid for the purpose for which I received them?' Rather, 'What is lacking to my orders, which I must receive before I may be invited to minister in other communities?' My desire in God's sight, whose ordained minister I believe myself to be, is to be in a position to minister everywhere. Therefore I am prepared to accept at the hands of each community that will unite with me, whatever it thinks it can add to me, provided that it will also receive from my community what we think we have to offer.[84]

The Appeal to Christendom was for Weston an expression of true Catholic spirit. The unity of the episcopate would not hinder each communion from retaining 'its own customs, methods and ways of worship, as far as is compatible with life in a universal fellowship that professes one faith, possesses one episcopal ministry, and uses sacraments common to all'. He warned Anglo-Catholics against picking holes in the language of the Appeal, and held up the Uniate Churches as a model of that unity in diversity which he saw as the direction in which, with acceptance of episcopacy, it would be possible to move.[85] Inevitably there were Anglo-Catholics who were suspicious that Weston had sold out to a Protestant lobby, but the vision of unity which he pointed to is one which has had an enduring influence on subsequent ecumenical ventures.

If the Church was the agent of God's reconciliation, and that was the ground and imperative of unity, then the mission of the Church was also to protest against injustice and oppression. In one particular scandal Weston was especially active, and enlisted the help of Archbishop Davidson. This was the matter of government endorsement of forced labour by Africans, a matter which had been encouraged by a memorandum from the bishops of Mombasa and Uganda who had urged the regulation of unscrupulous private practice in this regard by a law favouring some form of compulsion for work of national importance. Weston was irate, both because of the Government's policy and because of the complicity of the Church with it. His friend Cripps was preoccupied at the same time with the question of native reserve lands in Rhodesia, writing that 'this unawakened race does not perceive yet the injury that has been done it. But one day it will arouse itself, become articulate . . . and then . . . ? But this is for the next act in this sombre drama.'[86] Weston in a pamphlet, *The Serfs of Great Britain*, called attention to the social ills caused by the uprooting of Africans from their community by forced labour schemes, and later joined with J. H. Oldham and others in a memorandum to the

Government, which Davidson presented in December 1920 and which led in the course of the next year to a change of government policy.

It was the combination of incarnational and sacramental theology and social concern which was the keynote of Weston's concluding address to the Anglo-Catholic Congress in 1923 in words which have become justly quoted. His devotion to Christ in the Sacrament was central to his own faith. He believed that that sacramental focus gave a reality to Christ's presence and power that nothing else could. 'The one thing England needs to learn is that Christ is in and amid matter, God in flesh, God in sacrament.' And so he concluded:

But I say to you, and I say it with all the earnestness that I have, if you are prepared to fight for the right of adoring Jesus in His Blessed Sacrament, then, when you come out from before your tabernacles, you must walk with Christ, mystically present in you through the streets of this country, and find the same Christ in the peoples of your cities and villages. You cannot claim to worship Jesus in the tabernacle, if you do not pity Jesus in the slum.

Archbishop Davidson, when he heard of Weston's speech, commented to the Bishop of Salisbury, 'I feel very Protestant today'.[88] Certainly the reference to tabernacles did not speak of peace to a church divided about the legitimacy of reservation.

The other controversial issue was the sending of a telegram to the Pope in the name of the Congress, which was a spontaneous gesture by Weston. There were angry letters in the press, and Davidson brought pressure to bear on Lord Halifax to cancel a meeting on the theme of reunion with Rome in the light of the Malines Conversations. Weston was unrepentant: 'Were the Pope our enemy, Christ would still bid us love him!' And he cited the Appeal to all Christian People as justification for his telegram.

I humbly submit, as a member of the Lambeth Conference of 1920 that the priests were then given a glorious opportunity, by some 250 English Bishops, of accustoming their flocks to a vision of a reunited Christendom with the Pope as a central figure; and they appear to have missed it! May I, as humbly, suggest that before the telegram be quite forgotten, the Lambeth Appeal, in its relation to reunion with Rome, be explained to the people concerned?[89]

Some sixty years later that vision, though more officially recognized, still needs to be explained.

There is no doubt that the identity of Anglicanism was powerfully shaped by the influence of the Oxford Movement in the growing churches overseas. In that context the issues raised by Establishment were seen more sharply, and synodical forms of government evolved. In a missionary situation the pattern of the early Church could gain an especial relevance. The outstanding personalities and holiness of life of bishops such as Patteson, Selwyn, and Weston exerted an enormous influence and had an attractive power. As the Church of England grew into the Anglican Communion so questions of unity inevitably pressed themselves. If Patteson would not have shared Weston's approval of reservation and Benediction, he would none-theless have been at one with him in his sacramental emphasis and his understanding of episcopacy as the apostolic ministry. Selwyn and Gray were equally convinced of the autonomy of the Church overseas, and of the importance of synodical government. All were bishops who stood for the Catholic identity of Anglicanism.

IX. The Catholic revival and ecumenical endeavour

THE OXFORD Movement began as an assertion of Anglican identity and an affirmation of that identity as being found in the continuity of the Church of England with the Church of the Fathers. Keble's Assize Sermon protest against the right of secular authority to suppress bishoprics and so interfere with the order of the Church was grounded in the conviction that the apostolic ministry of the Church was divinely ordained and was no mere arrangement or organizational convenience. Apostolic ministry, episcopal succession, the sacraments as effective means of grace, and the creeds and liturgy as embodiments of the teaching authority of the Church formed an organic whole. The letters of Ignatius of Antioch and the teaching of Cyprian provided strong support for the Tractarian position, which also looked back (not always accurately) to the Caroline divines and the non-jurors.

This emphasis of the Tractarians seemed to many contemporaries to be provocative and divisive. Very early on they came into conflict with Thomas Arnold, a former fellow of Oriel, whose reaction to the attacks on the Church in the early 1830s was to propose a broad scheme of comprehension by which the Dissenters would be permitted to use the parish churches and be brought within the compass of the Establishment so that the 'National Church should be rendered thoroughly comprehensive in doctrine, in government and in ritual'.[1] Much of what Arnold wrote, about the division of dioceses, about an episcopacy which was genuinely local, about the need for councils and consultation, was far-sighted though unrealistic at the time. It was, however, a national rather than an international view of the Church, and in the view of the Tractarians treated important matters of faith and order as no more than convenient arrangements. For Arnold, whose indignation at what he saw as Tractarian narrowness led him to categorize them publicly as 'the Oxford malignants', the understanding of Church order taught by *Tracts for the Times* was a new Puritanism. Writing to Provost Hawkins in 1834 he made his views plain.

To insist on the necessity of Episcopacy is exactly like insisting on the necessity of circumcision; both are and were lawful, but to insist on either as *necessary*, is unchristian. . . ; all forms of government and ritual are in the Christian church indifferent, and are to be decided by the Church itself, pro temporum et locorum ratione, 'the Church' not being the clergy, but the congregation of Christians.[2]

Four years later, in a letter to A. P. Stanley, he drew strong parallels between the Tractarians and both the Jesuits and the non-jurors. It was not surprising, he suggested, that in the turbulence of the times, 'the elements of Toryism and High Church feeling at all times rife in Oxford, should have been moulded into a novel form by the peculiar spirit of the place—that sort of religious aristocratical chivalry so common to young men, to students, and to members of the aristocracy'.

The same cause produced the same results after the Reformation, in the growth and spread of Jesuitism. . . . So, again, the Puritans led to the Nonjurors; zealous many of them, and pious, but narrow-minded in the last degree, fierce and slanderous, . . . their party bears on it all the marks of a heresy and of a faction, whose success would have obstructed good, and preserved or restored evil. Whenever you see the present party acting as a party, they are just like the Nonjurors,—busy, turbulent, and narrow-minded; with no great or good objects, but something that is at best fantastic, and generally mischievous. . . . Their cause is one and the same—a violent striving for forms and positive institutions, which, ever since Christ's Gospel has been preached, has always been wrong—wrong, as the predominant mark of a party. . . . If this same spirit infected the early Church also . . . shall we dignify their error by the specious name of the 'Consent of Antiquity' and call it an 'Apostolical Tradition' . . . ?[3]

Arnold opposed the Tractarians because he believed them to be limiting the comprehensiveness of the Church of England at a time when that comprehensiveness needed to be affirmed. He saw in the Tractarian understanding of the faith and order of the Church the seeds of a narrowly partisan and ultimately sectarian view of the Church, looking as he did to ways in which Dissenters might be comprehended within the National Church. It might also be said that his criticisms reveal a lack of appreciation of sacramental theology, and show the tendency, so often questioned by Newman, to consider religion as dealing only with inner states and mental acts.

Nonetheless there is force in Arnold's concern about the potentially partisan attitude that could be inculcated by the Oxford 'apostolicals'. At the same time that Arnold was writing to Hawkins, F. D. Maurice also expressed his fears that the Oxford leaders might forget that the Church was catholic even while they were in the act of pleading for its catholicity.[4] Maurice was one who welcomed the recovery of the sense of the universal Church by the Tractarians, as he welcomed their strong sacramental emphasis and their awareness of the priority of God's grace, of the Church as a divine society and the ministry of the Church as an apostolic ministry, as well as their conviction 'that we belong to the Communion of Saints, and need not seek for another'. He was at one with the Tractarians in their repudiation of that Liberalism which 'resolved truth into an opinion', knowing that such Liberalism had no gospel for the multitudes 'who do not live upon opinions or care for opinions'.[5] But for all that Maurice had in common with the Tractarians, he was as critical of what he saw as their placing of the church, its ministry and sacraments, before God, as he was of the sectarianism of Evangelicals.

Maurice and Arnold were concerned with the National Church. The Tractarians were concerned with the identity of the Church of England with the Church of the Fathers. Stressing the elements of Catholic continuity they were inevitably accused of being Romanizers and crypto-papists, but, in the early years at least, there was as strong a criticism of Rome as of Protestantism. The theology of the Anglican *via media* as maintaining the 'Catholic consent' of antiquity was defended as free from the Roman distortions of an unwarranted usurpation of authority and over-systematization in theology. Newman continued to regard the Papacy as anti-Christ until the beginning of the 1840s, even though he was forced to re-assess the status of the definitions of the Council of Trent. In Tract XC, having been forced to reconsider the theology of the *via media*, and so the position of the Church of Rome, Newman argued that the supremacy of the Pope could not be regarded as belonging to revelation. 'The Papacy began in the exertions and passions of man; and what man can make, man can destroy. Its jurisdiction, while it lasted, was "ordained of God"; when it ceased to be, it ceased to claim our obedience; and it ceased to be at the Reformation.' Citing an article of his own in the *British Critic* Newman attempted to express an Anglican ecclesiology, which allowed to the Bishop of Rome only a primacy of order.

The Anglican view of the Church has ever been this: that its portions need not otherwise have been united together for their essential completeness, than as being descended from one original. They are like a number of colonies sent out from a mother-country. . . . Each Church is independent of all the rest, and is to act on the principle of what may be called Episcopal independence, except, indeed, so far as the civil power unites any number of them together. . . . Each diocese is a perfect independent Church, is sufficient for itself; and the communion of Christians one with another, and the unity of them altogether, lie, not in a mutual understanding, intercourse and combination, not in what they do in common, but in what they are and have in common, in their possession of the Succession, their Episcopal form, their Apostolical faith, and the use of the Sacraments. . . . Mutual intercourse is but an accident of the Church, not of its essence. . . . Intercommunion is a duty, as other duties, but is not the tenure or instrument of the communion between the unseen world and this. . . . Bishop is superior to bishop only in rank, not in real power; and the Bishop of Rome, the head of the Catholic world, is not the centre of unity, except as having a primacy of order. Accordingly, even granting, for argument's sake, that the English Church violated a duty in the sixteenth century, in releasing itself from the Roman supremacy, still it did not thereby commit that special sin, which cuts off from it the fountains of grace, and is called schism. It was essentially complete without Rome, and naturally independent of it. . . .

There is nothing in the Apostolic system which gives authority to the Pope over the Church, such as it does not give to a bishop. It is altogether an ecclesiastical arrangement; not a point *de fide*, but of expedience, custom, or piety. . . .[6]

Newman himself came to abandon this understanding of the Church, and in part this was the consequence of pressure from W. G. Ward and younger adherents of the movement, who had little interest in the historical questions which so exercised Newman. For Ward increasingly came to maintain that the contemporary Church of Rome was the pattern for all churches, arguing that the Reformation had to be undone, the ascetic ideal of holiness restored within the Church of England, and 'as Catholic spirituality was cultivated and preached, Roman doctrine would normally follow as its natural correlative'.[7] In *The Ideal of a Christian Church* (1844), in which Ward gave full and provocative expression to these views, Ward argued that the establishment of such a Catholic ethos within the Church of England would be the way in which union between Anglicanism and the Church of Rome would eventually be effected. 'It should be taken', he wrote, 'as a first principle by all Catholic-minded men, that the true Catholic character *exists*, is irresistibly attracted towards the image of itself. If then holy living and orthodox faith actively flourish in the Roman Church . . . it is plain that to implant it in our Church is to take the merest possible means of effecting a real and lasting union.'[8]

Ward may be taken as the precursor of what might be called the tradition of Anglo-papalism within the Catholic movement in Anglicanism, but it should be noted that he himself joined the Church of Rome only months after the publication of the *Ideal*, and that many of the Tractarians and their successors failed to be convinced by Ward's arguments. However much might be learnt from Catholic devotion and liturgy, and however great the appreciation of Catholic theology, there were many who could not dismiss the historical questions as easily as Ward. Pusey, for instance, steadfastly maintained that Rome had added to the primitive faith; that the existence of the Eastern Churches could not be overlooked in any assessment of the claims of the Church of Rome; and that the grace of Baptism united all in the Body of Christ, not only Roman Catholics and Anglicans, but Orthodox and Nonconformists. Although the Church was divided it was not fundamentally disunited.

Holding . . . one Faith, united by the same Sacraments, administered by the successors of the Apostles, to the One Head of the Church, the Eastern, Western, our own Church, is one, although it has not that intercommunion which it ought to have. A family is one, although it have misunderstandings or grievances. A limb is part of the body, although it be mangled. . . .
Unity involves the duty of love and of unity of will, of which the highest expression is inter-communion. But inter-communion does not make union; it is an act of love. It is that in the Church which mutual communication is in a family. A family in which there is dissension is one, although not 'at one'. . . .[9]

The cultus of the Virgin Mary in its practical devotional expression, the claims of the Papal supremacy, and, later on, the doctrines of the Immaculate Conception and Papal Infallibility, were all for Pusey barriers to reunion with Rome, much as he longed for the restoration of full communion. Of the younger generation of Tractarian leaders, Pusey's disciple, Liddon, shared his hesitations. 'The note of Unity', he wrote in 1868, 'like the other notes of Sanctity and world-embracing Universality, has been only partially realised in history'.

The note of Unity is, historically speaking, modified, if you like, obscured; just as are the notes of Sanctity and Universality. Wherever there are the Sacraments, and the Succession, and the Oecumenical Faith, there is Christ; there, too, is the capacity for reunion of other portions of the Body which retain these things. Unity in potentiality, as distinct from Unity always visible in fact, is our Lord's own historical interpretation of His promise hitherto; that it will always be so, is not what we should expect, but a point beyond the present discussion.[10]

For Liddon the Eastern Churches were both an historical argument and a contemporary objection to Roman absolutism. 'If the East did not run out like a jetty, breaking up the advancing wave of the Roman argument, our position, I admit, would be a much less defensible one.'[11] 'The real question', Liddon wrote, 'is: What is the evidence for the Roman doctrine of *the Supremacy* (not the Primacy in order) of the Pope?'

This is the real point on which the question of conduct hinges, and not on any *a priori* theory of unity. If the Romans are right about the Supremacy, all follows; if wrong, then either Constantinople is the centre of the Catholic world, or the Unity of the Church is dynamic, and there is room within its pale for the English Episcopate, as well as for the Bishops who communicate with the Pope.[12]

A later letter of Liddon's, subsequent to the 1870 definition of Papal Infallibility, cited a dictum of Pusey's that 'If St. Augustine had believed about the Pope as Cardinal Manning does, his conduct would have been very sinful'. The Fathers did not give support to the doctrine of Papal supremacy, and only a doctrine of development could weigh in its favour, but for Liddon 'development' was 'a dangerous guide which may lead us as easily to Infidel conclusions as the Roman ones'.[13]

Another critic of the Roman claims from the Tractarian tradition was the church historian, William Bright, the author of the two great eucharistic hymns, 'And now, O Father, mindful of the love' and 'Once, only once, and once for all'. Undoubtedly Catholic in his theology, Bright was pessimistic about hopes of unity between the Church of England and the Church of Rome. He wrote in 1895:

I regard all theories of possible corporate reunion with Rome as the merest illusion. If the history of the last fifty years has taught us nothing else, it has surely taught us *that*. It is not merely a question of Papal supremacy; it is the whole mass of Roman obedience and usage, of Roman principle and standpoint, the whole atmosphere, theological and ethical, in which Roman Catholic life energizes, that constitutes for us the impossibility of reunion. We dare not accept responsibility for Romanism as it is, and as, except for some inconceivable revolution in Latin Church opinion, it is likely to continue. Even if the bare letter of the Tridentine Decrees were all that we had to do with, it would form a barrier insurmountable. But behind and around that stretches all that is covered by the *magisterium* of the Latin Church, and that those who submit to her must assimilate.... We have no right to indulge in dreams which are dissipated by facts.[14]

The views of Pusey, Liddon, and Bright which have been quoted underline the point that the Oxford Movement did not endorse an uncritical acceptance of Roman Catholic theology and practice. The Tractarians indeed laid claim to the Catholic inheritance that had all too frequently been disregarded and dissipated. They recognized a common sacramental understanding with the Church of Rome, even whilst they criticized the theological categories of transubstantiation. The catholicity of the early centuries of the Church was the standard to which they appealed, even though the later generation of ritualists was prepared to learn from the seventeenth-century French Church and from contemporary Catholic practice in such areas as parochial missions. But there is no doubt that the vision of unity with the Church of Rome, however impracticable it might be thought, became and remained part of the aspirations of the Catholic movement within Anglicanism, however much doctrinal definitions of the Immaculate Conception. Papal Infallibility, and the condemnation of Anglican Orders by the Bull *Apostolicae Curae* might seem to make it a 'dream dissipated by facts'.

There were a number of significant moments in the nineteenth-century quest for a way forward in the relationship between Anglicans and Roman Catholics, even though those actively concerned with that quest were a small minority, and it has been rightly said that it cannot be characterized as a reunion movement.[15] From the ecumenical concerns and romantic dreams of the Catholic layman Ambrose Phillipps de Lisle sprang eventually the Association for Promoting the Unity of Christendom in 1857. Amongst the Anglican founders were the Provost of Perth, Knottesford-Fortescue; Lowder; Frederick George Lee; John Oakley, later Dean of Manchester; and George Nugée, who served as Secretary. In 1869 Lee claimed that the

Association had begun with forty members and had grown to some 13,000, but T. T. Carter gives a more sober estimate for 1864 of 7,000 Anglicans, 1,250 Catholics, and 360 from the Eastern Churches; 1864 was the year in which the Holy Office, encouraged by Manning, forbade Roman Catholics to belong to the APUC. In 1877 de Lisle was also involved in the aspirations of the Order of Corporate Reunion, the intention of which was to introduce into the Church of England orders recognized by Rome. To which end F. G. Lee, T. W. Mossman and, possibly, also J. T. Seccombe, were consecrated bishops in a boat off Venice, and then reordained a number of Anglican clergy. The story is a bizarre one and, though not without foundations, is shrouded in mystery.[16]

If the APUC in the 1860s marked a concern for reunion between Anglicans, Roman Catholics, and the Eastern Churches, the same decade was also a time of anxiety for Anglicans who looked for hopeful signs from Rome as the Ultramontane party gained more and more of an ascendancy. Bishop Forbes's brother, George, was told by a French Catholic priest that the Ultramontanes had simplified matters greatly:

They have reduced the Creed to a single article 'I believe in the Pope'; the Bible to a single verse, 'Thou art Peter', and duty to a single rule—in every difficulty consult the sacred congregation at Rome and obey it exactly.[17]

Gladstone, in a letter to Forbes, viewed the impending Vatican Council with foreboding. It was all too likely that 'much might be done to *widen* the breach' between Anglicans and Roman Catholics.[18] Pusey, who travelled in France in 1865, was also anxious. The object of his journey was to draw the attention of a number of French bishops to his first *Eirenicon*, in which he had attempted to narrow the distance between the Church of England and the Church of Rome by carefully distinguishing the formal teaching of the Church of Rome from popular devotions and unauthoritative theological statements, following the line of Tract XC in stressing that the protest of the Anglican articles was against a practical system not the decrees of Trent. On his return Pusey reported to Bishop Forbes that he had some encouragement from Archbishop Darboy of Paris:

He acknowledged our Succession and the grace of our Sacraments. I can hardly be mistaken in thinking that he acknowledged that we are a branch of the true Church, *enté sur le tronc, qui est Jésus Christ*, that we had the *sève*, since we had life.[19]

If Darboy was encouraging, other French Bishops were not, and back in England Pusey learnt to his disappointment that Newman was unhappy with the *Eirenicon*, feeling that the instances of extravagant devotional language Pusey had cited were calculated to produce hostility and misunderstanding. In attempting to make the intention behind his *Eirenicon* clear to Newman, Pusey emphasized that he was not only concerned with the excesses of popular devotion, but the way in which the promulgation of the doctrine of the Immaculate Conception provided a dangerous precedent for the development of doctrine.

It seemed to me that, on the principles and with the object upon which and with which the Immaculate Conception was made matter of faith, any other popular belief might be made matter of faith. Here was already a fresh difficulty in the way of the reunion of the Eastern Church as well as our own.[20]

Newman's *Letter to Pusey* endeavoured to place many of the instances of Marian devotion to which Pusey had taken exception in context, stressing with his usual realism that popular religion was always liable to corruption, and gently but firmly hinting that Ultramontane writers were not to be taken as spokesmen for English Catholics. In many ways Pusey and Newman had similar concerns, and although Newman objected to the impact of Pusey's catena of Ultramontane quotation on English Protestant sensibility, Pusey's letter did have the effect of making it possible to draw the kind of distinction between authoritative doctrine and devotional expression for which Pusey had hoped.

There were others, however, in the Roman Church who did not welcome Newman's stance. Monsignor Talbot wrote to Manning that 'Dr Newman is more English than the English. His spirit must be crushed'. Manning replied:

What you write about Dr Newman is true. Whether he knows it or not, he has become the centre of those who hold low views about the Holy See, are anti-Roman, cold and silent, to say no more, about the Temporal Power, national, English, critical of Catholic devotions, and always on the lower side. I see no danger of a Cisalpine Club rising again, but I see much danger of an English Catholicism, of which Newman is the highest type. It is the old Anglican, patristic, literary, Oxford tone transplanted into the Church. . . . In one word, it is worldly Catholicism, and it will have the worldly on its side, and will deceive many. Now Ward and Faber may exaggerate but they are a thousand times nearer to the mind and spirit of the Holy See than those who oppose them. Between us and them is a far greater distance than between them and Dr Pusey's book.[21]

Another Ultramontane, E. R. Martin, attacked Newman's cautious criticism of Marian devotion in a letter to the *Tablet*:

To see one's mother dragged down to a mere intellectual conceit, may well make a man bold. Newman has put our Mother in a public place, and taken her prerogatives to pieces, not reverently, not lovingly, not devotionally, but coldly, dogmatically and drily.[22]

It was no wonder that Newman told a correspondent that 'to write theology is like dancing on a tight-rope some hundred feet above the ground.'[23]

At the end of 1866 Pusey returned to Oxford from a Long Vacation spent in the cholera-stricken parish of Bethnal Green to take up again some of the issues raised by his *Eirenicon* and the reaction to it. This included assisting Bishop Forbes of Brechin in the preparation of his *Exposition of the Thirty-Nine Articles*, which was part of Forbes's endeavour at this time to build bridges with continental Catholics through correspondence and personal visits.[24] This in turn led to further correspondence with Newman in an attempt to elucidate some of the points of controversy between Anglicanism and Rome. Newman replied to the first of a series of letters on transubstantiation that he disliked considering questions of scholastic philosophy 'because partly I do not understand them, and partly distrust premises which many take for granted'. He preferred to discuss eucharistic theology in Greek Patristic terms rather than in Latin scholastic ones.[25] But he was prepared to probe the Latin definitions further with Pusey and by November 1867 they had reached a common mind on the interpretation of the Tridentine formulae on the Eucharist in a way that Pusey believed to be compatible with Anglican teaching.[26]

There was also an important exchange on the position of the Papacy, doctrinal authority, and doctrinal definition. Newman maintained, drawing out themes discussed much earlier in the *Lectures on the Prophetical Office of the Church* and the *Essay on Development*, that papal jurisdiction was 'not so much a *practice* as a *doctrine*— and not so much a *doctrine* as a *principle* of our system'. By maintaining that it was a principle, Newman placed the magisterium of the Bishop of Rome in the area of that which belonged implicitly to the inner dynamic of the Church. By the principle, he wrote 'I mean something far more subtle and intimately connected with our system itself than a doctrine, so as not to be contained in the written law, but to be, like the common law of the land, or rather the principles of the Constitution, contained in the very idea of our being what we are.' The papal office emerged from the prophetical tradition of the Church and was implicit in the Church's claim to be the proclaimer of an authoritative and saving revelation of God. Whereas Pusey and Forbes were concerned to isolate areas of doctrinal definition on which there could be agreement, consigning other areas of popular faith and practice to the category of that which might be properly ignored or repudiated, for Newman, for all his criticism of the tone and temper of Ultramontane teaching, this was an unacceptable 'minimist' attitude, which was cutting the nerve between the worshipping life of the Church, with all its inadequacy, and the process of theological reflection and definition.

It has always been trusted that the received belief of the faithful and the obligations of piety would cover a larger circuit of doctrinal matters than was formally claimed, and secure a more generous faith that was imperative on the conscience. Hence there has never been a wish on the part of the Church to cut clean between doctrine revealed and doctrine not revealed.[27]

Faith was in a living community not in a written code. 'The act of faith . . . must ever be partly explicit, partly implicit.' Applying this in a second letter to then undefined doctrine of Papal Infallibility, Newman wrote:

A man will find it a religious duty to *believe* it, or may safely *dis*believe it, in *proportion* as he thinks it probable or improbable that the Church might or will define it, or does hold it, and that it is the doctrine of the Apostles. For myself . . . I think that the Church *may* define it (i.e. it possibly may turn out to belong to the original depositum), but that she *will* not *ever* define it; and again, I do not see that she can be said to hold it. She never can simply *act* upon it (being undefined, as it is), and I believe never has;—moreover, on the other hand, I think there is a good deal of evidence, on the very surface of history and the Fathers in its favour. On the whole then I hold it, but I should account it no sin if, on grounds of reason, I doubted it.[28]

Newman felt that Pusey and Forbes had not fully grasped the dogmatic understanding of Catholicism, and that in consequence their pursuit of an eirenical minimum of doctrinal agreement was a chimera.

It sems to us false, and we must ever hold, on the contrary, that the object of faith is *not* simply certain articles, A B C D, contained in dumb documents, but the whole word of God, explicit and implicit, as dispensed by His living Church. On this point I am sure there can be no Irenicon; for it marks a fundamental, elementary difference between the Anglican view and ours.[29]

Newman concluded his letter with a reiteration of his distinction between doctrine and principles.

Doctrine is the *voice* of a religious body; its principles are of its *substance*. The principles may be turned into doctrines by being defined; but they live as necessities before definition, and the less likely to be defined, *because* they are so essential to life.[30]

There are echoes of Newman's earlier position that the highest (and most vital) state of the Church is one in which there is no doctrine, and Pusey's own contention that it is not the things which we know clearly but the things which we know unclearly which are of the greatest significance.

The efforts of Pusey and Forbes met with little success, though Pusey responded to Newman's *Letter* on his first *Eirenicon*, with a second *Eirenicon*, endeavouring again to set Ultramontane Marian doctrine against a scriptural and patristic background. Pusey concluded this letter with a moving appeal for unity, regretting that there were 'in the Roman Communion those who wish to exaggerate differences, who decry "explanations" under the term of "concessions", who think that it is beneath its grandeur to enter into negotiations with those whom they account as rebels', and who wanted Ultramontane devotions to grow and flourish. There were signs, Pusey believed, even with all the discouraging reaction he had encountered, that unity might yet be achieved. 'The first crack of the ice is not so sure a token of the coming thaw, as love, infused by God, is of larger gifts of love.'[31]

Among Catholics Forbes's *Exposition of the Articles* met with a warm response from the German theologian, J. J. I. von Döllinger. With the news of the summoning of the Vatican Council of 1870 Döllinger was apprehensive of an Ultramontane victory, and told Forbes that he wished Pusey had more clearly objected to the Ultramontane position. They refuse, he wrote, 'to see the beam in their eye, and talk constantly as if they were invulnerable and immaculate, and as if the Oriental and the Anglican Churches had only to say with contrite heart and mien, 'mea culpa', and to submit unconditionally to every error in theory and every abuse in practice'.[32] Following the definition of Papal Infallibility the 'Old Catholics' who refused to accept the dogma, of whom the most notable was Döllinger, linked themselves with the old Jansenist Church of Holland. In 1872 the Old Catholics met in congress at Cologne, a meeting attended by the Bishop of Lincoln, Christopher Wordsworth, and the Bishop of Ely, Harold Browne. Two years later there was the first of the reunion conferences in Bonn, at which representatives from the Old Catholic, Orthodox, and Anglican Churches assembled, Liddon being amongst the Anglican representatives. Bishop Harold Browne hoped much from these gatherings, commenting that 'Döllinger and the great body of Old Catholics have no greater difference of theological opinions from an old-fashioned and moderate English Churchman than such as English Churchman would discover between himself and the adherents of the three extreme parties at present existing in England.'[33] Friendly relations were maintained with the Old Catholics from this point on, though at the Lambeth Conference of 1888 Archbishop Benson was cautious in promoting closer relationships until the Dutch Old Catholics in particular had clarified their understanding of Anglican orders.[34] Eventually in 1925 there was a formal recognition of Anglican orders by the Old Catholics, which was followed in 1931 by the Bonn agreement on intercommunion, which stated that, whilst each Communion recognized the catholicity and independence of the other and agreed to admit members of the other Communion to participation in the sacraments, intercommunion did not require from either Communion 'the acceptance of all doctrinal opinion, sacramental devotion, or liturgical practice characteristic of the other, but implies that each believes the other to hold all the essentials of the Christian faith'.[35] Opposition to Ultramontanism and concern for Catholic unity thus led eventually to a union which was seen as bridging the Reformation.

In 1889 a fortuitous, or as some would say, providential meeting on the island of Madeira between a French priest, Fernand Portal, and the president of the English Church Union, Charles Lindley Wood, Viscount Halifax, led to the opening of a new chapter in the relations between Rome and Canterbury, an opening which was in part possible because Leo XIII had succeeded Pius IX in 1878, and at Canterbury Archbishop Benson was personally more sympathetic than his predecessor, Tait, to such ecumenical possibilities. Portal's encounter with Halifax introduced him to a Catholic-minded Anglican, and led him to a study of both Anglican history and contemporary works on ecclesiology and church history, including the Russian Khomiakoff's *The Latin Church and Protestantism*, and Duchesne's *Les Origines du culte chrétien*. By the end of 1890 he was urging Halifax that there was a need for information about Anglicanism to be disseminated amongst Roman Catholics, and by January 1892 he had come to the opinion that one important step which ought to be taken in order to advance the cause of reunion was to press for a reconsideration of the validity of Anglican Orders.[36] Under the pseudonym 'F. Dalbus', Portal wrote an account of Anglican Orders which attracted considerable attention, although it concluded that Barlow's consecration of Matthew Parker was doubtful, because of defects of intention. Subsequent ordinations had lacked the *porrectio instrumentorum* (the handing over of chalice and paten, or pastoral staff), which he held essential. Portal had in fact flown some intentional kites in the hope that there would be rebuttals of his arguments which would end in a favourable judgement for Anglicans, and so it proved from such scholars as Duchesne.[37] A visit to England in 1894 enabled Portal to go with Halifax to visit Archbishop Maclagan at York and Archbishop Benson at Addington, and this was followed by a summons to Portal to go to Rome, where he was received in audience by Leo XIII, though Portal failed to persuade the Pope to address a letter directly to the Anglican archbishops. He had to be content with a letter to himself from Cardinal Rampolla with instructions to let Halifax see it. Despite pressure from Halifax and Portal, Benson was reluctant to take any action which might appear to compromise his position or be misconstrued by sections of the Church, so no letter went directly from Canterbury to the Pope. On the Roman side Cardinal Vaughan, Manning's successor at Westminster, was hostile to Portal and Halifax's ecumenical vision, and took steps both in England and in Rome to ensure that no significant encouragement was given. In 1895 Leo XIII issued his encyclical *Ad Anglos* which spoke of his longing for union, but without making any mention of the Church of England. This provoked indirectly a pastoral letter from Benson in September of the same year in which he both noted the desire for reunion which was in the air and spoke of the Anglican Communion as having a special vocation in bringing 'the parted Churches of Christ to a better understanding and closer fellowship'.[38] In January 1896 Halifax, speaking at a meeting of the English Church Union, urged the bishops of the Church of England to recognize the opportunity of the moment and to declare 'that there is nothing they are not ready to do short of a sacrifice of truth to promote the reunion of Christendom, and that they would thankfully respond to any invitation which might be addressed to them to consider, with theologians named by the Pope, the differences which separate England from the rest of Western Christendom'.

You say it is too glorious a dream—that it is impossible. Why is it a dream? Why is it impossible? It is dreams that are realized. It is the impossible which does occur. . . . Let us keep the ideal of a reunited Christendom before our eyes, and let us not have the shame and confusion, the sting and reproach of conscience to learn, when it is too late, that all these things might have been in this our own day if our faithlessness had not hindered God's gracious purposes, if we had had eyes to see, and ears to hear, and souls so attuned to the guidings of God's providence as to discern the time of our visitation.[39]

The following month the Roman Commission was set up under the presidency of Cardinal Mazzella, and met three times a week from 24 March until 8 May. Two Anglicans, Father Puller of the Cowley Fathers and the Revd T. A. Lacey, made themselves unofficially available in Rome for the elucidation of any points the Commission cared to raise. Vaughan and the English Roman Catholics kept up pressure for a condemnation. In June a papal encyclical, *Satis Cognitum*, presented a view of the unity of the church which demanded an unconditional surrender to Roman claims. It offered little hope of a favourable decision from the Commission, whose findings were eventually embodied in the Bull *Apostolicae Curae* on 19 September, by which the Pope pronounced and declared 'that Ordinations carried out according to the Anglican rite have been and are absolutely null and utterly void'.

Vaughan, the Archbishop of Westminster, who had come to regard the movement for Corporate Reunion as something evil which only had the effect of delaying conversions, took the opportunity of delivering a strong speech following the Papal pronouncement.

The validity of Anglican Orders could never form even a single plank in the platform for either Corporate or Individual Reunion.

Reunion means submission to a Divine Teacher. When men have found the Divine Teacher and determined, at whatever cost, to submit to Him, there will be Reunion. Reunion with the Catholic Church can never take place on any other terms. . . . [Anglican Orders] stand alone, shivering in their insular isolation—and worse; . . .

Tarry not for Corporate Reunion. It is a dream, and a snare of the Evil One. We have all to be converted to God individually; to take up our Cross and follow Him individually, each according to his personal grace. The individual may no more wait for Corporate Reunion, than he may wait for Corporate Conversion.[40]

Portal and Halifax exchanged moving letters, Portal writing to his friend:

Our first thought was for you and for our friends in England. . . . The blow is so heavy and the grief so overwhelming that I am quite benumbed.

May Our Lord have pity on us. May He at least grant us the consolation of seeing with our own eyes that we have not done more harm than good. . . . To you, my dear friend, I owe my highest joys—to work and suffer for the Church. I give you the best that my soul had of affection and unalterable devotion. I feel over again your great grief, and I suffer more for you than for myself.

To this Halifax replied:

Your letter fills my eyes with tears; but it does me inexpressible good. Assuredly it was love of souls that moved us: we did not think of anything else. May something be done to put an end to the divisions among those who love our Lord Jesus Christ—those divisions that keep so many souls far away from Him!—so that those who love each other, communicating at the same altars, may love each other more; in short, so that the essential unity of the Church of Jesus Christ may be recognised by everyone. To bring that about we must come together in a spirit of love and charity, in a spirit also of penitence for all the faults committed on both sides; with a view to dispelling misunderstandings; to distinguishing what is of faith and what is merely a matter of opinion; to dispelling prejudice and, quite simply, to seeking the will of God. . . .

For our part, my dear friend, with what need we reproach ourselves? We tried to do something which, I believe, God inspired. We have failed, for the moment; but if God wills it, his desire will be accomplished, and if He allows us to be shattered, it may well be because He means to do it Himself. This is no dream. The thing is as certain as ever. There are some bitter things which are worth all the joys of earth, and I prefer, many thousand times, to suffer with you in such a cause, than to triumph with the whole world.[41]

Halifax, as John Jay Hughes has noted in his study of the events surrounding *Apostolicae Curae*, was a man consumed with an ecumenical vision. He thought both Cardinal Vaughan and Archbishop Benson had failed to rise to a moment of creative opportunity for the churches. He urged that the Church should recognize that 'with the passage of time . . . certain words, certain formulas, have not always the precise force that was once attributed to them, and that there is room for explanations which permit a rapprochement formerly thought impossible'. He asked for a Pope of large vision and ecumenical courage.

Have a little imagination, a little faith. We must be daring if we expect great results. To save the world God became man. It seems to me that for the sake of reunion the Holy Father could take steps that could be demanded of no one else. What won't a father do for the good of his children? Oh! we must cast aside conventions, fetters, everything that hinders those steps that people like to call folly, but which are the true wisdom. The age of miracles is not dead.[42]

In John XXIII's summoning of the Second Vatican Council and opening the ecumenical doors; in Paul VI's gift of his episcopal ring to Archbishop Ramsey and in his fostering of the work of the Anglican–Roman Catholic International Commission; and in Pope John Paul II's pilgrimage to Canterbury, Halifax's daring vision of 1894 has been in a measure fulfilled.

Towards the end of his life Halifax was once again a major inspiration in an ecumenical encounter between Anglicans and Roman Catholics, and again his friend Portal played a significant part. The Malines conversations sprang from the ecumenical concern of the Primate of Belgium, Cardinal Mercier, and the opportunity afforded by the Appeal of the Lambeth Conference of 1920 to all Christian people. Halifax and Portal visited Mercier in Malines in 1921, Halifax bearing a cautious letter from Archbishop Davidson, explaining that Halifax was in no sense an official ambassador of the Church of England but commending Halifax to Mercier. Agreement having been secured Halifax returned to Malines in December 1921, together with Father Walter Frere, the Superior of the Community of the Resurrection, and Dr Armitage Robinson, the Dean of Wells, and the first exploratory conversations took place. Sufficiently close relationships were established for the participants to look to a continuation of the conversations, and Halifax sought official authorization from Davidson. This Davidson did not feel able to give unless he had assurances for Mercier that the conversations were given a similar authorization by the Vatican. This assurance was given at the beginning of 1923, and in March of that year the second round of conversations took place, concentrating on an attempt to see what the practical steps towards a reunion of the Anglican Communion as a whole with the Church of Rome might be, always presupposing a previously reached doctrinal agreement. From this conversation emerged the following points which were to be submitted to the authorities for the participants' respective Churches:

1. The acknowledgement of the position of the Papal See as the centre and head on earth of the Catholic Church, from which guidance should be looked for, in general, and especially in grave matters affecting the welfare of the Church as a whole.
2. The acknowledgement of the Anglican Communion as a body linked with the Papal See in virtue of the recognition of the jurisdiction of the Archbishop of Canterbury and other Metropolitans by the gift of the Pallium.
3. Under the discipline of the English Church would fall the determination of all such questions as:
    The English rite and its use in the vernacular,
    Communion in both kinds,
    Marriage of the clergy.
4. The position of the existing Roman Catholic Hierarchy in England would for the present, at any rate, remain unaltered. They would be exempt from the jurisdiction of Canterbury, and, as at present, directly dependent on the Holy See.[43]

Davidson was alarmed by talk of Rome bestowing the pallium, and wrote both to Dean Armitage Robinson and to Mercier expressing his concern that the difficulties for Anglicans concerning the Papacy had been 'slurred over'. 'We are bound', he reminded Robinson, 'to disregard as untrue the theory that the Bishop of Rome holds *jure Divino* in the Church of Christ a position of distinct and unique authority, operative everywhere, and perhaps even . . . that, directly or indirectly, it is through that channel alone (at all events in the West) that the Ministerial Commission can be rightly or validly exercised.' In writing to Mercier he pointed out that 'the ambiguity of the term "primacy" is well known to us all' and that no good purpose was served by failing to face this question.[44] Other hesitations were expressed privately to Halifax by Bishop Gore, who was soon to become himself a participant in the conversations. Gore saw possibilities of union with both Protestants and Orthodox, but for him Rome was 'a very onesided development of Christianity into intellectual and moral despotism' requiring a profound reformation before any union would be possible. The most that could be hoped for, he told Halifax later, 'would be the formation of a Uniat English Church consisting of at most a few hundred priests and a few thousand people; and what would that do for the cause of Reunion? To my mind I fear that nothing presents itself as so great a hindrance to the Catholic movement in the C. of E. as a whole as the utterances of those who have been speaking in your sense.'[45]

Tensions in the Church of England over the revision of the Prayer Book, and the action of Bishop Frank Weston sending a telegram of greetings to the Pope from the Anglo-Catholic Congress increased Archbishop Davidson's nervousness over the conversations. If the conversations were to continue, he felt, the Anglican representation needed to be increased, particularly by the addition of Gore, whose caution over the enterprise would act as a restraint on the visionary Halifax. But Davidson was also aware that to increase Anglican representation would also appear as an increase in official backing for the conversations. The sensitivity of the issue is apparent in a memorandum written by Davidson in August 1923, after Gore and Dr B. J. Kidd, the Warden of Keble College, Oxford, had been added to the Anglican participants.

There is, I suppose, no conceivable subject of controversy so inflammatory as the position of the Church of Rome in English, Scottish, or Irish life, and red-hot Protestants on one side, or intractable and uncompromising Papists on the other would instantly distort and misrepresent, however unintentionally, any broken or isolated facts which might reach them.

But for all the difficulty Davidson recognized that 'the obligations . . . of Common Christianity and . . . of the special resolves and hopes' of the 1920 Lambeth Conference meant that the contacts must be pursued. He was no less certain that fundamental doctrinal matters must come to the fore:

The position and authority of Holy Scripture, the meaning and authority of Tradition, the existence or non-existence of a Supreme Authority upon earth, a Vicariate of Christ, and what it means as regards both doctrine and administration: then further the introduction of such dogmas as that of the Immaculate Conception, or again, and in another field, the definite teaching of the Church of Rome as to Transubstantiation and the attendant or consequent doctrines and usages [demanded discussion]. . . . It would be unfair to our Roman Catholic friends to leave them in any doubt as to our adherence, or large questions of controversy, to the main principles for which men like Hooker or Andrewes or Cosin contended, though the actual wording would no doubt be somewhat different today. What those men stood for, we stand for still, and I think that in some form or other that ought to be made immediately clear.[46]

The third conversation at Malines took place in November 1923, with Mgr Battifol and Père Hemmer added to the Catholic side to match the increased Anglican representatives. The conversations centred on the understanding of primacy, and Portal wrote to Halifax beforehand that a prime object of the meeting would be to convince Gore that 'an understanding in regard to the Primacy is not impossible'. He was also nervous about hesitations on Davidson's part, remembering Benson's attitude at the time of Leo XIII's Commission on Anglican Orders. 'We must also remember that Pius XI is a former librarian. . . . Politics and action demand other qualities than those required in a compiler of manuscripts.'[47] In their discussions of the issue of Petrine primacy, the Anglican representatives argued that all the apostles constituted the foundation of the Church: 'all have the keys of the kingdom, and all have the authority to bind and to loose. St Peter's special position, therefore, we hold to have lain, not in any jurisdiction which he alone held, but in a leadership among the other Apostles'. The Anglican representatives were willing to recognize five points: (1) that the Roman Church was founded and built up by St. Peter and St. Paul, according to St. Irenaeus; (2) that the Roman See is the only historically known Apostolic See of the West; (3) that the Bishop of Rome is, as Augustine said of Pope Innocent I, president of the Western Church; (4) that he has a primacy among all the bishops of Christendom; so that, without communion with him, there is in fact no prospect of a reunited Christendom; and (5) that to the Roman See the churches of the English owe their Christianity through 'Gregory our father . . . who sent us baptism'. What they were not willing to accept was any concept of universal jurisdiction, whether ascribed to St. Peter or to the Roman Church, Armitage Robinson being prepared to speak of 'spiritual leadership' or 'general superintendence', whereas Gore preferred the phrase 'spiritual responsibility'.[48]

Following this third series of conversations, Archbishop Davidson issued a Christmas Letter to the Anglican Metropolitans, which devoted a large section to the Malines conversations, but which underlined the tentative nature of what was being done from the Anglican point of view. 'The discussions', Davidson wrote, 'are still in a quite elementary stage . . . no estimate, so far as I can judge, can yet be formed as to their ultimate value, . . . there has been no attempt to initiate what may be called "negotiations" of any sort, . . . the Anglicans who have, with my full encouragement, taken part, are in no sense delegates or representatives of the Church as a whole.' The letter had been modified after correspondence with Mercier, particularly in regard to public mention of the cognizance taken of the conversations by the Vatican, but it nonetheless stirred up Anglican anxieties and disapproval, and there were also critics on the Catholic side. Mercier responded with a Pastoral Letter at the beginning of 1924, stressing like Davidson that the conversations were not 'negotiations' and reminding his critics that there was a need for breaking down preconceptions and for growing in trust, and that a Catholic bishop could not, having seen the wound of disunity, pass by on the other side.[49]

In May 1925 the fourth of the conversations took place, which explored further the relation between the episcopate and the papacy, and the limits of diversity. The most important contribution was a paper read by Mercier, but written by Dom Lambert Beauduin, which for the first time sought to expound a Uniat model for the reconciliation of Anglicans and Roman Catholics. The goal was an Anglican church, united to Rome but not absorbed by it, preserving its own liturgy, customs, and canon law, with the Archbishop of Canterbury having a function analogous to that of the Oriental Patriarchs. This paper was regarded as particularly significant in view of the continuing Anglican criticism of the absolutism and imperialism of papal authority, but because the memorandum had not been circulated before the meeting it was agreed that it should not be treated as one of the official documents of the conversations. It nonetheless sowed the seeds of an idea that has continued to prove fruitful in ecumenical discussion.

The implication in Beauduin's paper that unity did not mean an entire absorption of Anglicanism by the Church of Rome had some bearing on the paper which Gore read on the same occasion in which he pressed for distinction between fundamental doctrines (defined in terms of the Vincentian canon) and other articles of belief. Moreover, Gore went on, certain doctrines declared by Rome to be of the essence of the faith appeared to Anglicans to 'conflict with history and with truth'.

It seems to us illegitimate to yield that faith which we give to the fact of the virginal conception of our Lord, or His resurrection, or His ascension, to the immaculate conception of Mary. The former group of accepted facts rest upon original witness and good evidence: the latter on nothing that can be called historical evidence at all. But to believe in a *fact* on the mere ground of *a priori* reasoning as to what is suitable, without any evidence of the fact, seems to us to alter the fundamental character of the act of faith. It also makes ... a claim for the authority of the church, as centralized and absolute, which the ancient church never made. It frees from all those restrictions of universal agreement and unvarying tradition and scriptural authority—which in our judgement make the fact of faith rational.[50]

Reflecting on the conversations later, Kidd noted that Gore was less prepared to be open to arguments than the other Anglican participants: 'He had reached his conclusions and stood firm; so, when some point of importance arose he was apt to sound rather unyielding'. It was Frere, with his fluent French, his scholarship, and his quickness of mind, who was, in Kidd's opinion, the greatest influence on the conversations from the Anglican side. If the conversations had continued Kidd believed it possible that the two sides would have come closer together on the question of Papal Jurisdiction.[51]

This may well have been over-optimistic, but the whole future of the conversations was altered when Mercier died at the beginning of 1926, offering his life for the union of the Churches, and giving to Halifax his episcopal ring (now set in a chalice at York Minster). Six months later Portal died, and the final conversation in October 1926 was concerned solely with the preparation of the memoranda of the conversations for publication. Separate English and French reports were discussed, but it was not until 1928 that the report on the conversations appeared, following reluctance on the Roman Catholic side to authorize publication as a consequence of changed views at Rome resulting from pressure by Cardinals Bourne and Gasquet.[52] The important section of the report concerned with the primacy of the Pope explored issues which have since been taken further by the Anglican–Roman Catholic International Commission. 'The primacy of the Pope', the Catholic report stated, 'is not merely a primacy of honour, but it implies a duty of solicitude and of activity within the universal Church for the general good, in such wise that the Pope should in fact be a centre of unity, and a Head which exercises an authority over the whole'. From the various expressions of reservation put forward by the Anglican participants, the Catholic report concludes that 'what emerges from these expressions is the sense of a lofty mission attaching to the Pope, with the implication that to a "primacy of honour" there must be added a "primacy of responsibility"'.[53]

The same year as the report of the conversations was published the Vatican announced formally that there were to be no more conversations. Two years later, Halifax, frustrated by the failure to publish the individual papers in the report, and concerned at the distorted perspectives so many seemed to have as to what had transpired, published the original documents. He wished to destroy 'the conspiracy of silence which certain people in authoritative quarters had set up against the Conversations'.[54] The friendship and mutual understanding, if not doctrinal agreement, which had grown between the participants in the conversations were a sign of the unity they desired, and a foretaste of the work of patient understanding, the drawing together of hearts as well as the meeting of minds, which has been so much at the centre of all that has happened in recent years to bring Anglicans and Roman Catholics closer together.

At the beginning of Archbishop Davidson's primacy in 1903 Halifax addressed a long letter to him, in the course of which he wrote:

We are, I am convinced, on the eve of great changes. It is in more sense than one 'la fin d'un siècle.' There is a movement of unrest and expectation on all sides, The foundations are being shaken everywhere, and everything seems possible. There is a movement towards reunion at home and abroad which must bear fruit. Do not despise it, exercise great faith towards it, and, may I say it?—be brave about it. A price has to be paid, something has to be risked, for all things that are worth doing. There are defeats which are the necessary steps to victories; present failures which spell future successes.[55]

Halifax himself lived by the vision of unity, took risks, was disappointed, but sowed the seeds of much that has happened since in a world and in a church which has changed far more than he would have believed possible.

The picture presented so far of the ecumenical concerns of the Tractarians and their successors has focused almost entirely on relations with the Church of Rome. This is not surprising in view of the issues raised by the reaffirmation of sacramental theology and Catholic ecclesiology in the Oxford Movement. The Church of Rome was more immediate than the Eastern Churches with whom a kinship was also recognized, springing in particular from the important part played by Greek Patristic theology in the understanding of Newman and Pusey in particular. That perceptive precursor of the Tractarians, Alexander Knox, in the course of a long discourse addressed to Mrs Hannah More in 1806, had spoken of the Greek Church, of whom Chrysostom was the representative figure, as the supreme guardian of the tradition of Christian holiness. Admitting the contemporary lack of education in the Orthodox world, Knox nonetheless looked for great blessings for the whole Christian world from any revival in Orthodoxy. Looking to the Church of Russia in his day he saw real opportunities for revival as well as a deep kinship with Anglicanism.

With respect to Russia, in particular, hope becomes strengthened when one adverts to the increasing intercourse and connexion with England. It is striking to see this providential tie becoming more firm and close, for where else could it be formed with a shadow of like hopefulness? The English Church is most certainly at this day the only substantial representation of Christianity in the genuine Greek spirit. It displays this so identically, as to make it impossible not to see the close agreement, wherever the fact meets with a just faculty of discernment. What, then, can be more natural than that, as intercourse grows between the two countries, an understanding should also take place, at length, between the two Churches; that, as the . . . English writers on divinity (of the genuine kind) get into the hands of the Russian clergy, and our Common-Prayer-Book, in particular, catches their attention, a kind of ecclesiastical relationship should begin to be discovered.[56]

Knox was, however, too much a creature of contemporary Protestantism not to go on to suggest that Anglicanism possessed 'the features of their ancient and venerable Mother Church' more perfectly than the Russians, with the consequence that the Russians ought to 'regulate themselves and their public worship by what the English Church exhibits now'.[57] In a letter of some twenty years later he wrote that in going back to Chrysostom he had found 'the very religion which the Church of England at this day exemplifies in her services'.

Like the piety of our Prayer-book, he is equally free from the unballasted spirit of indefinite Protestantism, and the crouching servility of the Roman Catholic religion. His sober and deep retention of the Catholic faith and piety, distinguishing him as much as from the former, as his great, luminous, and soaring mind from the latter.[58]

It was to be many years before Knox's hope of a relationship between the Anglican and Eastern Churches was to be given any substance. When Newman and Froude made their Mediterranean journey in 1832–3, they saw something of Orthodoxy in the Ionian Islands but were not greatly moved. Newman spoke approvingly of some Greek devotional books he discovered, but feared that 'outward ceremonies are the substitute for holiness, as among the Jews'.[59] Froude gave a brief description of the Liturgy, which he attended once, commenting that 'in spite of the nasal twang, in which the chant was conducted, and the unintelligibility of the pronunciation, it was altogether very impressive'.[60] Although the influence of the Greek Fathers on Newman in particular was to be of such significance, it was not until the affair of the Jerusalem Bishopric in 1841 that any real attention was given by the Tractarians to relations with the Eastern Churches. The proposed Anglo-Prussian Bishopric at Jerusalem raised a number of ecclesiological questions— Anglican recognition of continental Protestant Churches in a way that implied there was no substantial doctrinal difference between them; the apparent intrusion of a bishop into an area where there were few Anglicans and Protestants, and in which, according to Tractarian ecclesiology, the Greek Patriarch of Jerusalem was to be recognized as the rightful bishop; and the prospect that Oriental Orthodox congregations, such as the Monophysite Syrians or the Nestorians, might be taken under the wing of the new bishop. Newman wrote to Keble that he had already read in the *Standard* of the 'necessity of our coalescing with the *Nestorians*; the Monophysites we have already heard of; in short before we know where we are, we shall find ourselves in communion with heretics'.[61] With Newman's sensitivity to Wiseman's comparison of Anglicans with the early Monophysites, this prospect may well have influenced him in his attitude as much as his opposition to the Lutheran association of Bishop Alexander, and the Protestant comprehensiveness of the scheme. Dr Arnold certainly recognized that the bishopric proposals endorsed the position he had maintained in his *Principles of Church Reform*.

The idea of my Church Reform pamphlet which was so ridiculed and condemned, is now carried into practice by the Archbishop of Canterbury himself. For the Protestant Church of Jerusalem will comprehend persons using different liturgies, and subscribing different articles of faith, and it will sanction these differences, and hold both parties to be equally its members. . . . Of course it is a grave question what degrees of difference are compatible with the bond of Christian union: but the Archbishop of Canterbury has declared in the plainest language that some difficulties *are* compatible with it; and this is the great principle which I contend for.[62]

Pusey, who had initially looked with favour on the scheme as a way of drawing the Prussian Church towards an episcopal order, was nervous about possible links with the Monophysites, and in the end protested to the Archbishop about insufficient safeguards against proselytism from the Greek Church.[63] In fact Archbishop Howley had written to the Eastern Patriarchs at the time of Bishop Alexander's departure assuring them that Alexander's appointment in no way carried the implication of an invasion of jurisdiction, and assuring them of 'his longing desire to renew that ancient love towards the ancient Churches of the East which has been suspended for ages' and which, 'if restored by the will and blessing of God, may have the effect of healing the schisms which have brought the most grievous calamities on the Church of Christ.'[64]

The Revd George Williams, whom Howley nominated as Bishop Alexander's chaplain, gained an enthusiasm for the Eastern Churches from his two years in Jerusalem, and the subsequent two years he spent as chaplain in St. Petersburg. Of Tractarian sympathies, Williams framed part of the historical background to Anglican–Orthodox contacts with his study of the relationship between the non-jurors and the Greek Church, and it fell to him to complete J. M. Neale's history of the Antiochene patriarchate after Neale's death. Along with Williams as an early pioneer of contacts between Anglicans and Orthodox must be set William Palmer of Magdalen College, Oxford, who visited the Russian Church in 1840. Palmer eventually followed Newman into the Church of Rome and it was only after his death that his account of his visit to Russia was published, edited by Newman. Newman's judgement, in a letter to Palmer's brother, Edwin, was that William Palmer had done 'a real work' in his encounter with the Russian church leaders. 'He introduced among them the idea and the desirableness of Unity, and made them understand that the action of the Anglican establishment was not the measure of the Catholic religious feeling in this country.'[65] It was clear from Palmer's narrative, Newman wrote, that 'the Russian ecclesiastics . . . had all but given up the idea of unity, or of the Catholicity of the Church'.[66]

It was John Mason Neale, as we have already seen, who played one of the most significant parts in making English Christians aware of the Eastern Churches, by his historical writings and by his translations of so many of the great liturgical hymns. It was through Neale's influence, and that of George Williams, that the Eastern Churches Association came into being in 1864. The Association had the support of Pusey at the outset, but he was later to withdraw from membership as so many of the enthusiasts for reunion with the Eastern Church seemed to him to sit lightly to the *Filioque* (the clause 'and from the Son') in the Creed.[67] When Neale died in 1866, Williams, then Secretary of the Eastern Churches Association, was visiting Syria, and he recorded how Neale was commemorated at an Anglican Eucharist, celebrated according to the Scottish Liturgy, in the ruins of the Church of St. Symeon Stylites.[68] It was a fitting context in which to pay tribute to Neale's influence.

In 1870 Archbishop Alexander Lycurgus of Syros and Tenos paid a three month visit to the Orthodox communities in England and the opportunity was taken for theological discussions, held at Ely under the auspices of the bishop, Harold Browne. The Archbishop also met a number of eminent English churchmen, and received honorary degrees at both Oxford and Cambridge. He returned well pleased with his visit to report to the Ecumenical Patriarch 'that in England there exists an intense desire to effect some approximation to, and, if it were possible, a union with the Eastern Church, I believe, cannot be doubted'. Recognizing that the work of unity would take time, the Archbishop nonetheless urged that the Orthodox should not only accord Christian burial to Anglicans dying in the absence of an Anglican priest, but that they should offer to baptize Anglican infants when no Anglican priests were available.[69] Archbishop Lycurgus was to figure again in ecumenical discussions with Anglicans, when he was one of the leading Orthodox participants in the second Bonn Reunion Conference in 1875. At this gathering an agreement between Anglicans, Old Catholics, and Orthodox was reached on the *Filioque*, a concordat which Pusey found deeply troubling, convinced as he was of the rightness of the Western formula.[70]

Official contacts with the Eastern Churches, which owed much to the advocacy of the relatively small group of Anglicans who were concerned to promote them, went hand in hand with the development of an international Anglican identity expressed through the growth of the Lambeth conferences. When the encyclical of the First Conference in 1867 was published it was sent to the Orthodox Patriarchs, and twenty years later the Conference of 1888 included a special committee under the chairmanship of Bishop Harold Browne on relations between Anglicans and Orthodox.[71] This in part reflected Archbishop Benson's own interest in the Eastern Churches, which he fostered with messages of greeting to the Russian Church when it celebrated the nine-hundredth anniversary of Christianity in Russia in 1888. He had earlier asked Athelstan Riley to collect information for him when he visited Mount Athos in 1884, and two years later he sent him to Kurdistan to investigate the condition of the Nestorians, one result of which was the founding of the Mission to the Assyrian Christians. Benson also saw the re-establishment of the Jerusalem bishopric—following the Lutheran withdrawal from the scheme which had aroused such Tractarian fury forty years earlier—as an opportunity for building relationships with the Eastern Churches in the Holy Land. This brought him under considerable suspicion from Liddon and other High Churchmen, who were aware that the new bishop's stipend was to be largely paid by the CMS and the Mission to the Jews, whose record in proselytism amongst the Orthodox was not in their view satisfactory. There was undoubtedly misunderstanding, for Benson commended Bishop Blyth, as one charged 'to give living tokens by his conduct and conversation of that fraternal desire for union between the Orthodox Church of the East and the Church of England'. Blyth was, with the full backing of Benson, to 'reprove and discountenance all attempts at proselytism from the Orthodox Churches of the East'. The Patriarch of Jerusalem responded enthusiastically to this commendation.[72]

The growing contacts between Anglicans and the Eastern Churches were considerably forwarded by the personal efforts of two Anglican laymen, both from the Catholic wing of the Church, Athelstan Riley and W. J. Birkbeck. Birkbeck's knowledge of the Russian Church was unrivalled, and he was relied on for advice by successive Archbishops of Canterbury. He accompanied Mandell Creighton, then Bishop of Peterborough, to Russia in 1896, and Archbishop Maclagan of York the following year. In 1903 he made a further trip with Charles Grafton, Bishop of Fond du Lac, and one of the leading Anglo-Catholic bishops in America.[73] These contacts, and the dissemination of information about Orthodox theology and practice, laid the foundations for even closer relationships after the 1914–18 War, when the collapse of the Ottoman Empire and the Russian Revolution created situations of considerable suffering and hardship for many Eastern Christians. Archbishop Davidson was called on to use his considerable powers of diplomacy to try and achieve some kind of security for Christians in the Middle East, and in 1921 became the first Archbishop of Canterbury to take part in a Greek liturgical service, when he read the Gospel at the funeral of Dorotheus, the then acting holder of the Oecumenical Patriarchate, who had died suddenly whilst on a visit to London.[74] In 1922 a further indication of a growing closeness was signalled by the appointment of Archbishop Germanos to reside in London as *apokrisarios* (ambassador) of the Oecumenical Patriarch to the Archbishop of Canterbury, and by the declaration of the Holy Synod of Constantinople that 'the ordinations of the Anglican Episcopal Confession of bishops, priests, and deacons, possess the same validity as those of the Roman, Old Catholic, and Armenian Churches possess, inasmuch as all essentials are found in them which are held indispensable from the Orthodox point of view for the recognition of the "Charisma" of the priesthood derived from the Apostolic Succession'.[75] In 1920 and again in 1930 there was a significant Orthodox delegation invited as guests to the Lambeth Conference.

The Russian Diaspora after the First World War was of great importance in bringing Anglicans and Orthodox closer together. Physical proximity was necessary for real understanding. But what was also important was the concern of Anglicans for closer relations with the Eastern Churches, and it was the Tractarian understanding of the church, expressed classically in the so-called 'Branch' theory, which led Anglicans to recognize in the episcopal, but non-papal, character of the Orthodox Churches a pattern of church order to which they also adhered. As a result of that conviction, romantic at times as it undoubtedly was, the Orthodox came to be drawn into a wider ecumenical movement, and the treasures of Orthodox spirituality came to be shared with Christians in the West. It was also true that it was easier for Anglicans of more central churchmanship to welcome contacts with the Orthodox, which did not have the same sensitive connotations as overtures to Rome. Thus not only Archbishop Benson, but a bishop much trusted by him, John Wordsworth of Salisbury, devoted much energy to the fostering of relations with the Orthodox world.

In a rather surprising way Anglican contacts with the non-Chalcedonian Churches developed even more quickly than with the Chalcedonian Orthodox. This was in part the result of the persecution of these Christian minorities, notably the Armenians and the Nestorians, in the Ottoman Empire, and in part the consequence of the fact that these ancient Churches did not, for the most part, claim to be the one true Church in the way that either the Byzantine or the Roman Church did. They witnessed in their way to a sacramental understanding of Christianity which was not Roman and Ultramontane.

Once again it was largely those touched by the Catholic revival who pioneered the way, though the Armenian massacres drew many others to a concern for Christian people of whom they would otherwise have had no knowledge. There was a division of opinion, however, concerning dealings with churches officially regarded as heretical, because condemned by the Councils of Ephesus and Chalcedon. Pusey and Liddon took a strict line, as they had done with the *Filioque* clause. Others endeavoured to help these ancient churches, whilst suspending judgement on the extent to which their present teaching was in fact to be treated as clearly heretical. George Patrick

Badger, who was sent on a Mission to the Nestorians in 1838 with an official commendation from Archbishop Howley, wrote a valuable study of their liturgy and contemporary condition, which was edited by Neale, who, however, added a cautionary note, warning that 'Mr Badger is throughout an advocate for the Nestorians'.[76] When in Benson's archiepiscopate a Mission to the Assyrian Christians was set up, the leaders of that Mission were A. J. Maclean, later a bishop in Scotland, and W. H. Browne, from the Tractarian parish of St. Columba's, Haggerston. Their willingness to live as Orthodox monks, sharing the common life of the Assyrian community made a great impression, and equally aroused the opposition of American Presbyterian missionaries, whose Board received a report that many Assyrians had been 'led astray by the Ritualist party, and the loose morals taught by their new teachers in regard to Sabbath observance, wine drinking, and other things'.[77] In Oxford William Bright corresponded extensively with Maclean about the theology of the Nestorian services which the Mission press was publishing.[78] Occasional travellers, like Liddon and Bishop John Wordsworth, seized the opportunity for theological discussions with the Oriental Orthodox, particularly with the Coptic Church in Egypt and the Armenians in Jerusalem. In Wordsworth's biography there is an amusing account of the bishop's wife finding him learning Armenian late into the night, and wondering in her diary, 'Do all Bishops sit down to learn Armenian after preaching tiring sermons in Westminster Abbey?'[79] Writing in commendation of an important account of the Syrian Church, Bishop Westcott summarized the appeal of the ancient Oriental Churches to Anglicans:

These independent Churches appeal with especial force to England and to the Churches of the Anglican Communion. They lie, it is true, under the imputation of contrasted heresies, dating from the controversies of the fifth century; but those most competent to speak are satisfied that ... the accusation rests on the misunderstanding of technical terms, and can be cleared away by mutual explanations. Meanwhile the rival Communions are eager for education. They desire to learn fully the teaching of their own ancient formularies and of Holy Scripture. They are not committed to any modern errors. Their very existence through centuries of persecution and temptation is a proof of the vitality of their faith. They are characteristically national Churches. They guard with the most jealous care their apostolic heritage, and are still able to express it through the power of their own life. . . .

The Anglican Church ... strong by apostolic order and catholic sympathy, can approach the Syrian Christians without threatening their independence or disparaging the primitive traditions of a Communion older than itself. . . . It is under no temptation to seek either submission or uniformity from those whom it serves. It acknowledges the power of the Faith to harmonise large differences of intellectual and ritual expression, answering to differences of race and history, within the limits of the historic creed. It can wait for the issue it desires, taught by some home experience that stable reform must come from within. It can with good hope prepare the way for reconciling divided Churches through considerateness and patience[80]

It was on that basis that Anglicans reached out to make important contacts with the Oriental Orthodox Churches, which have played a significant part in drawing them, like the Byzantine Orthodox, into the mainstream of the ecumenical movement, as well as doing something to counteract the effect of centuries of isolation. The Tractarian renewal of the Anglican vision of the undivided Church of the early centuries gave such outreach its main impetus.

Rome and the Eastern Churches were inevitably at the centre of the ecumenical concerns flowing from the Catholic revival in Anglicanism. As far as the Protestant churches were concerned, attitudes varied from hostility to misunderstanding and suspicion in the earlier period. Later, Bishops like Gore were able to foster close friendships with Free Church leaders, and the changing climate nationally led to a diminution of suspicion between Anglicans of a Catholic persuasion and Free Churchmen. The recovery of a more sacramental and ecclesial understanding in the Free Churches, in part derived, though indirectly, from the Oxford Movement, also contributed. All that having been said, however, it was the Catholic vision of a reunited, episcopally ordered, sacramentally centred Church, international in character, but to which local churches would contribute their particular genius and outlook, which was the inspiration of ecumenical endeavour. The horizons of unity stretched beyond those of Arnold's *Principles of Church Reform* and were more firmly grounded in the living tradition of the Church.

X.   Catholic and critical

IN AN often cited analogy in the *Essay on Development* Newman wrote of 'the history of a philosophy or sect', comparing it to a stream which became 'more equable, and purer, and stronger, when its bed has become deep, and broad and full'.

Its beginnings are no measure of its capabilities, nor of its scope. At first, no one knows what it is, or what it is worth. It remains perhaps for a time quiescent: it tries, as it were, its limbs, and proves the ground under it, and feels its way. From time to time, it makes essays which fail, and are in consequence abandoned. It seems in suspense which way to go; it wavers, and at length strikes out in one definite direction. In time it enters upon strange territory; points of controversy alter their bearings; parties rise and fall about it; dangers and hopes appear in new relations, and old principles reappear under new forms; it changes with them in order to remain the same.[1]

This is in many ways an apt illustration for the new bearings in the Catholic revival in Anglicanism represented by the theological work of Charles Gore, Henry Scott Holland, and the 'Holy Party'; by the social thought and action which they and others encouraged; and, at a later date, by the Liberal Catholicism of *Essays Catholic and Critical*. In a different way the theological debates of the Anglo-Catholic Congresses represent another line of development in a new era, which indeed demanded change in order that the vision might remain the same.

The problem of change and continuity in the Christian Church and in Christian theology was one which pressed upon the nine-teenth century and continues to be of central concern. A renewed attention to tradition in Newman's *Lectures on the Prophetical Office* and the wider ecclesiological interests of the Tractarians reflect this. Critical questions from Germany taken up in England led men to scrutinize the character of the Bible and re-assess the nature of its authority. The controversy over *Essays and Reviews* in the early 1860s focused this in a particularly sharp way. Pusey in 1861, cited a strong summary passage from the *Westminster Review* to the effect that the consequence of the *Essays* was for 'the word of God, the creation, the fall, the redemption, justification, regeneration, and salvation, miracles, inspiration, prophecy, heaven and hell, eternal punishment, a day of judgment, creeds, liturgies, and articles, the truth of Jewish history and of Gospel narrative' to have been discarded 'in their ordinary, if not plain, sense'. He saw the seriousness of the challenge. 'If any one cannot rest on the authority of the Universal Church, attested as it is by prophecy, nor again, on the words of Jesus, he must take a long circuitous process of answer.'[2] It would need 'books, not essays' to respond to what Pusey saw as the 'random dogmatic scepticism' of the essayists, whose ecclesiastical position, moreover, raised the issue of the Church's standard of faith and its relation to critical scholarship. As Liddon told John Keble 'it becomes a question of limits'.[3] How the Church was to set·those limits and reconcile the claims of historical investigation and scholarly criticism with doctrinal affirmations was to exercise churchmen from the 1860s onwards. With Gore's essay in *Lux Mundi* (1889) it became apparent that theologians in the Catholic tradition could no longer simply endorse the approach of an older scholar like Pusey. It pained Pusey's disciple, Liddon, deeply that Gore, the Principal of the House set up in Oxford as a memorial to Pusey, should have so abandoned Pusey's tenets. 'It is', he wrote to his friend, Lathbury, 'practically a capitulation at the feet of the young Rationalistic Professors, by which the main positions which the old Apologists of Holy Scripture have maintained are conceded to the enemy, in deference to the "literary" judgment of our time.'[4] To Gore himself Liddon set out the issue:

We are not opposed in *this* sense, that I hold all Criticism to be mischievous, while you hold it to be generally illuminating and useful. For Criticism is an equivocal term, and is applied to very different kinds of Textual or Exegetical work. Dr Pusey, in one sense, was a great critic; in another, Strauss, and Bruno Bauer, and Feuerbach were. What the young 'experts' . . . mean by Criticism now, is, I suppose, that kind of discussion of doctrines and of documents which treats the individual reason as an absolutely competent and final judge, and which had the most differentiating merit of being independent of Church authority. At least this would be, I fancy, the general sense of the term in that home of modern Criticism, Protestant Germany. Criticism with Dr Pusey was, of course, something very different. It was the bringing of all that learning and thought could bring to illustrate the mind of Christian Antiquity which really guided him. All Criticism, I suppose, *really* proceeds on certain principles, preliminary assumptions for the critic to go upon. The question in all cases is, Whence do the preliminary assumptions come? A Catholic critic would say, 'From the general sense of the Church.' But a modern 'psychological' critic (if that is the right word) would say, 'From his own notion of the fitness of things, or from the outcome of literature at large.'[5]

Lux Mundi represented the response of a younger generation of Oxford churchmen to the need to relate their faith to contemporary intellectual and moral problems. The 'Holy Party' of Henry Scott Holland, Edward Talbot, Aubrey Moore, R. C. Moberly, J. R. Illingworth, Francis Paget, and others, was closely knit by ties of friendship and churchmanship. There were particularly close links with Keble College, opened in 1870 as a memorial to John Keble, of which Talbot was the first, and extremely young, Warden. Another contributor to *Lux Mundi*, Talbot's brother-in-law, Arthur Lyttelton, was a former Keble tutor and Master of Selwyn College, the church college of a decade later than Keble in Cambridge. Education and the commendation of the Christian faith in a University gradually losing its old clerical character were shared concerns and led to the publication of the essays. Gore wrote in the preface:

We have written . . . in this volume not as 'guessers at truth,' but as servants of the Catholic Creed and Church, aiming only at interpreting the faith we have received. On the other hand, we have written with the conviction that the epoch in which we live is one of profound transformation, intellectual and social, abounding in new needs, new points of view, new questions; and certain therefore to involve great changes in the outlying departments of theology, where it is linked on to other sciences, and to necessitate some general restatement of its claim and meaning.[6]

Theology had to develop, but that meant neither innovation which failed 'to preserve the type of the Christian Creed and the Christian Church', nor 'a narrowing and hardening of theology by simply giving it greater definiteness or multiplying its dogmas'.[7] The collection was subtitled 'a series of studies in the religion of the Incarnation', an indication of the shift of emphasis in theology in the nineteenth century from *Christus Redemptor* to *Christus Consummator*, as well as continuing a central concern of the Tractarians.

Gore's own essay, which so disturbed Liddon, was on 'the Holy Spirit and Inspiration'. He began by commenting on the appeal to 'experience' in religion, an appeal which had often been viewed with suspicion by the Oxford Movement Fathers and others who were properly hesitant about the emotionalism of certain kinds of Evangelicalism. 'What is meant by the term', he wrote, 'is often an excited state of feeling, rather than a permanent transformation of the whole moral, intellectual and physical being of man.' The presence of the Spirit, which is at the heart of Christian faith, is an encounter with the life of God, which manifests itself socially in the Church, but no less in the particularity of each individual's vocation. It is found in nature, and is given through the material order. It works gradually, so that the Old Testament, for instance, is in many respects superseded by the New. 'It is of the essence of the New Testament, as the religion of the Incarnation, to be final and catholic: on the other hand, it is of the essence of the Old Testament to be imperfect because it represents a gradual process of education by which man was lifted out of depths of sin and ignorance.'[8] From this evolutionary perspective Gore was able, when he came to discuss the particular question of biblical inspiration, to admit the presence of myth in the Old Testament, and to find no difficulty in seeing the Genesis narratives before Abraham as unhistorical. He pointed out that the Church was not bound by any particular theory of inspiration, and suggested that the mystical interpretation of the Alexandrian Fathers had often led to a depreciation of the historical sense. Most significantly of all, he repudiated the argument that historical questions about the Old Testament could be settled by an appeal to the authority of Jesus.

Our Lord, in His use of the Old Testament, does indeed endorse with the utmost emphasis the Jewish view of their own history.... What is questioned is that our Lord's words foreclose certain critical positions as to the character of Old Testament literature. For example, does His use of Jonah's resurrection, as a *type* of His own, depend in any real degree upon whether it is historical fact or allegory?[9]

Incarnation meant, Gore went on to argue, a sharing by God in the historicity of the human nature he assumed, with all its limitations of perception.

The Incarnation was a self-emptying of God to reveal Himself under conditions of human nature and from the human point of view. We are able to draw a distinction between what He revealed and what He used.... Thus He *used* human nature, its relation to God, its conditions of experience, its growth in knowledge, its limitation of knowledge. . . . He willed so to restrain the beams of Deity as to observe the limits of the science of His age, and He puts Himself in the same relation to its historical knowledge. Thus He does not reveal His eternity by statements as to what had happened in the past, or was to happen in the future, outside the ken of existing history. He made His Godhead gradually manifest by His attitude towards men and things about Him, by His moral and spiritual claims, by His expressed relation to His Father, not by any miraculous exemptions of Himself from the conditions of natural knowledge in its own proper province.[10]

Gore's perspective was evolutionary, a gradual unfolding of revelation. Critical questions were to be asked, but the Christian's faith was in the presence of the Spirit in the Church who brought past and present generations of Christians together. As Dr Ellis has commented, in this respect Gore was more cautious than the contributors to *Essays and Reviews*, for he 'did not conceive of a radical cultural and intellectual difference between the biblical authors and modern man which the essayists so eagerly anticipated, and it was a serious weakness in his theory that the Old Testament contained a lower level of inspiration, so that far more critical work could be allowed on it than on the New'.[11]

The same themes of the immanence of God, his gradual self-revelation and, allied with this, his self-limitation, appear in other essays in *Lux Mundi* as well as in Gore's subsequent writing. In his Bampton Lectures of 1891 Gore wrote of the evolutionary character of nature reflecting the pattern of God's own revelation.

Slowly, we know, in the struggle for existence, by tentative advances, through painfully-secured results, has the end been realized and the developed product attained. There is harmony here, wonderful harmony, between the spiritual and physical methods of God; and the result of all we know of God's working in nature and in Christ is thus to modify some popular notions of the divine omnipotence. In accurate theology God has been generally regarded as inherent in nature as well as transcending it; as working out a divine purpose *in* the whole ordered system. The system, the laws, are regarded as, in a certain sense, limiting Him, only because they express His mind. God is limited by no force external to Himself, but by His own being; and the laws of nature are, therefore, limits in his working, only so far as they express something of that law of perfect reason, that fundamental law, 'against which,' says St. Augustine, 'God can no more work than He can work against Himself'.[12]

It was, Gore continued, 'the spirit of western imperialism, which led men to conceive of God externally, as the great unfettered monarch of all worlds'. The omnipotence of God has been understood to mean 'not His universal power in and over all things which works patiently and unerringly in the slow-moving process to the far-off event, but rather the unfettered despot's freedom to do anything anyhow'.[13] Gore took this understanding further in his *Dissertations on subjects connected with the Incarnation* published in 1895, in which he linked it more closely with his kenotic doctrine of the Incarnation:

All this line of thought—all this way of conceiving of God's self-restraining power and wisdom—at least prepares our mind for that supreme act of respect and love for His creatures by which the Son of God took into Himself human nature to redeem it, and in taking it limited both His power and His knowledge so that He could verily live through all the stages of a perfectly human experience and restore our nature from within by a contact so gentle that it gave life to every faculty without paralyzing or destroying any.[14]

Aubrey Moore, a brilliant contributor to *Lux Mundi*, who was to die prematurely young, in his essay on the doctrine of God again emphasized the close connection between religious experience and theological reflection. The tension between deism and pantheism was paralleled by the tension between a mechanical and an organic view of nature. Thus the immanentist trend in contemporary philosophy could be held to be inimical to belief in God, where that belief was framed on a particular understanding of transcendence. Religion, urged Moore, has no quarrel with the doctrine of immanence: 'the religious equivalent for "immanence" is "omnipresence", and the omnipresence of God is a corollary of true monotheism'. In the Logos doctrine of the Greek Fathers, and in their doctrine of the Trinity, the philosopher's acknowledgement of 'the immanence of reason in the universe, and the rational coherence of all its parts' is linked firmly with the revelation of God in Christ.[15]

The change of perspective represented by *Lux Mundi* had been noticed by Liddon in 1884, when he wrote to Henry Scott Holland that he feared that 'the younger Churchmanship of Oxford was undergoing a silent but very serious change. . . . the new cares less for authority, and relies more on subjective considerations, and expects more from fallen humanity, and attaches less importance to the

Divine organisation and function of the Church, than did the old'. To yield to such influences meant sooner or later 'some essentially Pantheistic substitute for the Ancient Faith'.[16] When *Lux Mundi* was published Scott Holland himself thought it doubtful that it would have any impact, as he told his friend Bishop Copleston of Colombo.

Poor old book! I look at it and wonder. I thought it so dreadfully heavy and dull when I first read it: I never thought that we should induce anyone to read it outside the circle of our aunts and mothers, and a few patient-minded clergy. The old book itself looked conscious of its own dead weight: and never dreamt of this stormy and excited career. . . . We ourselves seemed to ourselves to have been saying these things for years; and to have heard everybody else saying them. Now suddenly we find it all spoken of as a bomb, a new Oxford movement, etc., etc. We wonder who we are.[17]

Enthusiasm there certainly was as well as disturbance. The young Cosmo Gordon Lang, then a student at Cuddesdon, wrote to his father urging him to read the book at once; it marked 'the absorption of the best "Broad Church" thought with "High Church"'.[18] For Lang himself the 'firm sacramental teaching which was the kernel of the Oxford Movement' combined with 'the candour, freedom and breadth of view which marked Maurice, Kingsley and Robertson of Brighton' was what was needed, and *Lux Mundi* represented exactly that.[19] Westcott, interestingly, although he had had an influence on Gore as a Harrow schoolboy, and on Holland as an ordinand, confessed that he had 'purposely refrained from reading *Lux Mundi*', but went on in the same letter to say how he could never understand how anyone reading the first three chapters of Genesis could believe that they were literal history. 'Are we not', he asked, 'going through a trial in regard to the use of popular language on literary subjects like that through which we went, not without sad losses, in regard to the use of popular language on physical subjects?' But for Westcott poetry was 'a thousand times more true than history', and critical historical questions did not touch him so deeply as they did others.[20]

Lang viewed Gore's essay in *Lux Mundi* as representing the coalescence of Broad Church and High Church theology. Gore himself preferred the description 'Liberal Catholicism', not meaning by that an accommodation of latitudinarian views, but a serious endeavour to relate the faith revealed in Scripture and articulated dogmatically in the creeds to contemporary questioning. In his

Bampton Lectures he aligned himself with what he believed to be 'ancient and Anglican orthodoxy' that 'the creeds are simply summaries of the original Christian faith as it is represented in Scripture', and 'the dogmatic decisions of councils' were 'formulas rendered necessary for no other purpose than to guard the faith of Scripture from what was calculated to undermine it'. This position was distinguished from both contemporary Roman theories viewing the ancient decisions of councils as 'simply one stage in a gradual process, by which the rudimentary consciousness of primitive Christianity was gradually expanded into a great dogmatic system, covering a much wider area of positive teaching than the original Christian faith, and supplying a good deal of additional information', and from the latitudinarian view that the theology of the councils was 'a needless metaphysical accretion upon genuine Christianity which it would do well to get rid of'.[21] Gore remained committed to this position, defending dogmatic faith and arguing that there were limits to the speculative freedom of those with teaching responsibility in the ordained ministry of the Church, but also criticizing the intransigence, narrowness, and, as he often saw it, disloyalty to the Church of England of those Anglo-Catholics who gave an uncritical allegiance to all things Roman. As Bishop of Oxford he wrote in his *Diocesan Magazine* in 1915: 'If the Anglican Church has a real message and vocation, it is because it embodies these principles of a liberal or comprehensive Catholicism, which both accepts the fundamental dogmas and also severely limits the dogmatic requirement.' He could neither 'identify Catholicism with Roman doctrine and practice, or . . . treat much that belongs to Protestantism as if it did not also belong in some real sense to the Church'. For that reason it was vital that Anglicans should be concerned about their own theological coherence, for it was central to the Anglican vocation to witness to the comprehensiveness of the Catholic Church, and that vocation could not be fulfilled in a way which served to unite a divided Christendom without a greater theological and practical unity between Anglicans.[22] To this end Gore looked to a greater degree of self-government for the Church, which was to be realized in the setting up of the Church Assembly, though not according to Gore's wish that the franchise should be of the confirmed and not simply of the baptized.

In 1917 he viewed the state of the Church of England pessimistically, lamenting that his ideal of Liberal Catholicism seemed to have no attraction for either 'Catholics' or 'Liberals'. 'The advanced people', he complained to a friend, 'do not believe in the Church of England but only in their own organization, and they will not co-operate in any movement which tends to make a distinction between the creeds and what they call the Catholic doctrine of the Eucharist.'[23] Towards the end of his life, in a pamphlet entitled *The Anglo-Catholic Movement Today* (1925), he agreed with the proposition that the Anglo-Catholic 'must insist on being Catholic before he is "Anglican"'. but then went on to affirm that there was an obligation for the Anglo-Catholic to be loyal to the tradition in which he lived. He was under an obligation to follow the order and pattern of the Book of Common Prayer.[24] If doctrine and discipline, faith and order, went together, and were to be insisted upon with reference to Modernist teachers, then the same insistence was appropriate when it was not Modernists but Anglo-Catholics using Roman liturgical forms and sacramental devotions. Membership of a church imposed a corporate moral obligation, and to claim to be a Catholic meant the recognition of that moral obligation. As his biographer comments, this stern attitude earned Gore the nickname of 'the evening wolf' amongst some of the younger Anglo-Catholics.[25] Gore saw the need for coherence in Anglicanism; he also saw the need for liberalism, insofar as that meant a protest against the multiplication of dogmas. Firmly Catholic as he was in his affirmation that Christianity was not to be regarded as 'merely or primarily a doctrine of salvation to be apprehended by individuals', but as 'the establishment of a visible society as the one divinely constituted home of the great salvation, held together not only by the inward Spirit but also by certain manifest and external institutions', he was also alert to the distortions to which Catholicism was liable. There was a need to recognize the danger of 'formalism or materialism which has always dogged the steps of the sacramentalist, and the peril of subordinating moral to doctrinal considerations which has always dogged the steps of the dogmatist'. Some have doubted whether he ever really succeeded in reconciling the poles of coherence and comprehensiveness in his professed Catholicism, even when his greatness as a prophet and an apologist is recognized.[26]

Gore died in 1932, a year before the centenary of Keble's Assize Sermon. Six years earlier, in 1926, another collected volume of essays appeared, edited by Gordon Selwyn, with the title *Essays Catholic and Critical*. The writers consciously looked back to *Lux*

Mundi, of which Selwyn wrote in the preface that it was a book which had 'exercised upon many of them a formative influence and still has a living message'.[27] As the *Lux Mundi* contributors had been centred on Oxford, the *Catholic and Critical* essayists were centred on Cambridge. The essayists owed much to the Modernist theologians in the Roman Church; they were also aware that they were writing in a post-war situation which was less inclined to the easy evolutionary optimism of the late-nineteenth century. 'Liberal Catholicism', they wrote, 'appeals to . . . facts of religious experience as facts which, though embedded in history, cannot be adequately accounted for by historical science alone.' Repudiating 'evolutionary immanentism', the 'facts of human freedom and accountability, and the experiences of guilt and non-attainment' were emphasized. These pointed to the otherness of God, a redemption 'from above', and the Christian experience of such a redemption centred in Christ.[28] The institutional and worshipping life of the Church were not mere adjuncts to theology but integral to it. 'The oil and wine of the Christian life can only be preserved in vessels; and if creed and dogma provide the intellectual vessels, the Church's pastoral and worshipping system provides those needed for more common and day-to-day uses.' The essayists differed as to the degree of symbolism and ceremonial which was appropriate in worship, but there was no difference as to 'the desirability, or indeed necessity, of symbol and ceremony *in itself*'.

Symbolism in worship is an expression of a common faith and feeling, representing often more powerfully than words the religious experience and the mental attitude characteristic of the Christian revelation. It is thus a great safeguard against eccentricity of opinion and sentiment on the one hand and against a worldly and secularized worship on the other. It is one of the arteries of the *Corpus Christi*, by which the blood of the regenerate life circulates to all the members. It thus embodies and transmits in definite form that body of religious experience which provides Catholic theology with its subject-matter.[29]

This emphasis on religious experience is well illustrated by Wilfred Knox's essay on the authority of the Church. Knox characterized Christian experience as 'that apprehension of God through the person of Christ which is vouchsafed to all Christians who in any way attempt to live up to the standard of their profession'. Thus it must not be confined to the particular experiences of mystical prayer and devotion, though such experiences should not be neglected. In the development of Christian doctrine 'the general religious experience of the whole body of Christians has necessarily been of primary importance', and the importance attached to certain sees in the early Church was not linked to their possessing a body of apostolic doctrine additional to that witnessed to by the New Testament documents, but to the fact that 'the circumstances of their foundation and early history guaranteed that the Christian consciousness of those Churches had from the first rested on a basis of orthodox Christian teaching.'[30]

The whole sum of the Christian experience of the Church at any given moment must be an inarticulate mass of opinion comprehending in general the whole body of divine truth as revealed in Jesus; its only way of articulating itself will be its power to express approval of some particular statement of the faith as put forward by an individual theologian, unless the Church is to have some means of expressing its corporate voice.[31]

With the ending of persecution the Church was able to articulate her teaching and put into a coherent form 'the sense in which she interpreted in the light of Christian experience the original deposit of faith which she had received from her Lord'. Nonetheless, Knox noted, it was characteristic of those doctrinal statements that their aim was the exclusion of some doctrinal tendency believed to be fatal to the Christian life, rather than the promulgation of a truth not hitherto generally held. Summing up the character of doctrinal statements and their process of formulation, Knox wrote:

The organ through which the Church pronounces must be in a position to judge correctly what the Christian religious experience really is. This involves not merely intellectual capacity to understand the meaning of any doctrine and its relation to the rest of the Christian system, but also that insight into the Christian character which is only derived from a genuine attempt to live the Christian life.[32]

The man who lives the life will know the doctrine, but as the Christian life is not simply an individual matter but the life of the Church the Christian community, so 'the Catholic faith is an organic whole, the truth of which is guaranteed more by its intrinsic value as proved by past experience than by the oracular infallibility of certain isolated definitions'.[33] As Milner-White entitled a section of his essay, the Catholic Church is 'a Sacrament of Holy Spirit to the world'. Protestantism, he wrote, has an important critical function, but ultimately it is dependent upon the Catholic church. 'The Protestant bodies ... in their general meaning ... stand to the Church which is the formal sacrament of Holy Spirit to mankind as, in the sphere of Christian devotion, the sermon stands to the Eucharist or momentary prayer to age-long liturgy.'[34]

In the concluding essay of the book, on the Eucharist, Sir Will Spens, whose own earlier work *Belief and Practice* (1915) anticipated certain themes of *Essays Catholic and Critical*, attempted to meet some of the contemporary criticisms of Catholic sacramental theology. In writing on the Real Presence, Spens argued that just as in Jewish thought the presence of God was conceived of in nature, in the chosen people, and in the Holy of Holies in the glory of the *Shekinah*, and the last was not thought to be exclusive of the two former, so Christ is present in the Eucharist in a way which does not deny his presence to his Church in other ways. The bread and wine of the Eucharist may indeed be said to be changed by consecration, in that 'they acquire a new property, namely, that their devout reception secures and normally conditions participation in the blessings of Christ's sacrifice, and therefore in His life.' The receiving of Communion does not create the Presence, for 'the opportunity for reception and appropriation is afforded by the sacramental Gifts.' Just as a coin has certain natural properties and a certain purchasing power, and may be described as an effectual symbol, so, and to a far greater extent, are the Eucharistic elements effectual symbols.

The Eucharistic sequences and the natural sequences are both determined by the divine will. In and through consecration those complexes of opportunities of experience which we call bread and wine are changed, not by any change in the original opportunities of experience, but by the addition of new opportunities of experience which are equally ultimate and have far greater significance.[35]

Anticipating in a way the Eucharistic terminology suggested by Schillebeeckx, Spens commends the term 'transvaluation' as one which may be properly applied to the Eucharistic action. He goes on to argue that, if it is proper for Christ to be adored, then Eucharistic adoration is legitimate.

[The Eucharistic elements are] objects which are a direct expression of our Lord's being and nature; which exist in direct dependence on that being and nature as such an expression, and which enable us not only to participate in the blessings of His sacrifice but to be strengthened with His life, thus affording a relation to Him even more intimate than that which His natural body made possible.[36]

Writing at a time of considerable controversy over the reservation of the Sacrament, Spens goes on to maintain that if communion from the Reserved Sacrament is allowed, then adoration must also be allowed.

When this finds expression in devotional practices, what is involved is simply the transportation—in time, though not in thought, and for convenience though not in principle—of elements which are intrinsic parts of the Eucharistic rite. Thus, the devotional use of the Reserved Sacrament is not something independent of Communion and deriving from some separate conception. It is precisely because devout reception unites us to our Lord that the Reserved Sacrament is His body, that He is present in a special manner, and that He can thus be adored.[37]

Spens may thus be said to draw out the implications of Keble's words in his tract on Eucharistical adoration, that 'wherever Christ is there He is to be adored', and to share the perspective for which Von Balthasar has much more recently argued:

There is such a thing as 'spiritual communion' which is not intended to replace sacramental communion, but which, as it were, flows out from the latter on to all those who desire to share in the great banquet which the Father gives. And consequently there is, too, such a thing as the 'veneration of the holy of holies' wherever bread and wine from the celebration of the Mass are reserved, whether visible to the faithful or not. Such veneration is the act of the heart as it meditates on and thinks itself towards that point where the eternal love breaks into time and where time is broken open to the approach of eternal love.[38]

Ten years after the publication of *Essays Catholic and Critical*, and three years after the celebration in 1933 of the centenary of the beginning of the Oxford Movement, Michael Ramsey's publication of *The Gospel and the Catholic Church* developed further some of the characteristic themes of Anglican Catholicism. The book was intended as 'a study of the Church, and its doctrine, and unity and structure, in terms of the Gospel of Christ crucified and risen'. Not only was the Church to be seen as 'the extension of the Incarnation', it was to be closely related to the Passion of Jesus. Only a deep recognition of what this meant would provide a truly Christian understanding of the disunity of the Church and the quest for unity. 'If the problems about schism and reunion mean dying and rising with Christ', Ramsey warned, 'they will not be solved through easy humanistic ideas of fellowship and brotherhood, but by the hard road of the Cross.'[39] He wrote conscious of an impasse between Catholics and Evangelicals, the former thinking of 'the Church as a divine institution, the gift of God to man', emphasizing 'outward order and continuity and the validity of its ministry and sacraments' so that unity was 'inconceivable apart from the historical structure of the Church', and the latter seeing 'the divine gift not in the institution but in the Gospel of God', and so thinking less of Church order than of the Word of God and justification by faith. 'The two traditions puzzle one another. The one seems legalistic; the other seems individualistic.'[40]

The New Testament understanding of the death of Jesus and of the participation of Christians in that dying is first probed. 'Christianity', Ramsey wrote, 'is never solitary.' 'It is never true to say that separate persons are united to Christ, and then combine to form the Church; for to believe in Christ is to believe in One whose Body is a part of Himself and whose people are His own humanity, and to be joined to Christ is to be joined to Christ-in-His-Body.' Individualism, therefore, has no place in Christianity. It is 'through membership in the Body' that 'the single Christian is discovered in new ways and becomes aware that God loves him, in all his singleness, as if God had no one else to love.'[41]

Consideration is next given to the meaning of unity. This does not have to do simply with the present experience of Christian believers, it is apostolic unity, binding Christians to the original historical events from which the Church took its origin. In the New Testament the universal church is primary, and the local church is a manifestation of it, so the unity of the Church does not consist in the adding together of small societies. As P. T. Forsyth put it: 'it was one Church in many manifestations; it was not many churches in one convention'.[42] That unity is rooted ultimately in the unity of God, and the outward order of the Church is that which expresses that unity. In the struggle with Gnosticism the Christian writings and the succession of bishops are emphasized as the organs of the Church's unity and continuity, and so the organism of 'Sacraments, Episcopacy, Scriptures and Creeds' emerges as the pattern of church order.[43] But all these must be seen as belonging together. Given emphasis in isolation they distort the true catholicity of the Church.

Thus the Gospel may be seriously obscured by a piety which emphasises Christ's presence in the Eucharist and dwells too little upon His presence in the baptized; or by a use of the Creeds as scholastic definitions, which ignores their close relation to the Eucharist and to the scriptures; or by a reverence for Scripture, which ignores the ministry and the Creeds as organs of the society wherein Scripture grew.[44]

As far as the Papacy is concerned, a primacy might be allowed which was kept closely related to the organic unity of sacraments, episcopacy, scriptures, and creeds.

A Papacy which expresses the general mind of the Church in doctrine, and which focuses the organic unity of all the Bishops and of the whole Church, might well claim to be a legitimate development in and through the Gospel. But a Papacy, which claims to be a source of truth over and above the general mind of the Church and which wields an authority such as depresses the due working of the other functions of the one Body, fails to fulfil the main tests. This is where the issue lies; and the fuller discussion of the ministry, of the sacraments, and of authority must precede a fuller answer to the question of the Papacy in history.[45]

Ultramontanism is rejected, but the collegiality emphasized by the Second Vatican Council and the understanding of primacy put forward in the *Final Report* of the Anglican–Roman Catholic International Commission is anticipated here. The Church is to be understood as organism not as institution; it 'is defined not in terms of itself, but in terms of Christ, whose Gospel created it and whose life is its indwelling life.'[46]

Ramsey argued that episcopacy is misunderstood if it is isolated from the life of the Church, which is its context, for the function of the episcopate is to represent 'that general church life of which the prophets must know themselves to be a part, and that universal family in which all fellowships are made full'.[47] Again and again the stress is on the place of Eucharist, or episcopacy, or liturgical worship, or creed, in establishing the Christian in the wholeness of the

Gospel, whose heart is the death and resurrection of Jesus. Thus the Catholic creed frees the Christian 'from partial rationalisms, such as have identified Christianity with the Bible, or with some scholastic system, or with some humanistic shibboleth; and it delivers him into an orthodoxy which no individual and no group can possess, since it belongs only to the building up of the one Body in love'.

As he receives the Catholic sacrament and recites the Catholic creed, the Christian is learning that no single movement nor partial experience within Christendom can claim his final obedience, and that a local Church can claim his loyalty only by leading him beyond itself to the universal family which it represents. Hence the Catholic order is not a hierarchical tyranny, but the means of deliverance into the Gospel of God and the timeless Church.[48]

If the age of the Fathers is to be reverenced it is not from any motive of antiquarian imitation but because of the balance to be discerned in the worship, life, and order of the Church of their day.[49] When the Tractarians printed at the head of the *Tracts for the Times* the words 'OUR APOSTOLIC DESCENT' they did not mean, Ramsey went on, 'merely a doctrine about the status of the clergy, a revived clericalism, but a belief that the rites in English churches are not only acts wrought between Christ and Englishmen, but acts of Christ in His one universal Church in which Englishmen share through its representatives on English soil'.[50] Drawing on the ecclesiology of F. D. Maurice, with its strong links with St. John and the Greek Fathers, the unity of the Church, he argued, is to be seen in 'the dependence of all individuals, parties, movements, experiences, upon the one historical family founded by Christ'. 'The historic structure bears witness to this family, and Baptism, Eucharist, Creeds, Episcopate, Scripture are the "signs of the spiritual constitution", things not Anglican, nor Roman, nor Greek, nor Lutheran, nor Calvinist, but things belonging to the one people of God.'[51]

Summing up in a final chapter, Ramsey linked the quest for Christian unity closely with the deeper experience of the Passion of Jesus, wherein church order had its meaning. 'The unification of outer order can never move faster than the recovery of inward life.' Unity and holiness; order, theology, and spirituality belong together, as he was to emphasize many times during his archiepiscopate. The way to unity is difficult because it is the way of the Cross, and so although schemes of reunion may fail 'their failure may be no loss if men are thereby driven back to those issues of death and resurrection wherein the unity of God is found.'[52] The episcopate is 'the organ of unity and continuity' in the Church, it is not simply to be justified on utilitarian and functional grounds.

Its meaning is seen in the rites of ordination and in the ordering of every Eucharist. Every ordination and every Eucharist is the act of Christ in His one Body, and the Episcopate expresses this fact in outward order. The Eucharist celebrated in any place is the act of the one family as represented in that place; and the validity of the ministry and of the rite is bound up with its meaning as the act of the universal Church. Hence, when historic Christendom is divided, the meaning of its orders and of its Eucharist is maimed; no longer are they performed with the authority and the outward commission of the *whole* visible Church. . . . To seek unity apart from the historic order is to treat the Eucharist as a focus for groups of Christians in fellowship, rather than as the one λειτουργία into which all groups must die.[53]

Indiscriminate intercommunion is, it is suggested, an easy option: 'it can foster the idea that the one Body does not matter, and that groups of Christians can rightly join in one Eucharist and then return to their separate organisms'. The acceptance of the pain of disunity is one of the ways in which unity comes about, for through such pain there is a participation in the Passion of Christ. The same centrality of the death and resurrection of Jesus is what places the Church over against sentimental humanism. The cross is central. 'The Church can use and bless and learn from humanistic movements only if it also points them to the issues of the Cross.'[54] So, Ramsey concluded:

The question, whether the movement towards unity will or will not take Church order seriously, involves the deeper question;—whether unity is sought in terms of the historical death and resurrection or in terms of humanistic fellowship; and whether Jesus is known as the supreme example of our human values, or as the Messiah who came to die.[55]

The Gospel and the Catholic Church must be judged to be one of the most significant contributions by an Anglican theologian to an ecumenical ecclesiology, and that not least because its author as Archbishop of Canterbury was able, in a post-war situation and in a changed ecumenical climate, to forward the reconciliation of the churches on many fronts. The sympathy with the perspectives of the Greek Fathers contributed significantly to the dialogue with Orthodoxy in the theological conference in Moscow in 1956, when he noted the 'deep common understanding of the Church's being and its life in union with God, the Blessed Trinity',[56] and in the exchanged visits with the Eastern Patriarchs leading to the setting up of the Anglican-Orthodox Doctrinal Commission. No less significant were the ecumenical visits to Rome and the promoting of the Anglican–Methodist Conversations, even though the latter were not in the end found acceptable.

Michael Ramsey wrote *The Gospel and the Catholic Church* to interpret the Catholic and Evangelical traditions to each other and to affirm the biblical grounding of Catholic order. Faith was never the isolated response of the individual; it always belonged within the corporate context of the Church. That sense of the community of faith meant that alongside ecclesiological questions of faith and order went a concern for an understanding of the relation of church and society. In *Lux Mundi* W. J. H. Campion's essay on 'Christianity and Politics' urged the holding together of an emphasis on Christ as the fulfilment and restoration of the order of creation and on Christ as the redeemer who creates new and unthought of possibilities. Campion related political and social morality to the Trinitarian understanding of God and, following Coleridge and Maurice, emphasized the Catholic character of the Church and the human clue to that character being found in the family rather than the state.

The Church is essentially Catholic, and only incidentally national. It is their Catholic character so far as it remains, at least their Catholic ideal, which gives to the different fragments of the Church their strength and power. The 'Church of England' is a peculiarly misleading term. The Church of Christ in England is, as Coleridge pointed out, the safer and truer phrase. And this fundamental Catholicism, this correspondence not to one or another nation, but to humanity, rests on the appeal to deeper and more permanent needs than those on which the State rests. It is thus that the true type of the Church is rather in the family than in the state, because the family is the primitive unity of organized social life. Not in the order of time, but in the order of reason, the Church is prior to the State, for man is at once inherently social and inherently religious. And therefore it is only in the Church that he can be all that it is in his true nature to be.[57]

The same year that saw the publication of *Lux Mundi* also saw the founding of the Christian Social Union, giving practical expression to the theological perspective of the 'Holy Party'. One of its

members, Wilfrid Richmond, a former Keble tutor and subsequently
Warden of Glenalmond, was invited to give a series of lectures at
Sion College in London, and these were delivered the following year
under the title, *Economic Morals*. Scott Holland contributed a preface, lamenting that Christians lived 'as shuttlecocks, bandied about
between our political economy and our Christian morality'.[58] Under
Westcott's presidency the Christian Social Union took shape, and in
Gore's judgement it was Scott Holland who was at its centre.
Reflecting much that he shared in common with Holland, Gore
wrote that 'the Church is to express humanity at its fullest and best,
as a social organism or universal brotherhood'. A social understanding of the Trinity and a strong incarnationalism provided the theological grounding.[59]

The Christian Social Union was not the only indication of social
concern with which the *Lux Mundi* group and their associates were
linked. The 1880s saw new relationships being forged between the
universities, public schools, and slum areas, particularly in London.
Not all of these missions and settlements were the product of the
incarnational sacramentalism of the new generation of Anglican
High Churchmen, but the part they played was of major importance.
T. H. Green, an idealist in philosophy and with a strong concern for
the amelioration of the condition of the poor, influenced not only a
generation of Balliol men, but also many of the *Lux Mundi* group.
Samuel Barnett, the vicar of St. Jude's, Whitechapel, forged Oxford
links and drew undergraduates to experience life in the East End. In
1883 he preached in Oxford, and from meetings which followed
came the founding of Toynbee Hall, the young Cosmo Lang playing
a prominent part and so earning the rebuke of Jowett that his
business at Oxford was not 'to reform the East End of London, but to
get a First Class in the School of Literae Humaniores'.[60] Barnett
urged his undergraduate audience to recognize 'that little can be
done *for*, which is not done *with* the people'.

It is the poverty of their own life which makes the poor content to inhabit
'uninhabitable' houses, and content also to allow improved dwellings to
become almost equally uninhabitable. It is the same poverty of life which
makes so many careless to cleanliness, listless about the unhealthy condition
of their workshops, and heedless of anything beyond the enjoyment of a
moment's excitement.

'Such poverty of life', he went on, 'can best be removed by contact
with those who possess the means of higher life.'

Friendship is the channel by which the knowledge—the joys—the faith—the hope which belong to one class may pass to all classes. It is distance that makes friendship between classes almost impossible, and, therefore, residence among the poor is suggested as a simple way in which Oxford men may serve their generation. By sharing their fuller lives and riper thoughts with the poor they will destroy the worst evil of poverty. They will also learn the thought of the majority—the opinion of the English nation—and they will do something to weld Classes into Society.[61]

Gore maintained a close friendship with Barnett, acknowledging shared concerns in social reform and educational ideals, though noting that 'directly we touch religious observances or ecclesiastical attitudes to ritual we part company, and do not even try to sympathise with each other's point of view'.[62] For Gore and his friends the settlement principle, of the privileged identifying with and living amongst the poor, was the same incarnational principle which lay at the heart of Catholic sacramental worship and ecclesiology. Barnett's social idealism seemed to those who thought in this way to lack a deep theological root, and it was out of this concern that Oxford House was formed in Bethnal Green.

If Balliol was the Oxford home of Toynbee Hall, Keble was that of Oxford House. E. S. Talbot, the Warden of Keble, commended the House as founded on a basis which was religious and Christian, but the religion was 'to be a foundation and not a fence'. 'Men will be welcome to join in the work who could scarcely define their relation to Christianity or the Church of England.'[63] The first head was James Adderley, who looked to Gore as his theological and spiritual mentor. He was only there for three years, founding some six years later the Society of the Divine Compassion, along with a former Keble undergraduate, H. E. Hardy, who, as Father Andrew, was to have a notable pastoral ministry. The SDC was one of the first communities in the Church of England to look to Franciscan ideals for inspiration, but initially Adderley, like Lowder, was moved by St. Vincent de Paul.

S. Vincent was a Christian Social Reformer, and 'Christian Socialism' is in the air. . . . our most 'modern' and 'original' methods both in philanthropy and church work, were known and in full swing 250 years ago, and emanated from the brain of one man, and that man a poor peasant priest of the French Church.[64]

In 1888, at the instigation of Talbot, another Keble man, A. F. Winnington-Ingram, became Head of Oxford House, going on from there to be first Bishop of Stepney and then Bishop of London. He wrote that of the twelve churches in Bethnal Green only two had any congregations at all, and he recorded meeting a sad incumbent who after twenty-five years walked the streets of his parish unrecognized. It cost Winnington-Ingram £200 a year to keep the sick of St. Matthew's parish in milk and eggs.[65] Only one per cent of the population went to church, and he had to warn those who came to help him that the typical pattern of a Sunday for most men in the parish was to lie in bed until 11 or 12; a visit to the pub until 3; 'the great dinner of the week', followed by 'a lie down on the bed in shirt sleeves until five, with a pot of beer and *Lloyd's Weekly*'; then tea, followed by a walk, and an early night ready for work the next morning.[66]

Settlements, communities formal and informal and social theology sacramentally grounded, sprang from this new generation of churchmen. As J. R. Illingworth noted in a letter in 1912, it was a 'very interesting fact that when five of us started the first "Holy Party" . . . in 1875, it was the germ of the C.S.U.—of Mirfield, and of *Lux Mundi* and all the other writing of the party'.[67]

More strident than the CSU and the Settlements was Stewart Headlam's Guild of St. Matthew, founded in Bethnal Green in 1877. The Guild was strongly sacramental, coupling with the aim of promoting 'frequent and reverent worship in the Holy Communion' the promotion of 'the study of social and political questions in the light of the Incarnation', as well as endeavouring to remove the prejudices of Secularists against the Church. The Guild advocated a more representative church polity; supported land reform; and had links with the Fabian Society, on whose executive Headlam served on three occasions. 'We are', Headlam proclaimed, 'socialists because we are sacramentalists.' It ought not to be forgotten that Randall Davidson, when serving as Archbishop Tait's chaplain, was elected as chairman of the Junior Clergy Society in which Headlam and his friends were active, and through that connection took part in meetings with Trade Union leaders. Headlam was enthusiastic for the work of Henry George, *Progress and Poverty*, which, it was reported, Davidson had induced Queen Victoria to read. She found it difficult.[68] With Davidson's predecessor as Archbishop of Canterbury, Frederick Temple, Headlam tangled when Temple was Bishop of London. This was in relation to another of Headlam's causes, the Church and Stage Guild, which Temple considered did not sufficiently oppose what he saw as the morally corrupting influence of the ballet. 'The Ballet', he wrote to Headlam, 'does suggest what had better not be suggested.' Headlam protested, only to be countered with the observation that 'when you have persuaded the ballet-dancers to practise their art in proper clothing the case will be altered.'[69]

After the 1914–18 War the theme of social concern was one of the strands which was taken up by the Anglo-Catholic Congresses, the first of which was held in London in 1920. The aim of the Congress was both evangelistic—'to bring men and women to a true realisation of our Lord Jesus Christ as their personal Saviour and King'— and ecclesial—'to demonstrate the place of Catholicism within the English Church'.[70] There were four speakers on the theme of the Church and social and industrial problems: Gore, G. K. Chesterton, Mr Moore of the Rubber-Workers Union, and E. K. Talbot. Gore urged the witness of Christian brotherhood, the witness of the religious life, and the witness of personal morality. He was critical of establishment Erastianism and equally critical of moves to make the marriage laws diverge from Christian standards. He strongly condemned birth control as the separation of 'the sexual relationship from its divine purpose in the procreation of children by mechanical means'. 'Both inside marriage and outside it, this practice is sinful and will ruin any nation in the long-run which adopts and allows it.'[71] It is a signal reminder of the change in Anglican moral theology in this area to read these words. Talbot summoned his hearers to the mission of reclaiming 'the secular order for the kingdom of God', lest the 'Catholic faith' became 'the hobby of a small coterie, instead of a force for laying hands on the whole world'.[72] The second Congress, in 1923, was the occasion of the moving appeal by Frank Weston of Zanzibar, which was as notable for its social gospel as for its devotion to the Blessed Sacrament. Weston pressed his point home forcefully:

If you are prepared to say the Anglo-Catholic is at perfect liberty to rake in all the money he can get no matter what the wages are that are paid, no matter what the conditions are under which people work; if you say that the Anglo-Catholic has a right to hold his peace while his fellow citizens are living in hovels below the level of the streets, this I say to you, that you do not yet know the Lord Jesus in his Sacrament. You have begun with the Christ of Bethlehem, you have gone on to know something of the Christ of Calvary—

but the Christ of the Sacrament, not yet. . . . If you are Christians then your Jesus is one and the same: Jesus on the Throne of his glory, Jesus in the Blessed Sacrament, Jesus received into your hearts in Communion, Jesus with you mystically as you pray, and Jesus enthroned in the hearts and bodies of his brothers and sisters up and down the country. And it is folly—it is madness—to suppose that you can worship Jesus in the Sacraments and Jesus on the Throne of glory, when you are sweating him in the souls and bodies of his children. . . .

You have got your Mass, you have got your Altar, you have begun to get your Tabernacle. Now go out into the highways and hedges where not even the Bishops will try to hinder you. Go out and look for Jesus in the ragged, in the naked, in the oppressed and sweated, in those who have lost hope, in those who are struggling to make good. Look for Jesus. And when you see him, gird yourselves with his towel and try to wash their feet.[73]

In 1925 the first Anglo-Catholic Summer School of Sociology was held at Keble College. This school, and those which followed, were to have a significant influence on Anglican social thinking, both directly and through the closely linked 'Christendom group'.[74] The ecclesiology of the Summer School was Anglo-Catholic; the speakers were drawn from a wider circle, and included Charles Raven, William Temple, Henry Slesser, Gabriel Gillett, Ruth Kenyon, T. S. Eliot, V. A. Demant, and others.[75] A notable contributor was W. G. Peck, a former Methodist minister ordained into the Church of England, whose Hale Lectures of 1933, *The Social Implications of the Oxford Movement*, set Christian thinking about the ordering of society in a firmly incarnational, sacramental, and Trinitarian context. The doctrine of the Incarnation, wrote Peck, 'constitutes the secure differentiation of Christian theism from deism, with its modifications in dualism and pluralism upon the one hand, and from all systems, whether of pantheism or of absolute idealism, which identify God and the Universe, upon the other'. The Incarnation is the affirmation of 'a new cosmic co-ordination of which man, cohering in the redeemed social relation, is intended to be the instrument'.[76] The doctrine of the Trinity affirmed that 'the personal-social principle' was God's very nature, and as it is the Trinitarian God who is man's creator and end, the very heart of man's spiritual life is to be found in this same personal-social mode. The Eucharist is the redemption of man's social life; the sacramental principle involves the notion of human cohesion, and 'sacraments are the characteristic functions of the Church', 'The Church acting in her Sacraments sets forth the principle of a co-operative fellowship in which society is thoroughly and completely personal, and personality is thoroughly and completely social.'[77] 'Catholic dogma', Peck wrote, 'must judge the burning of wheat and cotton and meat, not only as economic idiocy, but as an insult to the Blessed Sacrament', just as the description of the unemployed as 'superfluous' was an insult to the Incarnation.[78] Colonial exploitation of natural resources and of native peoples in the interests of capital investment were, he went on, 'a steady contradiction of the Gospel and a constant denial of the fellowship taught and offered by the Church'. 'The suggestion of racial superiority conveyed in a hundred open or disguised forms has traduced the Catholic Gospel of equality in Christ', and behind that imperialism of race lay an economic system which fuelled it.[79] Peck was well aware that the Tractarian leaders were often accused of a cloistered academicism and a narrowly religious vision. He argued, however, that that criticism could be overplayed and that it was necessary to establish the central principles of doctrine and ecclesiology expressed in sacramental worship if the mission of the Church in society was to be fulfilled. So, he insisted:

We do not approach an understanding of the Oxford Movement unless we see in it the resurgence of another conception of the basis and purpose of world-order. The Oxford Revival did not merely remind men of spiritual reality. It reminded them of the Church, which is a specific social form supernaturally founded and shaped. And our thesis is that only upon the principles of that Divine Society can the true elements and fruits of modern culture be rescued from the waste and frustration now threatened as the result of their misuse, and made available as an unprecedented means to the spiritual end.[80]

Although this social gospel was a genuine mark of Anglo-Catholic thinking and of the Congresses, it was by no means the only one. At the first Congress in 1920 there were papers on biblical criticism and contemporary philosophy; on problems of church authority and ecclesiastical discipline; on Christian unity and corporate and personal religion. In 1923 the Congress was on the central theme of the Gospel of God, in 1927 on the Eucharist, and in 1930 on the Church. The speakers were intellectually distinguished and the papers, though designed for a general audience, were of a high calibre. So we find amongst the speakers in 1920, C. H. Turner, A. E. Taylor, Lionel Thornton, N. P. Williams, Milner-White, Frere and Darwell

Stone; in 1923, Gore, Kenneth Kirk, E. G. Selwyn and T. A. Lacey; in 1927 B. C. Butler, Nevill Coghill, Evelyn Underhill, Sir Edwyn Hoskyns, E. O. James, H. L. Goudge and A. E. J. Rawlinson.

In 1933 the centenary of the Oxford Movement was marked by a special Congress, with a total membership of 70,000, the climax being a Pontifical High Mass in the White City Stadium attended by a congregation of 50,000, probably, as the Centenary Report notes, the largest Anglican congregation which had ever assembled for worship.[81] Preaching at Oxford on the anniversary of Keble's Assize Sermon, Father E. K. Talbot reminded his hearers that the Tractarian leaders 'did not propose to give the Church a Catholic character, that they were sure it had always possessed', their confidence coming from the conviction 'that it is the Catholic Church which presents itself to the English people in the creeds, the sacraments, the ministry, the worship of the Church of England.'[82] In another paper Kenneth Kirk discerned five truths which the Tractarians revived or recovered for the Church in their reaffirmation of the Catholic identity of the Church: sacramental character; the social mission of the Church; the personal holiness of the genuine Christian; the pastoral (not penal) authority of the Church; and the Church's spiritual independence.[83] N. P. Williams took up Talbot's theme that the Oxford Movement began 'not in order to make the English Church Catholic, but because they were convinced that it was already Catholic'.

> They did not conceive themselves as inviting it to adopt a foreign system, or as endeavouring to foist alien ideas upon it; the last thing in the world which they thought of themselves as attempting was the task of tricking out an Anglican jackdaw with feathers borrowed from the Roman or any other peacock.[84]

The ecclesiology they professed was, Williams went on, one shared with the Orthodox and the Old Catholics. Anglican self-understanding was not simply that of being poor relations of the Church of Rome, and not even recognized as such. He appealed for a repudiation of the 'provincial and sectarian misuse of the great word "Catholic" which restricts it to ecclesiastical and sacramental doctrine, and by implication labels the foundation truths of the gospel as "merely Christian"'. 'Catholicism is not a mere *extra* superadded to Christianity; it is Christianity itself in its most intense and concentrated form.'

It follows, further, that we shall naturally shrink from anything that may look like a harsh and censorious denial of the name of ('Catholic') to any Christians of our own communion who with us firmly hold the glorious truths of the Trinity and the Incarnation, even though their apprehension of the preciousness of the sacraments and the splendour of the Church's historic worship may seem to us to be defective.[85]

He exhorted his hearers to think of themselves, 'not as a rigidly organized party or sect, but as a diffusive influence and an unseen tendency, the streams whereof make glad the whole city of God', for the ultimate object of the Catholic Movement was to 'secure its own disappearance, in that glorious day when the Church on earth shall have become visibly one and the kingdoms of this world shall have become the kingdom of our Lord and of his Christ'.[86]

Williams in speaking thus was aware of narrow and sectarian attitudes on the part of many Anglo-Catholics, in part the product of the long years of the ritual controversies and the breakdown of ecclesiastical discipline because the lines were too narrowly drawn and legalistically conceived. He knew of the tensions between adherents of the Western Rite, taking Rome, as W. G. Ward had done, to be 'the ideal of the Christian Church', and those emphasizing an English Catholicism, sometimes antiquarian in nature, exemplified by Dearmer's *Parson's Handbook* (1899) and to some extent by the *English Hymnal*.[87] It was, after all, the time of controversies over reservation of the Sacrament, and not so long after the Prayer-Book revision crisis of 1927–8. Behind these lay the continuing problem of Anglican identity. The Anglo-Catholic Congresses themselves were a symptom of the enthusiasm of a new generation following the First World War, and for a time there was tension with the much older Society, the English Church Union, with Lord Halifax at its head. It was to be one of Halifax's last services to the Catholic revival that he succeeded in uniting the English Church Union and the Anglo-Catholic Congress. The new society came into existence on 1 January 1934. Just under three weeks later Halifax died at the age of 94.[88]

Following the centenary year of the Oxford Movement the Sixth Anglo-Catholic Congress was planned for 1940, the culmination of seven years evangelistic work in the parishes. It was to coincide with a Lambeth Conference year. The Second World War meant that both were postponed until 1948, and when they met they met in very different circumstances from those originally envisaged. Congregations were struggling; churches, including a number of famous shrines, had been destroyed; costs of printing and administration had risen sharply. Even so 11,000 attended for a series of papers springing from the themes of the Lambeth Quadrilateral of 1888, of the Bible, the creeds, the ministry, and the sacraments, in their relation to the general theme of the Church—a reflection of a concern about the Church of South India unity scheme, which figured prominently on the Lambeth agenda. The speakers included Michael Ramsey, Gabriel Hebert, Gordon Selwyn, Gregory Dix, Robert Mortimer, Donald MacKinnon and E. L. Mascall. Michael Ramsey welcomed the new Biblical Theology as witnessing to the fact that 'the Bible is the record not of man's evolutionary religious progress but of God's word of judgment and self-revelation to man.' A 'shallow and optimistic liberalism' had been countered by a recovery 'of those stern and catastrophic elements in the Bible—wrath, judgment, election, and resurrection', which the Liberal-Catholic synthesis had tended to smooth away. But he was at the same time critical of the imbalance of that same Biblical theology.

Through its intense concentration upon 'the Word' and 'the hearing of faith', it sometimes makes speaking and hearing exhaust the whole relation of God and man; and there is in the Bible a great and many-sided theme—concerning man as creature and worshipper, man in his quest for sanctification with the Beatific Vision as his goal—which the Reformed biblicism mutilates or ignores. . . .

The recovery of the fulness of the truth of Scripture in the Church demands that we shall all link together the return to the living God in the Bible with the appeal to the tradition of the Catholic Church—the ancient fathers, the liturgy, the sacramental life, the visible order of the visible Church. Only thus do we recover the fulness of the Bible, for only thus was the fulness of the Bible first given.[89]

On the ministry, Gregory Dix urged that episcopacy was not to be commended for reasons of expediency, but for its apostolic character, but he reminded his hearers that in England that apostolic character was distorted by the role of the State in the nomination of bishops.[90] In the section on the sacraments Robert Mortimer stressed the corporate context of sacramental worship, his paper being indicative of the growing influence of the liturgical movement. Donald MacKinnon spoke movingly of the Eucharist and the

Passion deploring as 'fundamentally uncatholic a eucharistic theology which developed a doctrine of "the real presence" in abstraction from the sacrificial direction of the eucharistic action', thinking of consecration 'as a device for bringing Christ into the bread and wine' and ignoring altogether 'the theological character of the *act*'.

Where we differ from the men of the Reform is in our conviction that our words and action at the altar effectually embody the words and action, the effectual words and redeeming action, of the Christ himself. So we construe our ritual as a truly sacrificial performance, a veritably effectual remembrancing—effectual not because of our feelings of devotion, but because thus and thus has he willed that we should echo his words, and draw our flickering fidelity to its true home in his redeeming disposition towards the Father.[91]

Similar echoes are found in Mascall's paper, where both 'psychological and atomistic' and certain 'social' understandings of the sacraments are criticized. 'The Church', he wrote, 'has many functions *in* society, but it can never become a mere function *of* society, for it *is* a society—the Society of God, the life of the Holy Trinity communicated to men.' 'It is in fact in simply being itself and living its own supernatural life that the Church performs its greatest service to the world.'[92]

The Sixth Anglo-Catholic Congress was also the last. The postwar world was very different from that of twenty years earlier. New questions were being posed; new communications meant closer contact with the world church; changes which were affecting the Roman Church were to issue in the 1960s in the Second Vatican Council, whose impact on all the churches was to be incalculable. Energies were demanded for reconstruction after the war, and for responding to a much more consciously secular society. Yet many of the insights, Catholic and critical, to which the Catholic movement witnessed had been absorbed and become part of the lifeblood of the Church. If it is difficult to write the history of the Catholic Movement in Anglicanism after that date, it is partly because this is the case, though partly also because of a certain theological failure to reinterpret the Catholic tradition in a living and creative way. The Catholic revival in Anglicanism must, like all movements, as Newman discerned, change in order to remain the same.[93]

XI. Epilogue

PREACHING IN the University Church at Oxford in 1933, where John Keble had preached his Assize Sermon on 'National Apostasy' a century earlier, Father Edward Keble Talbot of the Community of the Resurrection noted that the significance of the Oxford Movement was 'not exhausted by its immediate reference'.[1] It was born in response to a threat to the Church of England, and was at one and the same time a defensive reaction to protect the Church from interference at the hands of political reformers and an affirmation that the identity of the Church was very much more than the religious aspect of English society. The threat to the Church was both greater and smaller than Keble and his friends supposed. The suppression of Irish bishoprics, and Erastian legislation, and the emergence of ecclesiastical pluralism is England, were not the immediate harbingers of the dissolution of the Church of England, or even of its Establishment, but were rather indicators of a much broader process of secularization over a much longer period, a process in itself difficult to define precisely and even more difficult to interpret.

Professor Chadwick has warned against using the word 'secularization', as religious men often do, 'like a lamentation of Jeremiah; as a way of harking back, of yearning for a promised land which they once occupied and from which they are expelled'. To do so is to refuse to recognize that the change in perception which it betokens has brought in some degree 'a clearer apprehension of the world and its independence'.[2] Newman was conscious of both this change in perception and its religious ambiguity when he looked back in 1879, in a speech made on the occasion of his receiving his Cardinal's hat from Leo XIII, linking this process with the spirit of 'Liberalism' in religion, which he had so long endeavoured to oppose. Not that such 'Liberalism' was to be condemned out of hand, for its spirit was one he acknowledged to be widely and properly influential, simply because there was so much in it which was good and true: 'the precepts of justice, truthfulness, sobriety, self-command, benevolence . . . are among its avowed principles, and the natural laws of society'.[3] But alongside that recognition—and the darker and more apocalyptic character of the twentieth century has shaken such optimistic assumptions—Newman was sharply aware of the solvent character of 'Liberalism' on the corporate character of Christianity. The end of the process was a privatization of religion.

> Liberalism in religion is the doctrine that there is no positive truth in religion, but that one creed is as good as another. . . . It is inconsistent with any recognition of any religion as *true*. It teaches that all are to be tolerated, as all are matters of opinion. Revealed religion is not a truth, but a sentiment and a taste . . . and it is the right of each individual to make it say just what strikes his fancy. . . . Since, then, religion is so personal a peculiarity and so private a possession, we must of necessity ignore it in the intercourse of man with man. . . . Religion is in no sense the bond of society. . . . It is a private luxury, which a man may have if he will; but which he must not obtrude upon others, or indulge in to their annoyance.[4]

Great movements start from particular occasions and moments of time in which perceptive spirits recognize, even if obscurely, larger changes than those to which the occasions themselves bear witness. Keble's Assize Sermon, which, for all its datedness and limitation, is a response to the same process delineated by Newman in his 1879 speech, reflects an awareness that the Christian religion was ceasing to be regarded as 'the bond of English society'. That could only be regretted by all who believed that Christian faith enshrined God's saving truth and pointed men and women to their true destiny. In such circumstances it was imperative that Christians should not simply be content to compromise and accommodate their faith to whatever might prove to be acceptable to a changing society, without first being confronted with the character of that primary society to which they belonged by virtue of their baptism. What did it mean to claim that the Church was 'one, holy, catholic, and apostolic' and that such was the character of the Church of England? The doctrine of the Church was thus central to the Oxford Movement, and Talbot rightly reminded his 1933 congregation that 'what gives continuity to the Movement is the conviction common to the Oxford leaders and all their successors, that the Church is central to the Christian faith and religion, and that the English Church is a true part of that supernatural society which derives from Christ and his Apostles'. It was, Talbot went on, an incarnational, christocentric vision.

> Here is the soul of Catholicism—a corporate experience controlled by the insight which divines the whole light, life and love of God incarnate once for

all in Christ, offered continuously to the world and entering the life of man through the fellowship of the Spirit. This insight is shared in greater or lesser degree by the simplest Christian believer with the whole worshipping community. It is as eliciting and training this central insight that the Scriptures have their enduring significance: it is as interpreting and justifying the experience of the community that the creeds have their authority: and it is to translate into the terms of the human intellect the truths implicit in faith's original divination that the theologian fulfills his proper and never completed function. And penetrating the Christian insight and experience is the sense of revelation: of love and light bestowed, and not searched out: of being found, rather than of finding: of being known of God, rather than of knowing. Hence in the Catholic consciousness the recognition of mystery. . . . Hence also inevitably the note of authority in Catholic Christianity. For the content and significance of the Christian experience transcend all individual apprehensions and defy all final intellectual analysis. Authority is the influence upon the individual of an insight more adequate than his own to the object of faith.[5]

It was such incarnational, Catholic Christianity, which found expression in the renewal of eucharistic worship and of theological imagination, and equally in pastoral concern, the life of prayer, missionary endeavour, and a concern for unity with Christians who shared that corporate vision in both east and west.

Inevitably such incarnational faith was itself incarnationally expressed. The Oxford Movement and the Catholic revival were coloured and influenced by the particular circumstances of Victorian England: by the conservative reaction to threatened Anglican privilege and by fear of a changing social order; by the Gothic enthusiasms and romantic medievalism of architects and wealthy patrons who built and endowed churches; by Ultramontane attitudes which exalted ecclesiastical authority, in theory if not in practice, at Rome if not in Canterbury. The Church of England was ill-prepared for the challenge of reform in the 1830s because it inherited a medieval structure largely unchanged by the Reformation, a structure adapted to a rural, squirearchical society and not to the urban terraces and tenements of London, the Midlands, and the North. In somewhat the same way the powerful theological and devotional inheritance of the Oxford Movement had been cramped by its Victorian origins, of which the buildings are the most obvious sign. Catholic theology can be obscured by its Victorian setting. Great churches, once staffed by teams of clergy serving the urban poor in an age before the welfare state, are now stranded in many places like great Anglo-Catholic

whales in areas of urban re-development, where planning has removed the original community who nourished the remembrance of
faithful service. Religious houses, built with genuine piety and devotion, were too often constructed for the assumptions of Victorian
middle-class society. The same assumptions coloured the ideals of
priestly life and pastoral care, as can be seen clearly revealed in a
quite unconscious way in a fine essay by Liddon, where having
described the discipline, devotion, and duty demanded of the parish
priest, he concludes with the words: 'he will say Compline with his
servants'.[6]

The consequences of this inheritance can breed fear, and insecur-
ity, and loss of nerve, a clinging to the old ways when they have
ceased to give life, and a confusion between what is Victorian, or
Gothic, or even Baroque, and what is truly catholic. In this situation
the way ahead is not necessarily an uncritical adoption of whatever is
decreed in Rome, nor yet an equally unthinking determination to be
different. Likewise the polemics of party in the nineteenth century
and the early part of the twentieth, necessary perhaps in the reaffirmation of the catholic heritage and faith of Anglicanism, have
left a sectarian legacy which is the antithesis of all that is meant by
Catholicism. Father Talbot's 1933 reminder, that 'the leaders of the
Movement did not propose to give the Church a Catholic character
. . . that they were sure it had always possessed' is one that is still
needed.

It is easy to be nostalgic, to yearn for the promised land of the
heady days of the Catholic revival, but that is to miss the extent to
which the very 'success' of the Catholic movement has meant a
transformation of the self-understanding and self-expression of
Anglicanism, and what that in its turn has made possible in relation
to other churches. At the very heart of the Catholic revival was the
call to holiness and the sense of the Church as a divine society,
striving to live by the sustaining mystery of the love and grace of
God. That was a shared faith, in continuity with the faith of the early
centuries, and of the saints of God down the ages, and at its heart, as
Keble said in one of his last sermons, was the living Spirit of God.

In Him they now live a new life, which they have entirely from Him; a life
which is both His and theirs; whereby they are so joined to Him as to be
verily and indeed partakers of a Divine nature.

Yes, my brethren, this and no less was the mysterious Whitsun privilege and glory of those on whom the Holy Ghost first came down: a glory so high and inconceivable, that the Holy Fathers did not hesitate to call it Deification, and Christianity which teaches and confers it, they called 'a deifying discipline'.[7]

That, and no less, is the vision glorious by which so many strove to live; a vision which endures because it is the gift of eternal life.